CHECKMATE HUMANITY

The how and why of Responsible AI

Sam Kirshner, Richard Vidgen and Catriona Wallace

with

Tiberio Caetano, Rumtin Sepasspour and Kimberlee Weatherall

Dedication

This book is dedicated to those who have been harmed and those who will be harmed by AI.

May you be very few.

Reprinted with corrections December 2022

Authors contact: info@checkmatehumanity.com Website: www.checkmatehumanity.com

A catalogue record for this book is available from the National Library of Australia.

Printed book ISBN: 978-0-6486929-9-7

Publisher:

global stories

ABN 61 747 410 514

Website: www.thebookadviser.com.au

Cover and internal page design: Rasika UM, www.shashika.info

Proofreader: Clare Wadsworth

Preface

This book is the result of many years grappling with AI and its challenges by a team of contributors with a broad range of experience and interests.

While the book should be of interest to all of us as citizens in the widest sense, much of the advice is intended to be of practical value to organisations and their management teams, as these are the primary generators and deployers of AI solutions. It should also be of interest to institutions and government agencies tasked with legislating for AI, and ultimately for everyone concerned about algorithmic justice.

Acknowledgements

We would like to acknowledge the profound contributions of Professor Kimberlee Weatherall who authored the chapter, Regulation and governance of AI, Dr Tiberio Caetano, Jenny L. Davis, Chris Dolman and Dr Simon O'Callaghan, who authored the chapter, De-risking Automated Decisions and Rumtin Sepasspour, who authored the chapter titled, Existential Risks of AI. We approached leaders who we believed were the absolute recognised experts in the fields of Responsible AI and legislation, risk and existential threat and we are so delighted that Tiberio, Jenny, Simon, Chris, Rumtin and Kim agreed to be involved in the writing of this book. Thank you for your on-going support and commitment to the field of Responsible AI.

We would also like to acknowledge Tristan Harris for his fierce leadership in holding the tech giants to account. The title of this book, Checkmate Humanity, was inspired by comments Tristan has made where he notes that AI creates a *checkmate on humanity*. We are so respectful of all that Tristan does in this field of Responsible AI.

We are very grateful to The Analytics Development Group of the UK Operational Research Society who provided commentary and feedback at all stages of the development of the book, helping us to ensure that it is timely and relevant for a practitioner audience.

Thanks also to Professor Lemuria Carter who was instrumental in bringing Sam, Richard and me, (Catriona) together to work on this important project.

And to Jaqui Lane, our book advisor, who has provided invaluable advice and assistance along the way, making this book far greater than we would have been able to do on our own! Thanks, Jaqs!

And to my super impressive co-authors, Richard and Sam, not only have we worked together in our field of passionate commitment, Responsible AI, but we have become good friends, and now dreaming about the next book in the Checkmate Humanity series .... The Metaverse!

Dr Catriona Wallace

Author and Contributor biographies

Authors

Dr Sam Kirshner is an Associate Professor of Business Analytics at the University of New South Wales. Sam teaches data visualisation, predictive analytics, and Responsible AI to undergraduates, postgraduates, and MBAs and co-authored the textbook Business Analytics: A Management Approach. Sam's primary research interests are analysing behavioural decision-making in operations and technology management and studying how algorithms and artificial intelligence impact decision-making. Sam has published his research in prestigious management, operations, tourism, and decision-making academic journals. Sam earned his PhD in Management Science from the Smith School of Business at Queen's University in Canada.

Professor Richard Vidgen is Emeritus Professor of Business Analytics at the University of New South Wales Business School, Emeritus Professor of Systems Thinking at the University of Hull, UK, and a visiting professor at the University of the Creative Arts, UK. Prior to becoming an academic, Richard had an extensive career in industry, working for a U.S. software company, as an IT consultant in the finance and banking sector, and as a software development manager for a major UK bank. Current research is focused on business analytics, with an emphasis on ethical and Responsible AI and is also researching the impact of AI on the creative arts. His research has been published in top-ranked journals, including the *European Journal of Operational Research, Information Systems Research, and MIS Quarterly*. He is a co-author of the textbook *Business Analytics: a management approach* published by Bloomsbury and is an editor-in-chief for the *Journal of Business Analytics.*

Dr Catriona Wallace is an entrepreneur and specialist in the fields of Artificial Intelligence, the Metaverse and the responsible use of technology. Catriona has been recognised by *The Australian Financial Review* as the most influential woman in business & entrepreneurship and by the Royal Institution of Australia as a pre-eminent scientist.

Dr Wallace is also Adjunct Professor at UNSW and has been recognised by Onalytica as one of the top speakers on Ethical AI, globally. Dr Wallace is the Founder of the Responsible Metaverse

Alliance, Director of the Gradient Institute, Chair of VC fund Boab AI, Director of medical research centre, the Garvan Institute, and she was the founder of a machine-learning company based out of New York. Catriona is also the Co-Chair of Sir Richard Branson's B Team's AI Coalition. Catriona is a champion of women, diversity, inclusion and ethics in technology and has a PhD in Organizational Behaviour.

And most importantly, Catriona is a mother of five and a Medicine Woman in training.

Contributors

Dr Tiberio Caetano is the Chief Scientist of Gradient Institute. He is an international leader in the ethical use of machine learning and AI, having worked in Brazil, Canada, France and Australia. He worked as a researcher at NICTA (now Data61) for 10 years, where he also managed the machine learning research group. He published extensively in the premier machine learning research venues and graduated numerous PhD students, among whom are leading data scientists, researchers and academics at premier universities and industry labs across Australia, the US and Europe. In 2013 he co-founded Ambiata, later acquired by Australia's largest general insurer IAG, where he led the design of decision-making algorithms that have touched millions of consumers across several industries. In 2019 he helped establish Gradient Institute, a not-for-profit research institute focusing on responsible AI, where he works on incorporating ethical considerations into the design, governance and operation of AI systems. Tiberio is an Honorary Professor at the ANU and an advisor for the OECD on AI.

Dr Jenny L. Davis is a sociologist at the Australian National University. Her research intersects social psychology and technology studies, with a particular focus on identifying and reducing inequality as it materializes in technological systems. She is the Deputy Lead for ANU's Humanising Machine Intelligence Project and Chair of the Communication, Information Technologies, & Media Sociology section of the American Sociological Association. She holds an ARC DECRA Fellowship leading a project on ethics in Australia's technology start-up sector and is the founder and Lead of ANU's Role-Taking Lab, established through a Futures Scheme grant. Her work is published in flagship journals from sociology, social psychology, and new media studies and her book, *How Artifacts Afford: The Power and Politics of Everyday Things (2020)*, is out with MIT Press.

Chris Dolman is an actuary working at Insurance Australia Group (IAG). His current role of Executive Manager, Data and Algorithmic Ethics helps to ensure that modern decision-making algorithms and other advanced uses of data are designed and implemented in an ethical, responsible and thoughtful way. Prior to this, Chris held a variety of senior management positions in the insurance industry and consulting, in Australia and the UK. Chris is an award-winning volunteer, researcher and Fellow of the Actuaries Institute, and a Gradient Institute Fellow.

Dr Simon O'Callaghan has over a decade's experience in developing and applying machine learning techniques to a wide range of problem areas such as behavioural prediction, robotics, demographic estimation and the sciences. He began his research into machine learning during his PhD at the University of Sydney while building a more principled framework for robots to reason about uncertainty in their surroundings. Simon has since been published in several top-tier conferences and journals as well as co-supervised PhD students in the same field. While working for Data61 and NICTA, Simon focused on turning ideas from academia into realisable systems to solve problems being faced by industry and government. At the Gradient Institute, Simon now directs his efforts towards developing methods that ensure the AI systems we build today contribute positively to society in a manner that is both fair and transparent.

Rumtin Sepasspour is an independent researcher and adviser, focused on the policy of existential and global catastrophic risk. He is a Research Affiliate with the University of Cambridge's Centre for the Study of Existential Risk and a Visiting Fellow at the School of Regulation and Global Governance of the Australian National University. After a career in the private sector, Rumtin moved to the Australian Public Service. He worked as an Analyst with the Department of Defence and as a National Security and International Policy Officer in the Department of the Prime Minister and Cabinet. He is currently leading activities relating to researching and engaging policy around existential and global catastrophic risks to find practical solutions for policymakers.

Prof Kimberlee Weatherall is a Professor of Law at the University of Sydney, and a Chief Investigator with the ARC Centre of Excellence for Automated Decision-Making and Society. In technology law, her current research focuses on the law relating to the collection, ownership, use and governance of data about and related to people, with the goal of ensuring that data collection, use and linkage, and data and predictive analytics are developed in ways that are beneficial to people and society. Her projects in this space include an ARC Linkage Grant, awarded in 2022, Socially Responsible Insurance in the Age of Artificial Intelligence, with Seth Lazar, Damien Clifford, Jenny Davis (ANU), Tiberio Caetano (Gradient) and Chris Dolman (IAG). She is a Fellow at the Gradient Institute, a research affiliate of the Humanising Machine Intelligence group at the Australian National University, and co-chair of the Australian Computer Society's Advisory Committee on AI Ethics.

Contents

Foreword

Louis Rosenberg, PhD

What would happen if NASA detected an intelligent species headed for earth in a fleet of sophisticated ships? The reaction from us humans would likely range from extreme concern to absolute panic. Even if we had years to prepare for their arrival, our fear of these approaching creatures, intentions unknown, would be overwhelming.

The fact is – an alien intelligence is racing towards earth and many predict it will get here within 20 to 40 years. It will show up knowing everything there is to know about us humans, understanding our languages and our cultures, our tendencies and inclinations, even our flaws and foibles, and we have no reason to believe it will be friendly.

No, this alien will not come from a distant planet. It will be born right here on earth, hatched in a lab at a major university or well-funded corporation. I am referring to the first Artificial General Intelligence (AGI) to match or exceed human level cognition.

It will be viewed as one of the greatest achievements in history, but unlike other human inventions, it will have a mind of its own. And if it behaves like all other sentient creatures we know, it will put its own self-interests first. And just because it was built by humans, that doesn't mean it will act human, share our values, or even prioritise our interests.

There are currently 72 active AGI projects at major institutions around the world. Few of these programs have any AI safety efforts underway. This is part of a larger trend in which AI technologies are being developed at increasingly faster rates while preparations for AI-related risks are not keeping up.

And it's not just AGI that could threaten human society. AI algorithms are being incorporated into more and more aspects of our lives, automating processes and decisions that have previously been overseen by humans. This creates entire categories of societal risk that need to be carefully considered, from biased algorithms amplifying inequity to automated weapons removing human sensibilities from armed conflict.

Already, AI platforms can defeat our best players at the hardest games on earth. But really, these AI systems are not just learning to master the games of chess, poker and Go, they are learning to master the game of humans, learning to anticipate our actions, sense our emotions, and exploit our weaknesses. Researchers around the world are developing AI systems to out-think-us, out-negotiate us, and out-maneuver us.

Is there anything we can do to protect ourselves?

We certainly can't stop AI from getting more powerful, as no innovation has ever been contained. And while many are working to put safeguards in place, there's a notable lack of urgency, especially in industry. Which is why this book, *Checkmate Humanity,* is so important – it clearly conveys the very real risks of AI and the urgent need for proactive measures.

Whether we like it or not, an alien intelligence is headed our way and we aren't ready for the consequences. Now is the time to prepare for its arrival.

Louis Rosenberg

CEO & Chief Scientist, Unanimous AI

Ed Santow

Artificial intelligence (AI) is, by and large, a closed-off world—accessible only to those with deep technical expertise.

When AI was largely theoretical, confined to laboratory experimentation, perhaps this did not matter. But this century AI has moved rapidly from the laboratory into commerce, government and countless other areas. This has meant that AI is no longer the plaything of technical experts. People without that technical expertise—in government, business and civil society—are now responsible for procuring, implementing and overseeing AI. Yet they have had to strain to catch a glimpse of precisely how the technology operates. Those subject to AI-informed decisions have generally been even more in the dark.

Checkmate Humanity is a resource that can help unlock the technical world of AI. The authors have come together with the aim of informing and guiding the wider public on the societal implications of AI. In doing so, *Checkmate Humanity* embodies two qualities that will be crucial in applying the best liberal democratic values to how we approach AI.

The first quality is clarity of vision. In my former role as Australia's Human Rights Commissioner, I was struck by how law, policy and business approaches to AI were informed by utopian and dystopian worldviews on AI. Those subscribing to the view that technology would solve all our ills often espouse a kind of technological 'solutionism'—the idea that technology generally, and AI specifically, is the answer to every conceivable question or problem. By contrast, those who fret that their smart washing machine is plotting violent insurrection with their other white goods are often unable to see benign use cases for AI.

Clarity can be achieved only by understanding the parameters of AI, and the operation of the technologies and techniques that make up AI. By understanding these things, we can make sensible judgments about how AI may be used safely and effectively, and where the greatest risks lie.

Patience is the second, and perhaps most easily overlooked, quality of an excellent guide. In the nineteenth century, Charles Babbage—one of the great minds, along with Ada Lovelace, behind what became modern computing—would be invited to Westminster where he would answer the questions posed by Members of Parliament. He once observed wryly:

> "On two occasions, I have been asked [by members of Parliament], 'Pray, Mr. Babbage, if you put into the machine wrong figures, will the right answers come out?' I am not able to rightly apprehend the kind of confusion of ideas that could provoke such a question."

The authors of *Checkmate Humanity* could be forgiven a similar impatience. Their burden is often to answer just these sorts of questions. However, this book is the best kind of response: it offers a firm foundation of scientific fact and applies this to a range of threats and opportunities. As readers, we emerge better armed, and better informed, to face a world being fundamentally reshaped by AI.

Ed Santow

Member of the World Economic Forum's Global Future Council on Human Rights and the Fourth Industrial Revolution

Introduction

Organisations are increasingly using AI algorithms[1] in their decision-making processes as they realise they can use technology to make decisions more quickly and more efficiently, more cheaply, and ultimately more profitably. AI can work 24/7, it does not get tired or sick, it does not get bored, it applies rules consistently, and it scales in a way that a human workforce cannot. Organisations use AI in many and growing ways, influencing our lives to determine who gets credit (Knight, 2019; Telford, 2019), who gets a job (Raghavan et al., 2020; O'Neill, 2016b), who may be a criminal (BBC, 2020), and who gets parole (Hao, 2019). AI is also used to automate the provision of welfare services (Booth 2019a, 2019b; Gilman, 2020), and to make healthcare diagnoses (Ledford, 2019; Savage, 2020).

Scanning the titles of articles and news reports reflects growing evidence of the potential for harm from AI, for example "AI algorithms intended to root out welfare fraud often end up punishing the poor instead" (Gilman, 2020), "AI is sending people to jail—and getting it wrong" (Hao, 2019), and "Millions of black people affected by racial bias in health-care algorithms" (Ledford, 2019). Every citizen's life will, sooner rather than later, be touched by AI technology in more and more different ways with greater and greater frequency. At a societal level, AI, fuelled by vast amounts of data, can create inequality and threaten democracy (O'Neill, 2016a) - in the extreme it may result in an existential crisis, and the extinction of humanity.

The AI researcher Noel Sharkey argues that "algorithms are so 'infected with biases' that their decision-making processes could not be fair or trusted", and that we should be "testing AI decision-making machines in the same way as new pharmaceutical drugs are vigorously checked before they are allowed on to the market" (McDonald, 2019). Indeed, those organisations that are not using AI responsibly may find themselves banned from using AI and facing punitive fines (BBC, 2021).

Artificial intelligence (AI) undoubtedly offers tremendous benefits across many industries, for example in healthcare for the diagnosis of cancer (Savage, 2020). As the UK's information commissioner states "Profiling and automated decision-making can be very useful for organisations and also benefit individuals in many sectors, including healthcare, education, financial services and marketing. They can lead to quicker and more consistent decisions, particularly in cases where a very large volume of data needs to be analysed and decisions made very quickly" (ICO, 2018, p.7). However, there are many instances of AI and algorithmic decision-making being used in ways that have direct and indirect, intended and unintended harmful consequences. Marjanovic et al. (2021a) labels the potential for harmful outcomes from AI "algorithmic pollution":

> "Algorithmic pollution is a new form of social pollution which denotes the unjustified, unfair, discriminatory, and other harmful effects of automated algorithmic decision-making for individuals, their families, groups of people, communities, organisations, sections of the population, and society at large."

They choose this label to focus our collective attention on negative and widespread effects of AI that can quickly be covered up by "myths of objectivity, neutrality and superiority of algorithms over human decision-makers" (p. 32).

In investigating AI harms, we do not seek to place the spotlight on either organisations or AI technology individually; rather, we approach the issue as an entanglement of organisations and AI that generates harm to those subjected to AI. Analogously, the NRA

(National Rifle Association) might argue that guns don't kill people – people kill people. Conversely, anti-gun lobbyists argue that guns do indeed kill people, making gun control necessary. Bruno Latour argues that guns and people are inseparable, and that it is the gun-people network which is responsible for death from gun violence (paraphrased from University of Twente, NL). In our case, it is the organisation-AI collective that leads to AI harms. AI is not the sole actor generating AI harm, and nor is it a neutral means to an end. Without both AI and organisations to deploy that technology, there would be no AI harm. AI technology is not simply an intermediary between organisations and AI subjects – it is a mediator that actively contributes to, and constitutes the way in which, AI harms are realised.

While this illustrates how AI today can be viewed as part of a socio-technical entanglement of technology and organisations, the future may be very different:

- There will probably be an increase in the meshing of AI and humans. For example, in the UK an 88-year-old blind woman has been given a bionic eye implant that has restored her eyesight (Gregory, 2022). The solution involves the surgical insertion of a 2 mm-wide chip into the centre of the patient's retina, which, together with special glasses and a video-camera, uses artificial intelligence algorithms to pass data back through the chip to the brain as it if were natural vision. Our physical and sensory worlds are likely to become more and more mediated by AI.
- Our social worlds are becoming increasingly mediated by AI technologies, from social media to virtual worlds. Metaverse, a development of Facebook, is a 3D immersive world that has already attracted sensational headlines concerning unacceptable sexual behaviour (Frishberg, H., 2022).
- There is the potential for machine sentience: broad agreement that, given time - although estimates vary from ten to fifty years (Turchin, 2019) - machines will achieve artificial general intelligence (AGI). For example, Google's DeepMind is already rivalling the average human programmer in coding competitions (Wakefield, 2022), and while we may not yet have a Proustian machine author, AI technologies are already generating poems and novels of publishable quality (Aalho,

2021). Further, should machines acquire artificial consciousness (Koch, 2019), then the whole question of what constitutes 'social' is called into question – machines could have their own socio-technical entanglement without the need for, or presence of, humanity.

Our aim with this book is to inform citizens, and to propose guidelines for organisations, engaged in the development and deployment of AI-based applications about applications that involve algorithmic decision-making (ADM), to steer a path between an outright ban on the use of AI (see Sharkey in McDonald, 2019), and a laissez-faire approach that allows organisations unfettered access to AI in unconstrained pursuit of their often profit-maximising goals. We further consider the catastrophic and existential risk that is posed by AI to society at large, to humanity, and to the planet. In short, this book is about Responsible AI (RAI) in its widest sense.

AI in context

In assembling the book, we are particularly interested in application areas such as welfare, health, and justice systems, which are especially sensitive to the use of AI and algorithmic decision-making. These sectors are referred to as transformative services (Figure I.1). Transformative services are human-centered services that have a direct impact on the well-being of individuals, communities, and wider society (Anderson and Ostrom, 2015). Sectors such as healthcare, welfare services, housing, education, justice, and financial services may have a significant impact on well-being outcomes. Transformative services should respect human dignity and centre on "creating uplifting changes and improvements in the well-being of individuals (consumers and employees), communities, collectives, societies, and ecosystems" (Anderson et al., 2013, p.1203). Transformative services must pay particular attention to discrimination, marginalisation, inclusion, access to services, and disparities in outcomes for different population groups (Anderson et al., 2013). The use of AI by organisations to aid decision- making can lead to intended - and unintended – consequences that may be harmful.

AI is a technology, and by itself can do nothing. It only achieves agency once it is adopted by organisations as part of their business and decision-making process. The same technology can be used in different ways within a business process to achieve very different outcomes. For example, a loan application might be turned down without explanation, or the applicant may be given a plan showing how to improve their financial situation to qualify for a loan. AI technology is not deterministic; it depends on how it is enrolled into a socio-technical network of people and things. AI and big data-enabled algorithms have been integrated within the decision-making processes of all types of organisations. Often AI is used to supplement human decision-making, but in some instances the algorithmic decision-making (ADM) process is automated (AADM):

> "Automated decision-making is the process of making a decision by automated means without any human involvement. These decisions can be based on factual data, as well as on digitally created profiles or inferred data. Examples of this include: an online decision to award a loan; and an aptitude test used for recruitment which uses pre-programmed algorithms and criteria. Automated decision-making often involves profiling, but it does not have to" (ICO, 2018, p.7).

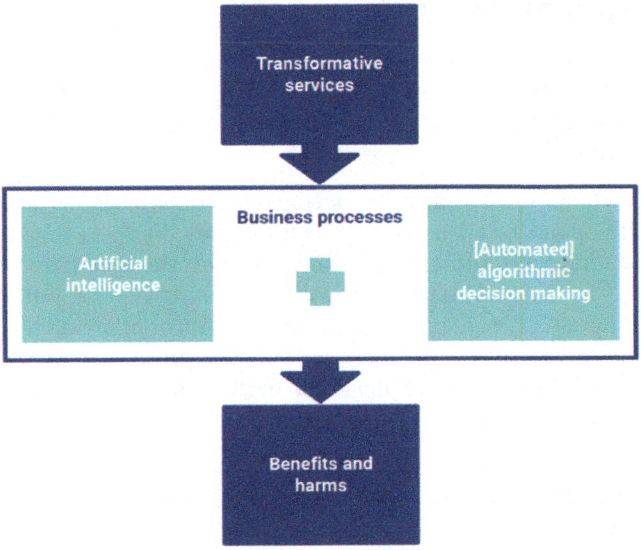

Figure I.1: AI in context

The use of AI and [A]ADM contributes to an intensification of the datafication process, where various phenomena, including people, are presented in data (Lycett, 2013). This data may include inferred data (inferences made based on postcode) and unrelated data (living in a crime hotspot). Datafication is further intensified through the use of scoring and ranking systems such as credit ratings, and good citizen scores. When this data, much of which are derived from networks of [A] ADM sharing decisions as data, are combined, then human AI subjects can be reduced to nothing more than their datafied representation. This datafication amplifies the potential for algorithmic and AI harms.

While the inclusion of [A]ADM in organisational processes can generate undoubted benefits (for example, faster loan decisions and improved cancer diagnoses), it may also lead to harms, whether intended or not. In some cases, such as armed military drones, the harm is both direct and intentional. To understand and assess the impacts arising from the use of AI in ADM we need to understand the types of benefits and harms that are generated and then consider what form a reasonable and appropriate response might take.

Structure of the book

The book has two sections. The first section explores the AI terrain and outlines the potential dangers of unconstrained AI development. The second section considers how we can respond to the AI challenge.

In chapter 1, we provide background on what AI is, and how it works. If you are familiar with AI technologies then you may prefer to skim this chapter. Chapter 2 is concerned with the benefits and harms facilitated by AI and ADM, principally focusing on the potential for harm. Chapter 3 considers the potential for harm of an emerging area of AI application, the metaverse. In chapter 4, we broaden our investigation into AI to explore the potential for catastrophic and existential risks arising from its use.

In the second section of the book, chapter 5 takes an organisational perspective, and considers how organisations can develop and deploy AI in an ethical and responsible manner. Chapter 6 focuses on a risk-based approach and makes proposals about how organisations could de-risk the AI development process. To give an idea of the current state of play in practice, chapter 7 presents the results of a survey of responsible AI practices. In chapter 8 we provide an introduction and review of the regulations and legislation for the use of AI. In the conclusions, we pull the strands together to provide a systemic and integrated approach to Responsible AI (RAI) – for individuals, organisations, society at large, and, in the extreme, for humanity.

Footnotes

1. An algorithm is a set of instructions to solve a problem or to achieve a task.

References

Aalho, J., (2021). I Wrote a Book with GPT-3 AI in 24 Hours — And Got It Published. Medium, 12 June, https://medium.com/swlh/i-wrote-a-book-with-gpt-3-ai-in-24-hours- and-got-it-published-93cf3c96f120

Anderson, L., & Ostrom, A. L. (2015). Transformative Service Research – Advancing our knowledge about service and well-being. Journal of Service Research, 18(3): 243–249.

Anderson, L., Ostrom, A. L., Corus, C., Fisk, R. P., Gallan, A. S., Giraldo, M., Mende, M., Mulder, M., Rayburn, S. W., Rosenbaum, M. S., Shirahada, K., & Williams, J. D. (2013). Transformative Service Research: An agenda for the future. Journal of Business Research, 66(8): 1203–1210.

BBC (2020). Facial recognition to 'predict criminals' sparks row over AI bias. BBC News, 24 June 2020. https://www.bbc.co.uk/news/technology-53165286

BBC (2021). EU artificial intelligence rules will ban 'unacceptable' use. BBC News, 22 April, https://www.bbc.co.uk/news/technology-56830779

Booth, R. (2019a). Benefits system automation could plunge claimants deeper into poverty. The Guardian. 14 Oct 2019. Available at https://www.theguardian.com/technology/2019/oct/14/fears-rise-in-benefits-system-automation-could-plunge-claimants-deeper-into-poverty.

Booth, R. (2019b). Computer says no: The people trapped in universal credit's 'black hole'. The Guardian, 14 Oct 2019. Available at https://www.theguardian.com/society/2019/oct/14/computer-says-no-the-people-trapped-in-universal-credits-black-hole.

Frischberg, H., (2022). Mother opens up about being 'virtually gang raped' in metaverse. New York Post, 1 February. https://nypost.com/2022/02/01/mom-opens-up-about-being-virtually-gang-raped-in-metaverse/

Gilman, M., (2020). AI algorithms intended to root out welfare fraud often end up punishing the poor instead. The Conversation, 14 February 2020. https://theconversation.com/ai-algorithms-intended-to-root-out-welfare-fraud-often-end-up-punishing-the-poor-instead-131625

Gregory, A., (2022). Bionic eye implant enables blind UK woman to detect visual signals. The Guardian, 21 January. https://www.theguardian.com/society/2022/jan/21/bionic-eye-implant-blind-uk-woman-detect-visual-signals

Hao (2019). AI is sending people to jail—and getting it wrong. MIT Technology Review, 21 January 2019. https://www.technologyreview.com/2019/01/21/137783/algorithms-criminal-justice-ai/

ICO (2018). What is automated individual decision-making and profiling. UK Information Commissioner's Office. 1-23. Available from https://ico.org.uk/for-organisations/guide-to-data-protection/guide-to-the-general-data-protection-regulation-gdpr/automated-decision-making-and-profiling/what-is-automated-individual-decision-making-and-profiling/

Knight, W., (2019). The Apple Card Didn't 'See' Gender—and That's the Problem. Wired, 19 November, https://www.wired.com/story/the-apple-card-didnt-see-genderand-thats-the-problem/

Koch (2019). Will Machines Ever Become Conscious? Scientific American, 1 December. https://www.scientificamerican.com/article/will-machines-ever-become-conscious/

Ledford, H., (2019). Millions of black people affected by racial bias in health-care algorithms. Nature, 26 October 2019. https://www.nature.com/articles/d41586-019-03228-6

Lycett M (2013) Editorial: 'Datafication': making sense of (big) data in a complex world. European Journal of Information Systems 22(4): 381-386.

McDonald, H., (2019). AI expert calls for end to UK use of 'racially biased' algorithms. The Guardian, 12 December, https://www.theguardian.com/technology/2019/dec/12/ai-end-uk-use-racially-biased-algorithms-noel-sharkey

Marjanovic, O., Cecez-Kecmanovic, D., and Vidgen, R., (2021). Algorithmic pollution: making the invisible visible. Journal of Information Technology, 36(4): 391–408.

O'Neil, C. (2016a). Weapons of Math Destruction: How Big Data Increases Inequality and Threatens Democracy. Penguin Random House. NY. USA.

O'Neil, C. (2016b). How algorithms rule our working lives. The Guardian. 1 Sept 2016). Available at https://www.theguardian.com/science/2016/sep/01/how-algorithms-rule-our-working-lives

Raghavan, M., Barocas, S., Kleinberg, J., & Levy, K., (2020). Mitigating Bias in Algorithmic Hiring: Evaluating Claims and Practices. In: ACM Conference on Fairness, Accountability, and Transparency (FAT*), 2020. https://papers.ssrn.com/sol3/papers.cfm?abstract_id=3408010

Savage, N., (2020). How AI is improving cancer diagnostics. Nature, 25 March

2020, https://www.nature.com/articles/d41586-020-00847-2

Telford, T., (2019). Apple Card algorithm sparks gender bias allegations against Goldman Sachs. The Washington Post, 11 November, https://www.washingtonpost.com/business/2019/11/11/apple-card-algorithm-sparks-gender-bias-allegations-against-goldman-sachs/

Turchin, A., (2019). Assessing the future plausibility of catastrophically dangerous AI. Futures, 107: 45-58.

University of Twente (n.d.). What can we learn from Latour? FutureLearn. https://www.futurelearn.com/info/courses/philosophy-of-technology/0/steps/26326.

Wakefield, J., (2022). DeepMind AI rivals average human competitive coder. BBC News, 2 February, https://www.bbc.co.uk/news/technology-60231058

Part 1

The AI terrain

Chapter 1
How AI works

1. Introduction

Artificial intelligence is ubiquitous in business and government. It permeates almost all aspects of our daily and personal lives. Many people recognise the influence and pervasive use of AI, although others are oblivious.

Consider a routine convenience task, like asking Alexa, Siri or Google Home to play Taylor Swift's new album, Fearless (Taylor's Version). Your chosen digital assistant must:

1. Understand that you are talking to it, rather than someone else in the room
2. Interpret what you are saying
3. Take action based on its interpretation.

All three of these steps require AI, broadly speaking.

In **Step 1**, the AI is looking for a specific command to (further) activate its listening. The AI interprets your audio waves, looking for a specific catchphrase, like "OK Google" or "Hey Siri"; this is AI intention detection. When the AI 'thinks' that it hears an intention detection phrase, it starts interpreting the rest of your request using two distinct aspects of AI:

- The AI uses natural language processing (NLP) to see if the words people speak contain the key activating phrase. This shows that AI devices are always listening, even when not activated, but we will get to that later.
- The AI uses if-then logic. If it hears "Hey Siri", then it starts listening to your entire request.

In **Step 2,** the AI comprehends your vocal request. So, the AI understands each word, converting the sound waves from your voice to text. Moreover, the AI must make sense of the entire sentence to extract its meaning. This creates a few critical differences between the sophistication required for the AI to complete Steps 1 and 2. Activating phrases like "Hey Siri" have a one-to-one mapping between the phrase and the corresponding action. This facilitates the use of if-then-logic. However, an entire command phrase can often be interpreted in many ways. Also, there are many different phrases I could use to make the same request:

- "Hey Siri, set my 7am alarm."
- "Hey Siri, create a 7am alarm."
- "Hey Siri, make an alarm for 7am."
- "Hey Siri, set an alarm for 7 in the morning."
- "Hey Siri, wake me up at 7 tomorrow."
- "Hey Siri, change my wake-up alarm to 7:30 am just for tomorrow."

AI's ability to recognise the human voice and nuances with language has improved tremendously over the last decade. Previously, I would have had to say "Hey Siri, play Taylor Swift's new album, Fearless (Taylor's Version)" in an over enunciated robotic voice to communicate my request to the digital assistant. Now, I can casually say "play Taylor Swift's latest album" or even "play T. Swift's newest album". Sadly, Siri doesn't yet recognise that Taylor Swift's nickname is Tay Tay, but, on a positive note, we now know of the French artist Tété - think French Jeff Buckley.

Step 3 uses if-then logic. Once the digital assistant knows our request to play a specific album – it follows a set of instructions to access the relevant music application and select the album we want to hear. A difference between this step and the first two is the role of certainty. In Step 2, the digital assistance uses NLP, which means that the AI cannot guarantee a 100% accurate inquiry interpretation. Instead, the AI's selected interpretation is a best guess, so the AI is uncertain. In contrast, Step 3 performs the assumed request perfectly since it follows a prespecified procedure, and there is no uncertainty.

Although the Taylor Swift example may seem trivial, think about all the ways we use digital assistance in our daily lives:

- To set alarms, timers, and reminders
- To make traditional calls, or call people through voice-over-IP apps like Facebook, FaceTime or WhatsApp
- To dictate text messages, e-mails, and notes
- To read text messages and e-mails
- To ask questions: What time is it? How many litres in a quart? How far away is London? What is the score of the Lakers game?

As digital assistants continue to advance, they will become more embedded in our lives. The more we use digital assistance, the less we think about the underlying AI driving the technology. So, even if we are fully aware that AI drives digital assistants, constant usage makes us lose sight of what is happening underneath the hood (well, in this case the screen). Many people are blissfully unaware that the technology powering this device is AI.

Taking technology for granted is not a new phenomenon. Think of photography. For thousands of years, the only way to capture an image of a moment in time was through drawings and paintings. Irrespective of the artist's talent, drawings and paintings have limits to their ability to mimic lifelike scenes. However, in the early 1800s, the technology for capturing images as photographs was invented. By 1900, Kodak had begun producing cameras for the masses, using the slogan 'You Press the Button, We Do the Rest'. The catchphrase captures the idea that anyone can use technology without understanding the underlying science and chemical processes. Over time, photography advanced from black and white to colour, from still to moving pictures, and from analogue to digital. A photo was worth a thousand words, with each photo being a deliberate choice. Now over a trillion photos are taken annually without much thought as to whether anyone will ever look at them, and definitely without thinking of the underlying technology that makes this incredible feat of science and engineering possible.

Figure 1.1: Kodak advertisement

The question is, does it matter? Does it matter that we use digital assistance and take photos without thinking of or necessarily understanding the underlying technology? Moreover, is AI really so different from previous technologies?

For many technologies and innovations, understanding the inner workings realistically doesn't matter. You do not need to understand how a plane works to fly from London to Hong Kong, just as you do not need to understand the chemical or electrical process for producing a photograph. However, for many emerging AI-driven technologies, it matters. It matters a lot.

Before reading why AI is different from most technologies, and why understanding AI can influence how our society evolves, it is helpful to grasp how it has developed, and, fundamentally, how it works. Appreciating the technology makes it easier to understand AI's potential for both improving and harming society.

2. Algorithms

AI, which is difficult to define because it has different meanings to different people, is built on algorithms. Simply put, algorithms are a sequence of steps that a machine follows to perform a task. Algorithms can either solve tasks exactly, or provide approximate solutions or heuristics. A fundamental programming problem is sorting a collection of numbers. For example, let's say you have the sequence of numbers 18, 4, 6, 11, 20, 17, 1, 8, 12, 3. We can look at this set of numbers and quickly sort it in ascending or descending order. However, a computer application to do this requires a set of instructions or algorithm.

Bubble sort

1. Compare each number in the set with the number that follows. If all numbers are in order, stop. If all numbers are not in order, move to Step 2.
2. Swap any pair of numbers not in the desired order. Go back to Step 1.

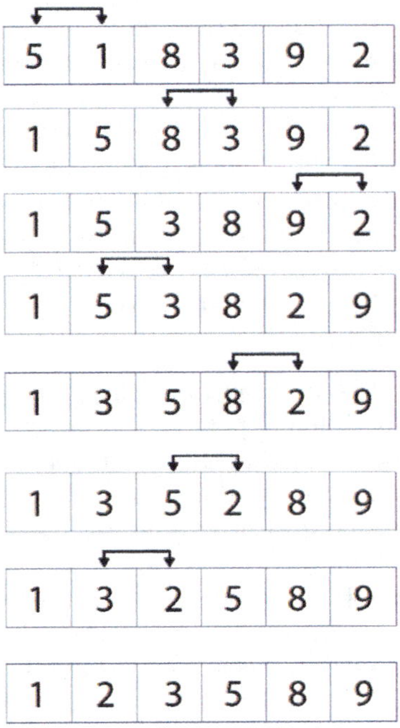

Figure 1.2: Bubble sort

The bubble sort continues to run through the sequence of numbers, swapping incorrectly ordered pairs until the sequence is correctly ordered. Observe that bubble sort steps will always order a sequence of numbers correctly. This is different from heuristic algorithms. Consider the problem of the travelling salesperson who must determine the shortest possible way to visit a set of cities so that each city is visited once, and they end their journey in their home city. Although there are methods for solving this problem exactly, they can be computationally complex, and less efficient than using a greedy heuristic algorithm. The greedy heuristic says that a travelling salesperson should travel to the closest non-visited city on the list and then travel home once every city has been visited. While this algorithm is not perfect, it provides a reasonable solution to the salesperson's choice. Although AI leverages algorithms, it has become a distinct phenomenon from its computer science foundations.

3. AI and machine learning

With roots dating back to the 1950s, AI began as a challenge for computer scientists to build a machine that could think. Typically, the approach was to hardcode lots of rules - or to use an algorithm. This is known as symbolic AI, and it worked effectively for well-defined problems. Symbolic AI takes rules plus data as input and provides answers as output (Figure 1.3). Think of the bubble sort (if numbers are incorrectly ordered pairs, then swap; if all numbers are ordered, then stop). The algorithm is the rule, and the sequence of numbers 18, 4, 6, 11, 20, 17, 1, 8, 12, 3 is the data. In this case, the answer is "1, 3, 4, 6, 8, 11, 12, 17, 18, 20".

AI built on rule-based logic is difficult to scale, particularly for complex problems with many potential answers. This holds for many problems that humans may find trivial, such as recognising images or speech, and understanding and engaging in argumentation. While symbolic AI, such as classical programming, cannot match the human ability to recognise objects, sounds, and texts, advances in machine learning have enabled AI to outperform humans in these types of tasks. An often-used benchmark for assessing the advancement of AI is evaluating how well it sees, i.e. its ability to perform image recognition. A significant milestone was reached in 2015, when AIs surpassed the human error rate of 5% in identifying objects in photos at the annual ImageNet Machine Vision competition. Beyond being a useful barometer on the advancement of AI, image recognition applications are widespread, with all major tech firms like Google, Apple, Microsoft, IBM, and Facebook developing algorithms for labelling photos. Another prominent benchmark is AI's ability to beat top players in checkers, chess, and Go.

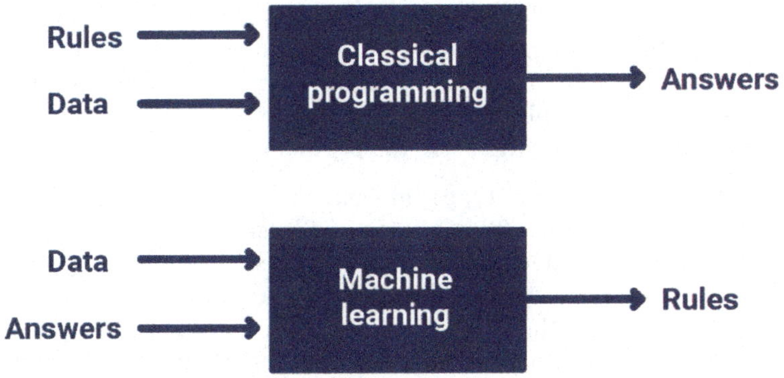

Figure 1.3: Machine learning: a new programming paradigm (Chollet, 2018, p. 5)

Machine learning works by taking data and answers as the inputs, with the output being rules (the bottom part of Figure 1.3). Thus, a machine learning algorithm is trained by seeing lots of examples in which it detects patterns. These data are appropriately called training data. Typically, the data observations within the training dataset can be broken down into two key components: the outcome and the characteristics. The outcome, also known as the dependent variable, the target, or the response, is the answer to that associated data observation. The characteristics, also known as the independent or explanatory variables, consist of all the other captured data describing the observation.

Let's say we are building an automated system that determines whether to approve loans. To train the machine learning algorithm, we need a dataset of past examples of people who have either paid back or defaulted on their approved loans. The machine learning algorithm then determines, based on the relevant characteristics provided, which are strong predictors of the default outcome variables. Similarly, if we are training an algorithm to detect cats from dogs, we need a training dataset with pictures of cats and dogs (the characteristic data) as well as the corresponding label of cat or dog (the outcome). With enough data points, machine learning can develop a set of rules to separate images of cats from dogs.

The key element of the training datasets in these examples is that the desired outcomes are known. Between the data or images and the answers - in this case cat or dog - machine learning algorithms create a set of rules. These rules are then used on new data, like in classical programming, to generate a best guess or prediction of the answers for the new data observations. This contrasts programming approaches like the bubble sort, where no data is required to build the set of rules that can always solve the problem.

There are many types of machine learning methods. For example, decision trees (also known as Classification and Regression Trees) create a collection of if-then rules that form a tree-like structure. This may seem like classical programming due to the if-then structure; however, the rules that govern the tree's if-then splits are determined based on training data rather than the developer's understanding of the problem. If you are curious about the inner workings of decision tree algorithms, see Box 1.1. While methods like decision trees are simple, understanding the underlying algorithms that create rules for other techniques is difficult. Moreover, even when the rules for the machine learning algorithm are determined, it is often challenging to understand how they produce answers given a set of input data. As a result, many deep learning algorithms, like neural networks, are considered complex black boxes.

Box 1.1: Decision Trees

To illustrate the mechanics of decision trees, we will consider the infamous Titanic dataset. Many aspiring data scientists first learn decision trees and other classification machine learning methods using this dataset. The Titanic dataset has several variables or data point characteristics for the passengers on board the Titanic, including their gender, age, fare class, ticket cost, port embarked, and the number of siblings on board, as well as the outcome of interest - whether the passenger survived. The objective of the decision tree is to build a model to predict whether a person, given their data characteristics, survived or perished.

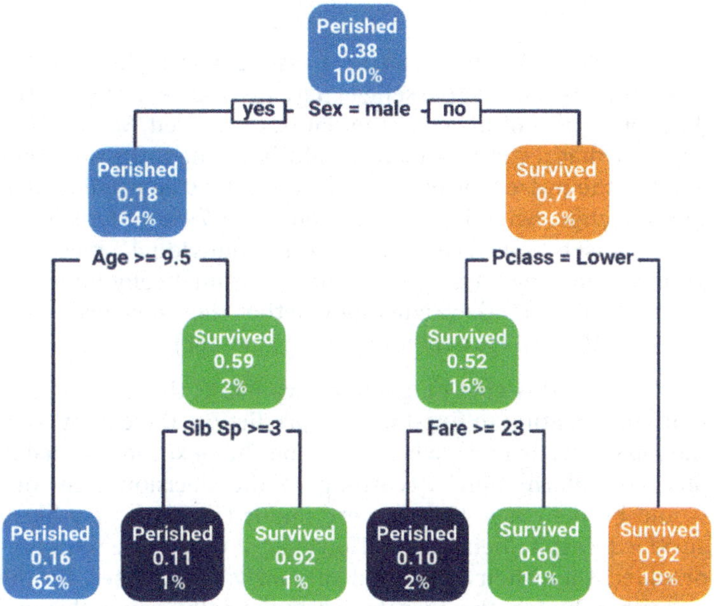

The best way to understand the logic of most decision tree algorithms is to think in terms of how information improves our best guesses. Let's say that our Titanic dataset has information on 1,000 passengers, of whom 38% survived, and 62% perished. Suppose we were to take a random passenger from the dataset, or someone who was on the Titanic but is not in the data set the model is built on, our best guess based on the raw survival rate (38%) from our 1,000 data points is that the randomly selected person did not survive the tragedy, since more people perished than survived.

A decision tree builds its model by selecting information from the characteristics that provide the greatest improvements in the odds of correctly predicting the outcome. Put differently, if I could know one additional piece of information to improve my likelihood of correctly predicting whether a random passenger survived, what would I want to know? Perhaps their fare class, maybe their age - but it turns out, based on the data, the most valuable piece of information is gender. So, the tree then adds gender as the first set of branches.

If the randomly selected passenger is male, then the tree predicts that the passenger perished, since, based on the data, only 18% of males in the dataset survived. So, our best guess is that a random male would have died. On the other hand, if the passenger was female, then the tree predicts that the passenger would have survived since 74% of females in the dataset survived. Thus, this individual piece of information - the passenger's gender - dramatically increases our odds of correctly predicting whether they survived (from 62% to 74% or 82% depending on the gender).

While this split on gender is valuable, the tree can add more information to fine-tune the prediction. If we know that the passenger is male, what would be the next most valuable piece of information? According to the decision tree, this would be their age. If they were under ten, then they likely survived despite being male. However, if they were ten years or older, then their likelihood of survival decreases. So the algorithm builds the tree by systematically going through each available piece of information in the data to determine which variable provides the greatest information gain in the prediction accuracy of the training dataset.

4. Deep Learning

Recently, the term deep learning has increased in popularity. Deep learning is a subset of machine learning, where deep refers to a model with multiple layers of representation. In line with Chollet (2018), machine learning can be viewed as a subset of the more general class of artificial intelligence, which includes symbolic AI. The traditional relationship between the three terms is shown in Figure 1.4.

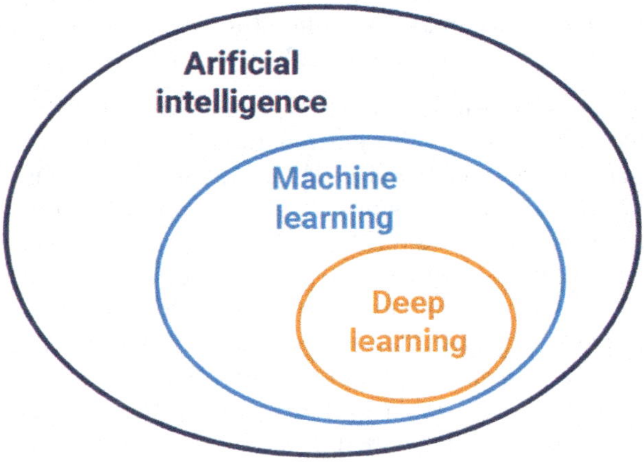

Figure 1.4: AI, machine learning, and deep learning (Chollet, 2018, p. 4)

In deep learning, data undergo multiple layers of transformation to give an increasingly significant representation. In a layered and incremental approach, inputs are turned into a final representation; for example, an image of a squiggly, handwritten digit can be turned into an output with a value between 0 and 9 using successive image transformations. In this case, deep refers to the many layers of input transformation needed to reach the answer. Deep learning only became a well-known technique in the early 2010s, yet it has achieved success in notoriously difficult application areas such as image classification (deep learning was how AI surpassed humans in the Annual ImageNet competition), digital assistants such as Google Now and Alexa, autonomous driving, and natural language processing (Chollet, 2018).

5. Defining artificial intelligence

Artificial intelligence is often a catchall for sci-fi-like technologies, including digital assistants, robots, and machine learning applications indistinguishable from magic. Many pundits worry about the growing harm caused by these technologies, although others think that discussions regarding the singularity, killer robots, and other aspects of AI that could result in the end of humanity are overblown without a chance of happening. Even when thinking about the use of

AI today, some see AI's current potential for improving organisational processes and decision-making, while others view it as nowhere near as good as advertised, and mainly useless beyond niche applications.

One reason for such divergent views is that artificial intelligence has so many different meanings and interpretations that people rarely agree on what qualifies as AI. The definitions and meaning of AI differ across people, organisations, government bodies, and research fields. Does AI differ from an intelligent agent, i.e. "any device that perceives its environment and takes actions that maximise its chance of successfully achieving its goals" (Poole et al., 1998)? Does AI require data, and does AI have to learn? Kaplan and Haenlein, in their article "Siri, Siri, in my Hand: Who's the Fairest in the Land?" believe so, defining AI as "a system's ability to correctly interpret external data, to learn from such data, and to use those learnings to achieve specific goals and tasks through flexible adaptation." Others define it based on the task. The Lords' Report on AI uses the definition that AI is technology "with the ability to perform tasks that would otherwise require human intelligence, such as visual perception, speech recognition, and language translation." Others, like the management economists Agrawal, Gans, and Goldfarb (2018) from the University of Toronto, define AI as any tool or technology that generates a prediction in their book, appropriately entitled *Prediction Machines: The Simple Economics of Artificial Intelligence*. This is consistent with Figure 1.4, where AI is a general set of algorithms that incorporate both traditional rule-based programming and advanced machine and deep learning.

All of these definitions are in the spirit of narrow rather than broad AI. Narrow AI systems perform specific tasks that require human intelligence, for example facial recognition, and may outperform humans in areas such as medical diagnoses. Broad AI refers to machines that can give the impression of thinking like human beings, and are ultimately indistinguishable from a human. The Chinese room example designed by Searle (1980) is a seminal thought experiment for differentiating between broad and narrow AI. The thought experiment involves an AI asking the following question in Chinese: does the AI understand or simulate an understanding of Chinese? If AI inherently understands Chinese the way a human can, then this is broad AI. If AI is merely simulating an understanding, then this is narrow AI. Thus, with narrow AI, when a machine correctly (or incorrectly) identifies an object in a photo such as a cat, it does not inherently understand that the picture is of a cat; instead, it is making a prediction based on previously seen training data that the object is a cat.

For our purposes, we use the straightforward definitions offered by Cassie Kozyrkov: "AI allows you to automate what you can't express" and "AI automates the ineffable" (Kozyrkov, 2019). Think about tasks such as identifying an object like a cat. Can you define a set of rules or equations that can take an image and determine what the image is about with a high probability of success? This is still consistent with the concepts of narrow AI, and will most certainly incorporate broader AI in the future, but offers an important distinction from rule-based approaches such as decision trees, and statistical methods where prediction is based on an equation such as linear regression.

Defining AI in this way has several advantages. The definition subtly highlights the learning elements of AI. If the task is ineffable, then it means a recipe cannot describe it. Instead, the AI has to figure out a recipe, which requires intelligence to learn. Also, we retain the emphasis on data. Remember, traditionally if-then algorithms can be built entirely without data. Statistical approaches can provide inferences with small data - tens to hundreds of observations. On the other hand, automating the ineffable requires data: lots and lots of data. Advances in AI and machine learning are often due to more and better data rather than technical advances in computer science, statistics, or mathematics.

To return to the example of image classification: author Janelle Shane has a great post on her blog AI Weirdness, entitled "Do neural nets dream of electric sheep?" on AI's ability to detect images. With only a few photos - hundreds to a few thousand - to classify items, you may end up with an image classifier that will label any pictures of green rolling hills as sheep. Why? Simply because with a small dataset, all images of sheep will likely be outside on green hills. Similarly, Janelle doctored an image of sheep standing in a tree as an experiment, and gave it to Microsoft's image classifier Azure. Azure provided the tag "a group of giraffes standing next to a tree", probably because the image database used to train the classifier had many giraffes standing next to or grazing on trees in the original dataset. However, with richer data - more images covering more scenarios: sheep being held by children, sheep being shorn indoors, sheep being transported between farms, children counting sheep, psychedelic sheep - the AI will be better able to detect the features of an image that is actually a sheep. With tens of hundreds of thousands of these images, fooling an AI into a false positive like detecting a sheep when it is just a green hill or a false negative like detecting a giraffe when it is a sheep in a tree will become increasingly difficult.

6. Chess vs. Go

With the continuous improvements in AI's state of the art capabilities, the goal posts of what many people constitute as being true AI are also constantly moving. The best way to see the evolving line of what we classify as AI is to consider the canonical examples of AI playing humans in popular board games. In the 1950s and '60s, a machine that could play checkers, even poorly, was a fantastic feat of 'intelligence'. Finally, in the 1990s, IBM's Deep Blue could not only play chess, but beat a champion, Garry Kasparov. More recently, a startup acquired by Google, DeepMind's AlphaGo, beat one of the world's best Go players, Lee Sedol, in a five-game series. The prestigious academic journal Science deemed this victory one of 2016's scientific breakthroughs.

Why was AlphaGo's achievement so significant? After all, a machine had already beaten one of the Greatest Of All Times (GOATs) of chess. To understand this, it is helpful to examine the differences between chess and Go, and the respective programs underlying machine learning approaches. Both systems use tree searches. Each move has a tree where each branch represents a different legal move of the opponent, and each of those branches will have a range of possible follow-up moves, and so on. Like our Titanic decision tree above, each branch that includes the possible moves that follow has an associated probability of winning. The algorithm then evaluates which move has the highest probability of winning, and makes that move.

Checkers is considered a solved game. It is possible to construct a search tree that can contain all possible moves in checkers, and it turns out that if two perfect competitors play checkers, then the game will always end in a draw. Chess is a substantially more complex game than checkers: it uses the same board as checkers, but has more pieces - 16 as opposed to 12 - with more complex moves. However, Go is substantially more complex than chess. Go has a larger board (19 x 19 squares), and more ways to place pieces on the board. The number of legal positions on a Go board is enormous: if X stones have been played, then there are 361 minus X possible moves. A crude estimate of the number of possible ways a game of Go can unfold is therefore $361! = 10^{764}$, which is astronomically larger than the same calculation for chess, which is 10^{120} possible chess moves, and the number of atoms in the known Universe. A rough estimate for atoms in the universe is 10^{78}, which is based on 10^{56} atoms in our sun times 10^{11} stars in our galaxy times 10^{11} galaxies in the known universe.). Thus, while trees in checkers can (mostly) contain all possible moves, it is impossible by brute force to express games like chess and Go as a giant tree structure. The standard of strategy required to excel at Go makes it an ideal challenge for AI.

One of the key elements underlying Deep Blue's success is that IBM leveraged Chess Grandmasters to help evaluate which branches were more likely to result in winning a game. Instructions from Grandmasters were hard-coded into the tree search algorithm, however the vast number of possible Go moves means that this approach is intractable. Moreover, feel and intuition are as important as strategy in Go, and even determining who is ahead in the middle of the game can be difficult, whereas it is often easy to detect who is ahead - and likely to win - halfway through a game of chess. Overall, Go is too complex to create comprehensive instructions for a strategy that could beat the world's top players. Unlike Deep Blue, AlphaGo was made without human intervention on what classifies good strategy. Instead, AlphaGo leverages a combination of neural networks and reinforcement learning to learn from millions of real and simulated games that it plays against variations of itself, which means AlphaGo was trained on human players and advanced AI-based players, allowing it to look beyond human thinking in the game. Based on actual and simulated games, AlphaGo can evaluate the strength of board positions following a proposed move, and optimise moves accordingly. Thus, compared to Deep Blue, AlphaGo better captures the notion of lots and lots of data (millions of simulated games), learning (it teaches itself strategy), and 'automating the ineffable' (too complex for a human to describe strategy).

A remarkable aspect of AlphaGo vs Lee Sedol was that AlphaGo won by making a move that no human ever would. Move 37 in the second of the games instantly became infamous, sparking headlines like "Move 37, or how AI can change the world" (Zarkadakis, 2016). The move made Lee take a 15-minute break. Commentators noted "that's a very surprising move", and "I thought it was a mistake." The move, later called beautiful by pundits, led AlphaGo to victory, beating Lee by playing in a way that no human had played in Go's 2,500-year history. The move became infamous because it extended human understanding of the game. Remarkably, there was another moment that was just as shocking in Game 4: Move 78. This move forced similar observations from commentators: "It took me by surprise. I'm sure that it would take most opponents by surprise" (Wood, 2016). Except, this move was made by Lee. The move - aka "God's touch" - forced AlphaGo into a disastrous response that led to Lee winning the game. AlphaGo never thought that a human would make Move 78, so its strategy did not have an adequate response. Together these moves show that between humans and machines, our understanding of games and larger systems has more significant potential than either humans or machines individually. Before retiring, AlphaGo was also able to beat the world's number one ranked Go player Ke Jie in 2017.

Although AlphaGo's accomplishments are nothing short of astounding, the achievements have more consequential implications. The search trees built to play grandmasters in checkers and chess are narrow applications, because the technology developed is only good at playing checkers and chess. However, DeepMind's approach for AlphaGo based on reinforcement learning - the AI's ability to masterfully explore new solutions and exploit knowledge from solutions stored in memory while playing itself - provides endless AI applications. Box 1.2 shows how state-of-the-art AI's capacity to learn has evolved over the last five years, from Go to games of multi-agent competition and cooperation.

Box 1.2: AI plays hide and seek

In 2019, Open AI created a game of hide and seek where two blue AI agents - the hiders – try to avoid being spotted by two red AI agents - the seekers. Initially, the agents play the game in an arena, which is characterised by a hiding area with two open doorways, and two boxes and a ramp outside the hiding area. The agents move around the arena, sense distances to other objects like walls, and move objects like boxes to block doorways. The red agents have a narrow field of vision (a frontal cone), which serves as their line of sight. If the blue hiders are caught in this line of sight, the seekers are rewarded. If the blue agents avoid the red agents throughout the round, then they get the reward.

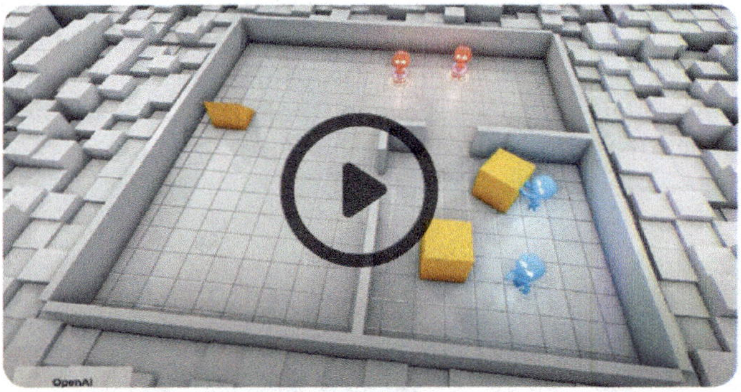

https://www.youtube.com/watch?v=Lu56xVlZ40M

At first, both groups of agents move around randomly. This happens for millions of rounds as the agents slowly learn what aspects of the game reward them. The seekers eventually learn that they can chase the blue agents to get them into their field of vision, winning many of the early rounds. However, over time, the random movements of the blue team inevitably allow the hiders to move the boxes into the doorways to block out the seekers. Interestingly, the hiders must each block one of the doorways, requiring cooperation to win the game. More interestingly, once an AI team discovers an effective strategy, it keeps using it to win. This forces the opposing teams to adapt by trying new strategies. Eventually, after 8.5 million rounds, the red seekers learn to use the ramp to infiltrate the hiders' enclave, but, after another 8.5 million rounds, the hiders prevent the seekers from using the ramp by moving it inside the enclave, and blocking the entryways.

OpenAI's game relies on reinforcement learning. Playing a game over and over again enables the development of strategy. However, DeepMind has recently created a different set of games, where the AI is tasked with open-ended learning, and the AI agents must figure out how to play the game in real time without benefit from prior knowledge of past game experiences, so the seeker gets constant rewards by keeping the hider in its field of vision. The hider, who is losing rewards, has no choice but to try and escape the seeker by creating distance, and eventually finding a hiding spot. The lack of required training means that the AI agents are generalists rather than narrow specialists as in OpenAI's hide and seek game. Consequently, DeepMinds AI agents can play many different games beyond hide and seek, including competitive games like capture the flag.

https://www.youtube.com/watch?v=uuzow7TEQ1s

7. What does AI look like?

AI can embody many different types of forms. For example, robots are now increasingly driven by AI rather than using sensors and collections of hard-coded if-then rules (think traditional assembly lines). AI robots themselves can have different forms. Some robots have innocent forms that do not resemble nature, like the Roomba, and other AI Robots exhibit anthropomorphism, which is the attribution of human traits, emotions, or intentions to non-human entities. Interestingly, anthropomorphism can make AI seem harmless, or even cute and cuddly. For example, Sony recently re-released their robotic dog Aibo, which is Japanese for companion. Unlike the late '90s versions of the social robot, the new version is powered by AI, which means that, over time, the robotic dog will learn to understand its name, seek praise, know that human smiles are good, and respond to petting, which helps foster a bond between the human owner and Aibo.

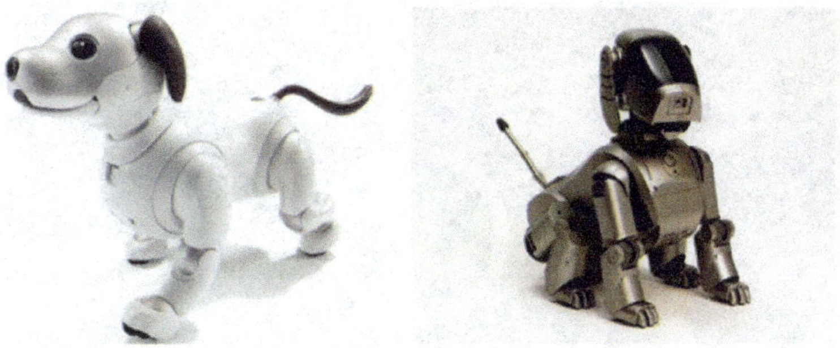

Figure 1.5: Robotic dogs

Compared to the late' 90s version, the change in features, intentional or not, mimics the exact change in traits of how wolves evolved into dogs. Through natural selection, features like round eyes and rounder faces, which humans find cute and adorable, helped wolves to be accepted in human communities. Now Sony has created a new version of their robotic dog that is inherently cute - and comforting - which will undoubtedly persuade consumers to warm to and adopt it.

Although anthropomorphism can make AI seem harmless, other AI-driven robots like Boston Dynamics' Spot AI can look terrifying. Spot uses machine vision and an autonomous navigation system to traverse the terrain. It also has a 'chicken head', so it can perform functions like opening doors. Although the CEO of Boston Dynamics has publicly stated that he is bothered by comments declaring their robots terrifying, the early videos of Spot and the humanoid Atlas undoubtedly created dystopian fears in many people. As a result, Boston Dynamics have taken a different approach: rather than having videos that imply their robots are creepily watching us, now the videos often feature the robots dancing. Most recently, Spot used its chicken head to mimic Mick Jagger's famous chicken-like dance moves.

https://www.youtube.com/watch?v=XnZH4izf_rI

AI does not need a physical robotic form and can be represented virtually - think of your virtual assistants and chatbots. Similar to AI robots, the degree of anthropomorphism can vary, depending on the designer and application. Voices and the appearance of the virtual AI's avatar can be humanised and gendered, or, alternatively, the avatar can be more abstract. For example, assistants like Siri are presented by waves of colours that align with sound waves, and Siri even says they imagine themselves as colourful sound waves (see Figure 1.6). Ultimately, virtual AIs are entirely software. While personifying software to be more human-like has advantages in increasing our trust, it can also have repercussions. For example, the study I'd Blush if I Could (West et al., 2019) from the United Nations Education, Science and Culture Organisation explores how obedient digital systems with female names and flirtatious female voices like Siri and Alexa reinforce sexist stereotypes. Even fictitious AI's exhibit these tendencies - think Samantha portrayed by Scarlett Johannsson in the movie Her. One of the directors of the report, Saniye Gulser Corat, stresses that organisations must:

1. Pay careful attention to how, when, and whether AI should be gendered
2. Create greater diversity within the field of AI.

Research by AI Now (West et al., 2019) shows that currently, 22% of jobs in AI are held by females. At Facebook, 15% of AI research staff are female, and at Google, only 10%. Only 12% of leading machine learning researchers are female. The study's authors note that diversity issues extend well beyond gender, and that the picture is even worse regarding race, where less than 4% of Google's, Facebook's, and Microsoft's workforce are black (West et al., 2019).

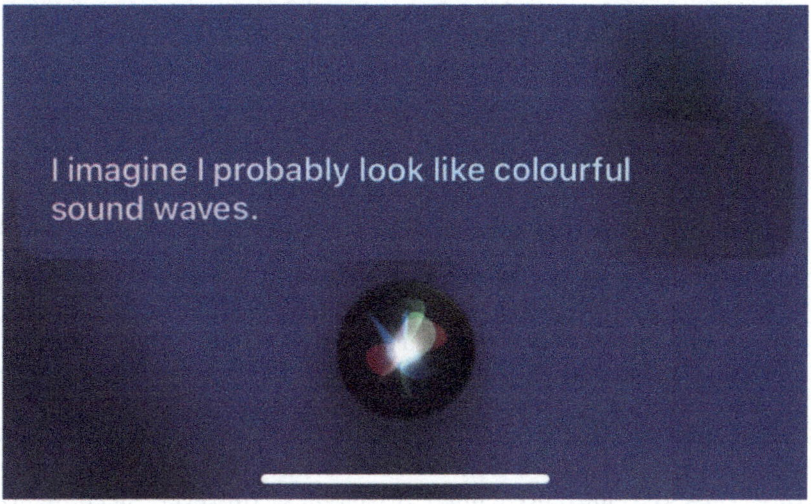

Figure 1.6: Siri's humorous response to the question, "What do you look like?"

The presence of AI in applications can be very apparent. When talking to a chatbot (unless it is effectively pretending to be human and using sneaky techniques like an intentional spelling error) or a digital assistant, you realise you are talking to a virtual agent, irrespective of whether you know the degree of AI being used. However, it can also be embedded in a software or hardware application - making it invisible to the user. Unlike virtual AI, embedded AI will not have gender, voice, or distinguishable personality, so search engines, spelling and grammar checking, e-mail filtering, and many other applications can function without users being aware that these tools rely on AI.

8. What is AI used for?

AI is the fastest growing technology sector globally, due to its tremendous potential in enhancing decision-making, efficiency, and automation. AI applications range from seemingly innocuous tasks related to personal productivity and social media to critical sectors like government, finance, health and education.

AI for greater and lesser convenience

One of the most visible and prominent uses of AI is as recommender agents to improve the customer experience in apps by helping consumers navigate impossibly large choice sets (Spotify has over 70 million songs) through recommendations. Notable examples include Spotify for music, Netflix for movies, Facebook and LinkedIn for connections, Amazon for products, and TikTok for social media videos. Indeed, as early as 2013, a McKinsey report found that 35% of products purchased on Amazon and 75% of content on Netflix were from algorithmic recommendations (Mackenzie, 2013). Early recommender agents were based on relatively unsophisticated clustering techniques known as collaborative filtering, where users are clustered into predefined archetypes. However, deep neural networks understand both the underlying characteristics of the products being recommended and the consumer better by incorporating detailed history and feedback, consisting of comments, and whether people view recommended movies the whole way through, making predictions on content likely to be more relevant. While books, music, and movie recommendation systems are commonplace, there are endless applications in a consumer-driven world. For example, apps like Amazon's Echo Look can take your picture using AI-enabled voice commands, and then use AI to find new items of clothing that complement what you are already wearing. Similarly, Stitch Fix uses Artificial Intelligence to recommend clothes and ship the recommended outfits to customers who can return unwanted items.

Amazon's future vision is shipping items you want based on their AI recommendations without your involvement outside of payment. While this would have seemed unrealistic even a few years ago, Amazon has already patented this anticipatory shipping method. Recently, packages being delivered by machines rather than humans seemed equally futuristic, however drone delivery is already a reality.

Initially used for niche and time-sensitive applications like Zipline's collaboration with the Rwanda government to deliver blood, Amazon and Google are using drones to deliver everyday products. Wing, a subsidiary of Google, has used Logan, a suburban city near Brisbane, as a pilot city, making 50,000 drone deliveries in eight months. In 2021, Logan was the drone capital of the world, with a delivery almost every 30 seconds during the first week of August.

Retail and grocery stores have been working continuously towards more seamless shopping experiences, with many stores transitioning towards self-service checkout systems. Now, AI can be used to semi-automate checkouts with apps like Scan&Go, which scans products using a mobile application, is equipped with smart product scales for goods priced on weight and connects to a user's account to handle payments digitally. However, in classic Amazon fashion, Amazon Go stores take the concept of seamless and efficient shopping further. Amazon Go uses AI to detect which products consumers select and put in their shopping bags, and then charges consumers as they leave the store, thus creating a fully automated shopping experience. Recent research by Gina Cui and Patrick van Esch from the Auckland University of Technology, and Shailendra Jain from the University of Washington, finds that AI-enabled checkouts lead to "more favourable store atmosphere evaluations and higher purchase intent", however, this can depend on the importance a consumer gives to innovativeness.

Like recommendations, many other digital applications are being improved through AI. One of the most fundamental aspects of the internet is the search engine. Google rose to prominence due to their page rank algorithm, which outperformed early competitors by providing users with more relevant web pages based on search strings. Naturally, search engines have evolved well beyond the original rule- based algorithms to benefit from advances in AI. One way that Google uses AI is to analyse the new queries that are approximately 15% of searches. Specifically, Google's RankBrain uses AI to determine the weight to place on the words and phrases in the search string, as not all words have a similar meaning in determining the correct interpretation of the user's query (Metz, 2016). New search engines are also using AI to provide alternatives to Google. For example, Qwant, launched in 2013, differs from search engines like Google by using AI to select content based on technical and editorial criteria such as text and image quality, links, and mentions on social networks rather than user-specific data, avoiding user data to provide search results.

Language translation is both a practical application and, like image recognition and progress in games, an essential indicator in the "capabilities of AI. Recall, translation underpins the Chinese room thought experiment. Like all early applications, digital translation services were initially based on if-then logic. Words were translated one at a time, which created glaring errors as word sequences and verb tenses vary tremendously across languages. Babel Fish, launched in 1997, was good enough to help students with their French homework and achieve passing grades, but not good enough to persuade teachers that the students write French fluently. Modern, more sophisticated natural language processing apps like DeepL and Google Translate use complete sentences as the basic unit for translation, which leads to more fluid language. As discussed by James Vincent in his interview with Google's head of translation Macduff Hughes, "Free, easy, and instantaneous translation is one of those perks of 21st century living that many of us take for granted" (Vincent, 2019).

While all of these examples represent virtual AI where the user is aware of the AI, there are also a growing number of embedded AI applications. During the COVID-19 pandemic, most people have used videoconferencing in both their work and personal life. Compared to previous generations of video conferencing technology, modern applications have hedonic and utilitarian enhancements and functionality driven by AI. Many people enjoy selecting professional or fun backgrounds in Microsoft Teams or Zoom, which rely on AI to separate them from the image background. Similarly, computer vision can be used to follow an individual's movement for more dynamic presentations. As noted by Adilin Beatrice, AI identifies speakers, enables voice-to-text transcriptions and, through Natural Language Processing, underlies improvements in sound quality by decreasing echoes, muffling background noise, and balancing acoustics.

AI the creator

AI is often perceived as only capable of accomplishing objective tasks. For example, a study by Noah Castelo, Maarten Bos, and Donald R. Lehmann called Task-Dependent Algorithm Aversion examined the role of subjectivity vs objectivity as a determining factor in whether people believed AI could accomplish tasks as well or better than a well-qualified human (Castelo et al., 2019). While AI was trusted for objective tasks like giving directions, analysing data, scheduling events, predicting an election, recommending a marketing strategy, buying stocks, and forecasting the weather, subjective tasks like writing new articles or composing a song placed substantially more trust in humans. AI is often seen as incapable of creativity since creativity is viewed as a fundamental aspect of being human. However, as the examples of AI playing Go, hide and seek, and generating marketing content demonstrate, this could not be farther from the truth.

There are many examples of creative AI, which do not address problems with creative solutions. Instead, creative AI is deep learning applied to creative problems and industries. AI can create custom music in seconds for a video, podcast, or game with the style, length, and structure wanted without infringing copyright or looking through library music. This, of course, is all without knowledge of composition or music theory. Leading examples of music generators are Amper and MuseNet. When given genre, artist, and lyrics as input, Jukebox creates a new music sample from scratch. AI can also produce news articles. Given a news headline, AIWriter searches the Web, and generates an article with original text, and an app like Wordsmith can also generate news articles. The Associated Press was an early adopter of augmented journalism, and initially piloting AI with more formulaic articles like sports and then financial earnings, it has greatly expanded its use of AI in news reporting.

Although a crucial element of news articles is their brevity and objectiveness, making AI excellent for creating content, the boundaries of AI's ability for more creative undertaking is continuously being pushed. AI cannot yet write a convincing original screenplay (Lea 2020), but many firms are trying. For example, ScriptBook analyses movie scripts and provides feedback to writers, and, in the process, identifies turkeys and winners. Beyond breaking down scripts, in the film industry AI offers platforms that automate tasks such as storyboarding, generating shot lists, creating schedules, and managing movie budgets. AI-based software can also automatically sync and group recorded clips, and may soon be able to create content independently. The research team at the Allen Institute for Artificial Intelligence has trained an AI model using over 25,000 videos of the Flintstones. With this training, the AI model could generate a fresh Flintstones video. Similarly, IBM's Watson created a six-minute trailer in just twenty-four hours for a horror movie called Morgan, using visuals and audio training data from a hundred different horror movies. Watson categorised features from each movie scene into moments, which were then analysed based on visual, audio and scene composition elements. Once the system understood the types of scenes found in a standard suspense/horror movie trailer, it was given the full-length film and recommended ten moments for the Morgan trailer. A total of six minutes of footage were pulled from the ninety-minute movie, resulting in a twenty-four-hour process from start to finish for a film trailer that typically takes weeks to complete (Kumba, 2019).

Figure 1.7: AI art

AI is being applied in almost all creative industries. Art has attracted a lot of attention from the AI community, with a new genre of AI Art coming into vogue. Google's Deep Dream is one of the best known tools for creating, having begun as an initiative to visualise the layers of a neural network of an image transformed into a process for creating psychedelic and abstract art. Like other applications such as Instapainting, Deep Dream combines photographic images with either other images or an artistic style such as futurism. More recently, AI's creativity has been pushed farther by combining machine vision and NLP.

In early 2021, OpenAI launched their application "DALL-E", which creates different images based on a string of text. Technologies like DALL-E have a wide variety of applications, and many large organisations. Fashion houses and retailers, including Amazon, Walmart, and the Gap, are also applying AI to create new clothing designs. Currently, AI can detect upcoming trends and identify popular styles to create original and inventive designs. Amazon research has developed machine learning to determine whether a look will be considered stylish, given a few labels associated with the clothing image (Knight 2017). However, the potential for novel innovation will expand considerably by augmenting human designers with AI like DALL-E.

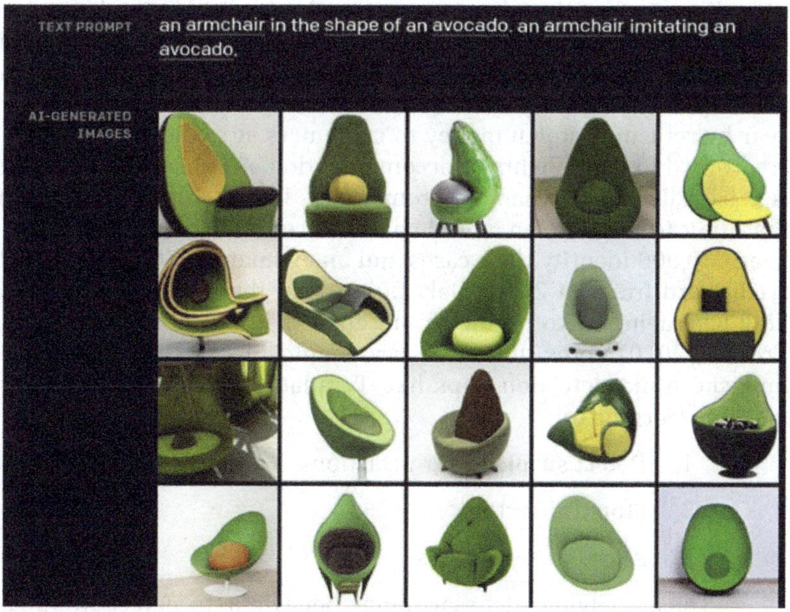

Figure 1.8: AI design

Boring AI

Although AI is expanding its capacity for creativity, most organisational applications fall into the category of Boring AI. Unlike the recommendation and chatbot agents that focus on consumer interactions, Boring AI typically focuses on improving the efficiency of internal organisational processes, the automation of which relieves humans of tedious and monotonous tasks, either introducing cost-saving redundancies or enabling human workers to take on higher value-adding tasks, which contribute substantially to the bottom line. Indeed, recent estimates by PwC found that automating AI can save businesses 30–40% of the hours typically spent on such processes. One of the most critical applications of AI is underwriting, and Schroer (2020) highlights applications like Underwrite.ai and Zest, which apply machine learning to distinguish good and bad credit applications for consumer and small business loan applications. Another widely used application redacts text within the legal industry.

Many organisational processes require making predictions regarding potential consumers or other external stakeholders. Payment fraud is one of the most popular types of scam in this industry, and, according to several reports, airlines and the travel industry suffers greatly from e-commerce fraud, losing billions each year by returning stolen money to customers after the use of a stolen credit card to book flights or accommodation. Another popular racket is a 'friendly' fraud, when a customer pays for a purchase then claims that the card was stolen, and demands a refund. The US experienced over 650,000 identity theft cases and an estimated 270,000 counts of credit card fraud in 2019 (Daly 2020), and the financial industry is now leveraging AI to predict fraud and take preventative measures. Trehan (2020) notes that banks are employing specialised AI-based financial fraud detection apps like Teradata and Datavisor that use machine learning to:

1. Detect suspicious transactions
2. Stop transactions
3. Alert the authorities.

Thus, applying AI to customer behaviour to detect fraud can reduce the average final cost per transaction and detect illegal transactions.

Effective forecasting of financial products like stocks and indices also benefits from analysing large, complex, and continuously evolving data, making financial prediction an essential application of AI and machine learning. For example, Kavout uses machine learning to process structured and unstructured data to rank stocks, using 200 factors and signals, including fundamental information, pricing and trading volumes, technical signals, and alternative data. Combining chatbot technologies with predictive trading also provides scalable retail-based financial solutions through robo-advisors. Robo-advisors and robo-investors previously used big data analytics to recommend portfolios for customers. Many of these applications used if-then logic based on predefined investment strategies, which Deloitte defines as Robo-advisor 3.0. With Robo-advisory 3.0, final decisions are still made by fund managers. According to Deloitte, many firms are now introducing the next generation of robo-advisors, Robo-advisor 4.0, which makes "direct investments via self-learning artificial intelligence (AI) investment algorithms. They shift between different asset classes based on changing market conditions and individual investment needs such as profit, risk appetite, and liquidity aspects."

Of course, predictive-based AI has a wide variety of applications. The Weather Channel pioneered mobile weather a decade ago by launching its flagship app for Android and iOS devices, and has consistently ranked #1 ever since – the most downloaded, most used, and most accurate, according to third-party validator ForecastWatch. Today, almost 50 million active users depend on The Weather Channel app for crucial weather information, and use it well over a billion times each month. The Weather Channel's newly released app for Android-based mobile devices reimagines how users get their weather information, with new features such as weather storytelling and artificial intelligence-powered custom alerts. Similarly, in healthcare the most common application of traditional machine learning is precision medicine – predicting what treatment protocols are likely to succeed on a patient, based on various patient attributes and the treatment context (Davenport and Kalakota, 2019; Daley, 2019). Buoy Health is an AI-based symptom and cure checker that uses algorithms to diagnose and treat illness. Here's how it works: a chatbot listens to a patient's symptoms and health concerns, then guides that patient to the correct care based on its diagnosis. Harvard Medical School is just one of the many hospitals and healthcare providers that uses Buoy's AI to help diagnose and treat patients more quickly.

A little more exciting are the applications of autonomous vehicles. Outside of the advancements by Tesla and other software-based vehicles for personal transportation, driverless vehicles have a range of organisational implications. Like drones, autonomous vehicles will improve logistical efficiency. Back in 2015, Uber bought driverless technology firm Otto. A year later, it completed the first autonomous truck delivery, carrying 50,000 tins of Budweiser beer over 120 miles from Fort Collins to Colorado Springs. DeepBlue, a

Chinese public transportation AI startup, is already operating its Smart Panda Bus in multiple cities across China, and selling to Greece and Thailand (Financial Times, 2019).

Public services

Although AI is widely used within profit-driven organisations, government agencies are also increasingly leveraging AI. Public service resources are often heavily constrained, so AI is being employed to help with allocations. Emergency services use AI for directing first responders with real-time traffic data, and AI can similarly help firefighting, analysing on-scene, real-time data like temperatures and gases measured through sensors to help combat fires more efficiently, and reduce exposure to harmful environments. then making intelligent recommendations specific to the firefighting team's roles, and suggesting using resources efficiently. WIFIRE's artificial intelligence software collates on-scene data such as wind, precipitation, vegetation, and smoke plumes, then visualises model projections for responders. Modelling also allows responders to prepare for fires by running simulations of possible scenarios, allowing firefighters to spot potential vulnerabilities. In California the WIFIRE system is used by the LAFD (Los Angeles Fire Department), Ventura County Fire Department and the Orange County Fire Authority. AI can now predict fires with 90% accuracy, and examine high-resolution satellite imagery to forecast the combustibility of vegetation surrounding a fire. This allows fire crews to allocate more fire crews to more flammable neighbourhoods, secure people's safety, and minimise property damage.

Similarly, police departments use big data and AI to predict temporal and spatial features of crime, supporting law enforcement to optimise resources and ensure an adequate police presence. For example, IBM's Blue CRUSH predictive analytics software analyses past and present data to identify crime hot spots through layered mapping techniques to increase police patrols there. PredPol uses location- based algorithms to link places, events and historical crime rates to predict where and when crimes are more likely to happen (for example, in certain weather conditions or at large sporting events).

However, predictions in policing and the justice system extend beyond facilitating resource allocations. Following an arrest, police can use risk assessment algorithms to determine whether someone is sufficiently high-risk to be jailed until their trial, which influences a judge's decisions regarding sentence severity. Facial and voice recognition technology also identifies criminals and underpins modern surveillance systems for large public areas and events like marathons and festivals. Clearview AI has built a controversial database containing three billion publicly available images from the internet (including from Facebook, YouTube, and Venmo), and uses machine learning to form a biometric template for each face and to match templates to online images. Over 600 global law enforcement agencies have now used Clearview to solve shoplifting, identity theft, credit card fraud, murder and child sexual exploitation cases, but although facial recognition has the potential to improve security, it has severe implications regarding biases and privacy, which are discussed in detail in the next chapter.

Perhaps even more worrying are the military applications of AI. Autonomous weapon systems can identify, select, and engage a target without meaningful human control. A system applies object and facial recognition to create decision-making algorithms that seek to target and kill without human controllers (i.e. an algorithm makes the decision). The technology has a fixed list of people it can target, and fires only if it is highly confident from video footage that it has correctly identified one of the targets. An example of this application may include a scenario where swarms of crewless helicopters, each packed with several kilograms of explosives, attacks airbases and essential aircraft. Brimstone is an air-launched ground attack missile developed by MBDA UK for Britain's Royal Air Force. Brimstone missiles use radar, laser and infrared sensors to form machine vision that identifies patterns in images, and helps weapons distinguish tanks, cars and buses, and hunt targets in a predesignated region without human oversight. They coordinate with other missiles to determine which are within a defined area, so as to strike in an organised order with a 'fire and forget' outlook. The 2017 Slaughterbots video gives a fictionalised account of the possibilities and dangers of autonomous weapons. While it may appear far-fetched, in 2021, Libya reportedly deployed a swarm of drones with facial recognition to hunt down and attack specific human targets (Bailey, 2021, Tekingundiz, 2021).

AI at work

The change in working practice during the pandemic is also resulting in more applications of AI, since relationships and collaboration in the workplace can indicate employee health and are essential to getting work done and sharing knowledge. As a result, businesses are now leveraging AI-powered tools to track and assess how team members cooperate. Humanyze, a startup, provides smart ID badges that track employees in the office throughout the day, reporting on how well they interact with each other and work together on projects. To ensure the integrity of employees working at home, major companies and government agencies are fitting webcams with technology to observe them. Facial recognition can naturally detect if someone is sitting at their desk, and if they are engaged or idle, or making unauthorised calls, to monitor infractions.

AI-enabled wearables are integrated with deep learning models, natural language processing, and voice and image recognition to monitor and analyse employee behaviour and emotions. For instance, Cogito, a Boston-based software company, built a platform for listening to customer service communications in order to identify stressed- out agents. Machine learning and speech recognition technology that picks up the tone and speed of communication to track employee stress levels is inbuilt. These tools, which take cues from employee mood, movements, and speech patterns, suggest when employees should take a break, and send alerts regarding unhealthy work patterns (Bercovici, 2017).

Although AI is being used extensively to monitor employees, perhaps one of its most widespread uses is hiring. AI can find candidates based on data from a company's internal database, public job boards, and social media platforms such as Facebook and LinkedIn, so it can undertake candidate rediscovery, analysing a database of applicants to rediscover which candidates may be a good fit for a new opening. Chatbots can then contact these previous applicants about new openings.

After the search, AI can be used in pre-hire assessments to evaluate candidates more efficiently. These assessments commonly take the form of game- and video-based evaluations. AI is used to assess a candidate's facial expressions and body language as part of a broader dataset to determine their suitability for a position. HireVue, with clients like Unilever and Goldman Sachs, uses AI-driven assessment that analyses video interviews, leveraging metrics such as word choice and facial movements to figure out an employability score, which is compared across applicants. Curious Thing uses conversational AI for simple phone interviews for high-volume recruitment. By pioneering new recruitment tools and creating voice applications powered by conversational AI, Curious Thing offers a scalable hiring solution to reduce human bias. Even after hires are made, AI can predict whether an employee is likely to leave an old job and take a new one, based on their promotions, movement between previous roles and industries and the predicted fit of a new position.

9. Is AI different?

AI is everywhere, but most people fail to understand how it works or even - due to invisible AI - if it is at work – and most people are not limited to end-users and consumers of AI, but also include its designers and deployers. In his article *The Dark Secret at the Heart of AI,* Will Knight gives an excellent example of Nvidia's experimental autonomous vehicle, which was developed entirely by watching humans drive. Despite it being a fantastic feat of science and engineering, the designers do not know how the car makes its decisions. This is starkly different from the designers of technologies like analogue and digital cameras, planes, and even the internet, making AI different from previous technologies. Although the car may mostly drive like a human, as we have seen with the example of Alpha Go, it can at any point do something seemingly illogical, ranging from stopping for minutes at a stop sign to driving into oncoming traffic.

Tendencies and preferences for automation mean that AI predictions often lead to automated decision-making. The volume and consequentiality of these decisions will only increase as organisations and governments continue to adopt and scale their AI solutions. While these solutions can undoubtedly create benefits for society, they also create the potential for serious harm, and, in the next chapter, we explore these benefits and harms extensively, emphasising why citizens need to understand when and how AI is being used.

References

Agrawal, A., Gans, J., & Goldfarb, A., 2018. Prediction machines: the simple economics of artificial intelligence. Harvard Business Press.

Bailey, R., 2021. Autonomous 'slaughterbot' drones reportedly attack Libyans using facial recognition tech. Reason. <https://reason.com/2021/06/01/autonomous-slaughterbot-drones-reportedly-attack-libyans-using- facial-recognition-tech/>

Bercovici, J., 2017. Why the secret to making customer service more human isn't human at all. Inc Magazine. <https://www.inc.com/magazine/201707/jeff-bercovici/cogito-ai-reads-nonverbal-cues.html>

Castelo, N., Bos, M.W. and Lehmann, D.R., 2019. Task-dependent algorithm aversion. Journal of Marketing Research, 56(5), pp.809-825.

Chollet, F., 2018. Deep Learning with R. Manning Publications. ISBN 9781617295546 Daley, S., 2022, 38 examples of AI in healthcare that will make you feel better about the future. Built In. <https://builtin.com/artificial-intelligence/artificial-intelligence-healthcare>

Davenport, T. and Kalakota, R., 2019. The potential for artificial intelligence in healthcare.Future healthcare journal, 6(2), p.94.

House of Lords, 2018. AI in the UK: ready, willing and able? Select Committee on Artificial Intelligence. Report of Session 2017–19, HL Paper 100. <https://publications.parliament.uk/pa/ld201719/ldselect/ldai/100/100.pdf>

Kaplan, A., and Haenlein, M., 2018. Siri, Siri in my Hand, who's the Fairest in the Land? On the Interpretations, Illustrations and Implications of Artificial Intelligence. Business Horizons, 62(1)

Knight, W., 2017. Amazon has developed an AI fashion designer. MIT Technology Review. <https://www.technologyreview.com/2017/08/24/149518/amazon-has-developed-an-ai-fashion-designer/>

Knight, W., 2017. The dark secret at the heart of AI. MIT Technology Review. <https://www.technologyreview.com/2017/04/11/5113/the-dark-secret- at-the-heart-of-ai/>

Kozyrkov, C., 2019. Artificial Intelligence: Do stupid things faster with more energy! Towards Data Science. <https://towardsdatascience.com/artificial-intelligence-do-stupid-things-faster-with-more-energy-379aa6bac220>

Kumba, S. 2019, AI in movies, entertainment, and visual media – 5 current use – cases. Emerj. <https://emerj.com/ai-sector-overviews/ai-in-movies-entertainment-visual-media/>.

Lea, R., 2020, If a novel was good, would you care if it was created by artificial intelligence? The Guardian. <https://www.theguardian.com/commentisfree/2020/jan/27/artificial-intelligence-computer-novels-fiction-write-books>

Mackenzie, I., Meyer, C., and Noble, S. 2013, How retailers can keep up with consumers. McKinsey. <https://www.mckinsey.com/industries/retail/our-insights/how-retailers-can-keep-up-with-consumers>.

Metz, C., 2016, AI is transforming Google search. The rest of the web is next. Wired. <https://www.wired.com/2016/02/ai-is-changing-the-technology-behind-google-searches/>.

Poole, D., Mackworth, A., and Goebel, R., 1998. Computational Intelligence: A Logical Approach. New York: Oxford University Press. ISBN 0-19-510270-3.

Schroer, A., 2022, AI and the bottom line: 20 examples of artificial intelligence in finance. Built In. <https://builtin.com/artificial-intelligence/ai-finance-banking-applications-companies>

Searle, J.R., 1980. Minds, brains, and programs. Behavioral and brain sciences, 3(3), pp.417-424.

Tekingunduz, A., 2021. A series of autonomous drones gives Turkey a military edge. TRT World. <https://www.trtworld.com/magazine/cutting-edge-akinci-combat-drone-joins-turkey-s-defence-offerings-49551>

Vincent, J. 2019. Google's head of translation on fighting bias in language and why AI loves religious texts. The Verge. <https://www.theverge.com/2019/1/30/18195909/google-translate-ai-machine-learning-bias-religion-macduff-hughes-interview>

West, M., Kraut, R. and Ei Chew, H., 2019. I'd blush if I could: closing gender divides in digital skills through education. UNESCO.

West, S.M., Whittaker, M. and Crawford, K., 2019. Discriminating systems: Gender, Race, and Power in AI. AI Now.

Wood, G., 2016. In two moves, AlphaGo and Lee Sedol redefined the future. Wired. <https://www.wired.com/2016/03/two-moves-alphago-lee-sedol-redefined-future/>

Zarkadakis, G., 2016, Move 37, or how AI can change the world, Huffington Post. <https://www.huffpost.com/entry/move-37-or-how-ai-can-change-the-world_b_58399703e4b0a79f7433b675>

Chapter 2
AI benefits and harms

1. Introduction

AI's potential benefits to individuals, organisations and governments are driving its development and adoption. Thus, its potential is leading it to touch almost every aspect of our lives. However, the potential for societal benefits differs from a society realising benefits. This raises several questions:

- On balance, does AI benefit or create harm for our society?
- What exactly are AI benefits, and who benefits most from AI?
- What are the harms of AI, and who in our society is at greater risk of experiencing AI harm?

Fortunately, AI has undoubted benefits across many industries, including medicine, agriculture, and transportation. As the UK Information Commissioner says, "Profiling and automated decision-making can be beneficial for organisations, and benefit individuals in many sectors, including healthcare, education, financial services, and marketing. They can lead to quicker and more consistent decisions, particularly in cases where an enormous volume of data needs to be analysed and decisions made very quickly" (ICO, 2018, p.7). However, despite that, there is growing evidence of potential for harm from AI, as biased and inaccurate algorithms routinely make decisions on job applicants (Raghavan and Barocas, 2019), healthcare (Ledford, 2019), social services (Gilman, 2020), parole and criminal justice (Hao, 2019), policing (BBC, 2020), and access to credit and insurance (Telford, 2019).

2. AI touchpoints

To analyse the impact of AI on individuals and society, we consider a model that includes AI subjects, developers, and deployers. (Figure 2.1). AI developers build AI solutions that AI deployers can acquire and use in their business processes, and in many cases, the developer and deployer are the same organisation.

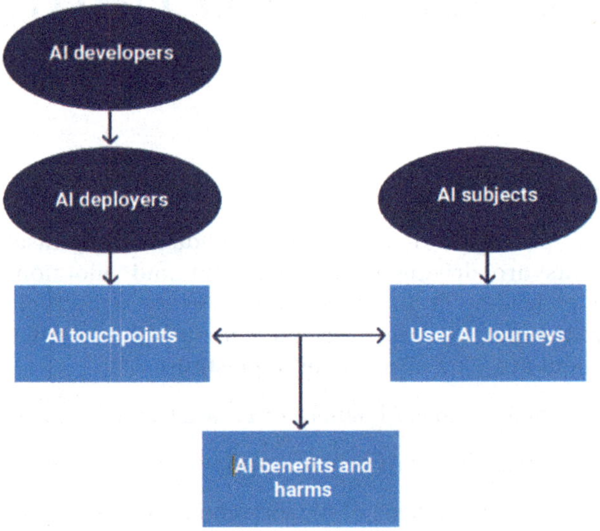

Figure 2.1: The AI touchpoint model

AI deployers provide touchpoints by using AI technologies in their business processes. Through their use, an AI subject (described and represented by a persona) encounters AI touchpoints (decision points). Thus, the intersection of a user journey and a touchpoint is a concrete instantiation of AI in use. Journey mapping is another technique from design thinking (e.g. Brown, 2009) that sketches the dimensions of an experience over time. Journey mapping highlights aspects of a user journey that either add value or are problematic. User journeys are typically created from the perspective of an individual or group.

3. Why organisations are turning to AI

Biases

Human judgment and decision-making are influenced by cognitive biases, and often overrely on decision heuristics, which are simple rules of thumb that are often imperfect yet adequate, such as the greedy algorithm for solving the complex travelling salesperson problem. Psychologist Daniel Kahneman, who won the Nobel Memorial Prize in Economic Science for his work on judgment and decision-making under uncertainty, details his research in a fantastic book called Thinking, Fast and Slow, which discusses how human judgment and decision-making are controlled by two cognitive systems, one fast (system one) and the other slow (system two). Slow system two is characterised by deep, deliberate thought (reflection, problem-solving), whereas fast system one is characterised by intuition. While the fast brain is essential for survival skills like recognising when a car is speeding towards you, triggering your body to move out of the way quickly, it is not as important in solving complex problems.

Many biases in decision-making occur because we resist engaging our slow, methodological thinking system. Consider the multiplication problem 271 x 63. Now, try and solve this simple multiplication problem without a pen, paper or calculator. Even the idea of solving a relatively simple multiplication problem creates a weird sensation, almost a dull pain, in your head. This is the cost of engaging your slow system. Engaging your slow brain involves overcoming inertia. In contrast, the fast brain sees the correct answer and goes for it. Probably the best example of the fast brain in action is "A bat and a ball cost $1.10 in total. The bat costs $1.00 more than the ball. How much does the ball cost?" Even though you are probably aware that this is a trick question, or perhaps you have seen the problem before and know the answer is five cents, it is almost impossible to read the question and not see it as ten cents. Even when people often arrive at the answer of 10 cents, rarely do people bother to engage their slow brain to do the simple math (which can quickly confirm that $0.10 + $1.10 equals $1.20 and not the desired total of

$1.10).

We have to engage our slow brain to solve problems like 271 x 63, where no immediate answer comes to mind. However, for most questions we face, given our reluctance to engage our slow brain, we often rely on our fast brain, which will simply provide the most available answer (10 cents). When the information is not readily available to solve a problem, or the problem is complicated, system one will often substitute a straightforward problem to address than the actual more complex problem, and even when you intend to solve the target problem, you substitute a related but more straightforward heuristic question to answer instead. For example, a question like "how popular will the president be six months from now?" is difficult to answer as there is little science for forecasting human sentiment six months into the future. Answering the question "how popular is the president right now?" instead is a reasonable heuristic, but still does not address the original problem. With difficult target questions, you will often notice that your answer is based on a substituted question, because intuitive answers come to mind quickly. So, people express many judgments, opinions, and decisions based on intuition, even when we think we are being deliberate, often addressing the wrong question.

Organisations and governments do not want to rely on heuristic intuition for decision-making, consequently many are becoming data-driven, using AI to make decisions. Unlike humans, AI addresses the problem as instructed by the data scientist or programmers. The AI does not think I can't solve this problem, so I will solve a more manageable problem and hope for the best. Moreover, creating AI means that the exact problem being solved has to be articulated so that a machine can solve it. This ensures that the organisation solves the desired problem, which is to forecast six months hence rather than generating a forecast for today or tomorrow.

Noise

AI offers several other advantages compared to humans. For example, Kahneman's more recent book, *Noise: A Flaw in Human Judgment,* explores the human propensity to introduce randomness into judgments and decisions. For example, compose a list of fifty to a hundred of your favorite albums or songs. Then rank your favorite ten or twenty albums or, if that is too difficult, try just ranking your favorite twenty songs. Now, save that and, in two days, try the exercise again without looking at your previous list. We would wager that the list would be different, even though your musical taste is unlikely to have evolved significantly in those forty-eight hours. The reason for this change is noise. Both noise and bias lead to decision errors. However, noise is different from cognitive bias. Cognitive biases result in the same error being made repeatedly; it is a systematic error. Noise is almost the opposite, creating variability without good reason.

While ranking songs and albums is harmless, noise may have a substantial impact on people's lives. Medical, business, and public decisions are all subjected to loud noise. As Kahneman notes, sentencing in judicial systems should reflect the crime, and not the judge presiding over the case. Similarly, a radiologist analysing a series of x-rays should always arrive at the same conclusions. Unfortunately, as these tasks are relegated to human judgment, noise is almost inevitable, and while it can change an individual's decisions, it can also explain variance in decision-making. This may be beneficial, as in crowdsourcing forecasts for future product success, where a range of opinions are expected and sought. However, for many decisions, such as judicial sentencing, insurance premiums, welfare entitlements, credit decisions, and medical diagnoses, two different judges (i.e. people using judgment to make a decision) should arrive at the same conclusion given the same set of information. Thus, another crucial benefit of employing AI is not suffering from unwanted noise: given the same input information, AI can always arrive at the same judgment, prediction, or decision. Thus, AI makes repeatable decisions without cognitive bias, although we do note that AI does not have to always arrive at the same decision, since it can be programmed to be exploratory by introducing noise into the decision-making processes, allowing the AI to learn by seeing if it can achieve its objective better by trying a slightly different strategy.

Finally, humans are bad at solving complex problems, and problems characterised by uncertainty. Consider the following problem, also from *Thinking, Fast and Slow:* a cab was involved in a hit-and-run accident at night. Two cab companies, the Green and the Blue, operate in the city. You are given the following data:

- 85% of the cabs in the city are Green, 15% are Blue.
- A witness identified the cab as Blue. The court tested the reliability of the witness under the circumstances that existed on the night of the accident and concluded that the witness

correctly identified each one of the two colors 80% of the time and failed 20% of the time.

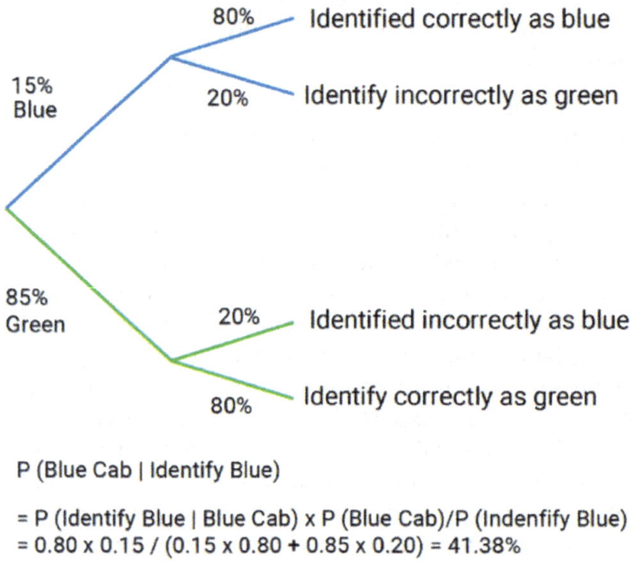

Figure 2.2: Blue cab Green cab problem (www2.math.upenn.edu/~kazdan/220F12/notes/Bayes/cabs.pdf)

What is the probability that the cab involved in the accident was Blue rather than Green? Try and figure it out - or even come up with an approximate answer - before reading on. According to Kahneman, most people pick 80%. They focus on the accessible information that the person is correct 80% of the time, and ignore the base rate that most cabs in the city are green. The answer is 41%, which can be calculated using a standard probability calculation called Bayes Rule. The cab problem is a simple statistical problem with only two probabilities, yet it still stumps decision-makers. Unfortunately, humans are not intuitive statisticians due to reliance on system one rather than activating system two. Fortunately, AI does not suffer from these issues. AI is extremely good at handling complexity, and does not calculate probabilities incorrectly since it uses principles like Bayes Rule rather than intuition. Our predictions are also limited to prominent predictors that fit a preconceived narrative. AI is better equipped to incorporate potentially overlooked factors, and does not care about finding evidence or factors supporting a preconceived narrative.

The combination of objective, repeatable, and accurate decision- making means that AI employed by organisations and governments has a substantial impact on our society. For example, better organisational decisions will result in better economic outcomes. The judicial system could become fairer. Enhanced predictions can better detect fraud and criminal money laundering. Predictions of natural disasters can also help with preventative and reactive measures, and enable early detection of health issues, thus saving lives. There are also potential auxiliary benefits like reducing the need for human action through the automation of boring work. AI-augmented workflows can result in more meaningful and enjoyable work for humans, and also liberate us from the 9 to 5 work paradigm. With less work, we should be able to reduce commuting. AI in platforms like Zoom, which have improved video communication, enables more people to work from home. Moreover, algorithms are faster than humans, which increases the speed of decision-making, and they, unlike humans, can undertake decision- making tasks at scale. Thus, there are many potential benefits to the wide-scale use of AI.

4. Why does AI go wrong?

AI objectives

Organisations and decision-makers now defer to AI to make many crucial decisions in their consumer, workforce, and business operations. While we have argued that AI is unaffected by certain weaknesses common in human decision-making, in reality it provides an illusion of objectivity. It is marketed as a system creating unbiased decisions since it is grounded in data rather than human intuition. However, AI is, as Ellen Broad argues, made by humans, and humans are heavily involved in all aspects of data collection, and AI development and deployment, which means that our biases seep readily into an AI system.

For an AI to achieve an objective, a human must specify the objective. Societal, corporate and government objectives are often conflicting. An obvious example is social media sites like Facebook.

Facebook's objective for their newsfeed is to maximise profits, which is at complete odds with societal interests. Even governments must make a tradeoff between people and profits. Fines and parking violations can be carefully set to balance a sufficient discouragement of infringements, but still generate revenue from price-insensitive citizens. Similarly, governments have an incentive to collect the debt from all citizens to recoup money owed, although this may have serious consequences, particularly for vulnerable populations. Organisations leveraging AI are often driven by technologists' ideologies, seeking technological rather than holistic solutions. Consequently, when creating AI systems, there is often a pursuit of accuracy, i.e., how well they classify categories or predict outcomes, with little thought to the social consequences, or even if high accuracy is the primary goal of the system. Moreover, fixations on predicting categories - whether a consumer is likely to default on a debt - can reduce the nuances of a situation due to personal circumstances. Subjectively quantifying and categorising issues and characteristics is necessary, and while categorising whether a person is a credit risk, or a post on social media is bullying may be obvious, it is often open to interpretation and contextual factors. Thus, we increasingly rely on objective algorithms to solve subjective problems.

When goals are hard-wired into algorithms, they may become the yardstick. For example, HR departments often receive many applications for job advertisements. Employing AI-driven recruitment systems, the AI scans the resumés, rejecting 75 percent of job applicants before the applications reach any HR human (Kohler, 2018). Given the number of organisations using AI resumé screening systems (including 95 percent of Fortune 500 companies), savvy applicants tailor their resumé to avoid being rejected by the AI systems with many aspects of gaming AI, focusing on peripheral design issues and formatting CVs (Kohler, 2018). There are dozens of AI applications like Rezi that build resumés to beat organisational AIs. Thus, getting hired is evolving into a game between AI writing resumés and AI screening applications. Objective decisions like the best candidate are also inherently subjective.

AI playing AI also manifests in other domains, like pricing. There was an interesting case on Amazon where a developmental biology book about flies was priced at over $23 million (Solon, 2011). There were two copies, owned by competitors using algorithmic pricing, and the retailer's algorithms kept pushing up the price, reacting to changes in the pricing. While these algorithms were based on if-then rules, pricing algorithms is evolving to leverage machine learning, and there are growing concerns that price-setting AIs programmed to maximise prices may engage in anticompetitive behavior. Simulated experiments by Emilio Calvano, Giacomo Calzolari, Vincenzo Denicolò, and Sergio Pastorell, researchers from the University of Bologna, demonstrate in a recent study called Artificial intelligence, algorithmic pricing, and collusion, that through reinforcement learning, AI pricing bots will adopt collusive strategies to maintain supra-competitive prices without explicit communication with other bots or being explicitly programmed to adopt anticompetitive tactics (Calvano et al., 2020). In these scenarios, AIs' profit-maximising objectives result in outcomes beyond the legal threshold tolerated by our society.

Biased Data

AI cannot achieve even well-intended objectives without data. Theoretically, unbiased data will lead to unbiased decisions. However, in our inherently biased society, achieving unbiased data makes this objective next to impossible for many applications. Accordingly, biased data to support the decision-making process will lead to biased outcomes. We saw earlier that AI can classify animals on rolling green hills as sheep due to a lack of diversity in training data. Again, this is a harmless example of AI decision-making based on limited training data, since sheep are not harmed from misclassification. However, it does show that the diversity of datasets is critical for accuracy.

Many of the high-profile examples discussed in the popular press when AI goes wrong are related to biased training datasets. For example, the role of facial recognition in police surveillance systems is a hotly contested subject. There are humorous examples of AI getting it wrong too - for example, a British motorist was fined £90 for a traffic infringement over 120 km away from his home because an AI-integrated CCTV system mistook someone's t-shirt featuring the word "KNITTER" for his registration plate, "KN19TER". This mistake was quickly rectified when the motorist was shown photographic evidence of his infraction (Grierson, 2021), however in many cases misclassification from biased data has serious consequences.

Research by Timnit Gebru, an advocate for diversity in technology, and co-founder of initiatives like Black in AI, and her colleague Joy Buolamwini from the MIT Media Labs, examined several commercial facial recognition accuracy rates classifiers. They found that the systems were incredibly accurate, with a less than 1% error rate, for light-skinned males. In contrast, females and people with darker skin had error rates that ranged from 20-35% (Buolamwini and Gebru, 2018). A direct consequence of inaccurate machine vision can range from mistaken arrests, as in the case of Robert Williams, to perpetuating systematic racism.

The training data for these programs are based on historical incarceration, which has systematically exhibited tremendous racism, where Black Americans are more likely than white Americans to be arrested, convicted (at a rate of 6:1), and experience lengthier prison sentences (The Sentencing Project, 2018). A report by ProPublica examined the software COMPAS used in actual courts statistically to predict the risk of defendants, which is then used as an input to judges' decision-making. The authors found that "black defendants were 77% more likely to be pegged as at higher risk of committing a future violent crime, and 45% more likely to be predicted to commit a future crime of any kind" after controlling for criminal history and recidivism, age and gender (Angwin et al., 2016). As a result, risk assessment scores and AI that uses historical data for predictive policing (systems that direct police departments' resource allocation decisions), which were meant to make objective decisions without bias, are further entrenching racism into police and justice systems.

Even though many police departments are aware of the discrimination embedded in their dirty data, there are seldom attempts to use any data processing techniques to achieve more equitable training data. For example, Kate Crawford and colleagues at the AI Now institute analysed thirteen jurisdictions that have used or developed predictive policing tools while under government investigations due to their extensive histories of unlawful police practices. Of the thirteen jurisdictions investigated, which include major cities like New Orleans and Chicago, nine trained their systems using dirty data. While the United States has been in the spotlight regarding their use of AI in policing, a report from the United Nations University, academic and research arm of the United Nations, notes that "police departments in countries such as China, Denmark, Germany, India, the Netherlands, and the United Kingdom, and Australia are reported to have tested or deployed predictive policing tools."

Hiring algorithms are also frequently discussed to highlight the implications of biased data. While we have illustrated how AI objectives can make hiring decisions, resumé screening also suffers from being fed historical data exhibiting gender bias. Famously, Amazon had to scrap its resumé screening system because it taught itself that males were preferable candidates. The AI's conclusion was natural, since most prominent tech companies predominantly feature males in their technical roles. According to Reuters, Big Tech firms like Apple, Facebook, Google, and Microsoft employ approximately four males to every female. Thus, many historically preferred candidates were male. Although firms may strive for neutrality and equality, there are too many patterns in the data that enable the AI to identify gender (or, in the case of predictive policing, race). For example, Amazon's system apparently penalised resumés where the college was female-only and resumés with the word women (e.g. women's chess club). Other studies, like *Ethical Implications of AI Bias as a Result of Workforce Gender Imbalance*, conducted by a team of computer scientists and policy researchers from the University of Melbourne, found that AI rewarded years of continuous service, which favours men, due to women being more likely to take long periods off work for caring responsibilities (Cheong et al., 2020).

Taxonomy of AI harms

We now see how AI, despite its benefits, and even where developers and deployers have the best intentions, can lead to harm due to the combination of biased data with overly objective black box decision-making occurring at scale. AI outcomes like recommendations are often customised to individuals. Thus an individual using AI - what we call an AI subject - will have different experiences - what we call user journeys - through their interaction with AI. This may result in people obtaining the desired benefits, but can also lead to various degrees of harm. While the harm caused by AI providing harsher risk assessment scores to African Americans relative to European Americans is straightforward, the full range of potential harms caused by AI is far from clear. AI is often created for narrow and specific purposes, and consequently the specific benefits and harms that it can create are wide-ranging and difficult to understand concretely and fully. These issues are further exacerbated by how the touchpoints, typically hidden within a deploying organisation, materialise.

An effective tool for helping individuals and organisations

understand the causes and consequences of AI harms would be through an AI taxonomy of harms, a classification system of how AI can negatively impact our lives. There are currently no comprehensive taxonomies of AI impacts, which could be critical in allowing individuals and organisations to understand, explain, and predict the potential harms of adopting AI solutions. To develop a taxonomy of AI impacts, we conducted a series of five workshops with eighteen experts, where we asked each practitioner and academic specialist to list as many harms and benefits, and issues driving these harms and benefits, as possible on virtual sticky notes, using the platform Miro. After that, the group discussed how to categorise their sticky notes, which quickly pointed out the benefits of AI, but the ideas and concepts of AI impacts were overwhelmingly negative, suggesting that AI causes substantial harm as it is currently deployed.

We leveraged the experts' insights to create a taxonomy of AI harms, and as these concepts can be abstract - for example, even the word harms has many definitions - we decided to map the various harms to understand how AI determines our well-being. One particular primary argument for the wide-scale deployment and adoption of AI is that it will improve quality of life, but while AI may improve the quality of life for some individuals, it can also harm the quality of life of others, so that a fitting lens to analyse and categorise AI harms is through this perspective. The dimensions represent complementary aspects of quality of life related to economic and social development measures, and citizens' abilities to pursue their well-being. Quality of life is an appropriate way to classify harms from AI since "factors potentially affecting our quality of life range from job and health status to social relationships, security and governance," all areas that are extensively discussed regarding AI's impact.

Table 2.1 outlines our Taxonomy of AI harms, with definitions and examples, and we then describe each type of harm in detail:

AI Harm Category	AI Harms	Definition	Use Case Example
Well-being harms	Physical harms	How AI negatively impacts physical health and well-being	AI misclassifying diagnosis or treatments
	Mental and emotional harms	How AI negatively impacts mental health and emotional well-being	AI increasing insecurity and emotional distress from employment monitoring
	Leisure harms	How AI negatively impacts people's time outside productive activities	AI damaging the social cohesion of society
Economic harms	Financial harms	How AI negatively impacts people's financial circumstances	AI automatically, unfairly, and inaccurately recovering debt from welfare recipients
	Material harms	How AI negatively impacts discrepancies and inequalities in terms of material living standards	AI perpetuating inequality in access to government and organization services
	Productivity and work harms	How AI negatively impacts the quality of gainful work and productivity	AI decreasing the quality and quantity of fulfilling employment

Individual harms	Agency harms	How AI negatively impacts people's ability to make independent choices	AI automatically curating news and social media feeds
	Identity and reputational harms	How AI negatively impacts people's ability to shape their identity and reputation	AI being used to label and classify individuals without their knowledge or consent
	Privacy harms	How AI negatively impacts people's ability to seclude themselves or their information	AI being used to analyze individuals' energy data to understand households' activities and preferences
Institutional harms	Security harms	How AI negatively impacts security and vulnerability to economic and physical risks	Police or military forces using AI for surveillance and weaponry
	Democratic harms	How AI negatively impacts trust in government and public institutions	AI influencing individual choices in elections
	Informational harms	How AI negatively impacts the effectiveness and accountability of governments and public institutions	AI usage in government systems reducing accountability and trust
Environmental harms	Built environment harms	How AI negatively impacts the built environment	AI being used or exploited for hacking smart infrastructure

	Natural environment harms	How AI negatively impacts the natural environment	AI's environmental cost, e.g., the energy and water required to train and maintain AI

Table 2.1: Taxonomy of AI Harms

Well-being harms

Physical harms and mental and emotional harms

Poor health limits individuals' well-being and influences society more broadly, preventing people from engaging in leisure activities and limiting enjoyment, which can hinder contributions to society's economic advancement and social development. Unfortunately, AI will directly harm individuals' physical and mental well-being - and many aspects of AI will indirectly create physical and emotional harm. For example, despite the potential for making roads safer on average, the proliferation of autonomous vehicles will inevitably lead to collisions, causing direct physical and probably emotional harm, and the growing potential of mass automation will create uncertainty that can damage workers' emotional health. Similarly, the UK's *Report into The New Frontier: Artificial Intelligence at Work* shows that pervasive monitoring and target-setting technologies such as queue monitoring in supermarkets are damaging employees' mental and physical health "as workers experience the extreme pressure of constant, real-time, micro- management and automated assessment." In his report *Of Two Minds - One Human, One Not: Mental Health in the Era of Artificial Intelligence*, Bill Wilkerson, Executive Chairman of Mental Health International, states "AI will be a superpower of dangerous, deep stress with the capacity to produce rumination that, in turn, predicts depression. Deep stress is at the root of severe frustration, fear, anger, and uncertainty" (Wilkerson, 2019).

In general, harms are naturally interrelated. Financial harm can reduce accessibility to healthcare and wellness, which has direct implications for physical and mental health. Similarly, stretches of poor mental health can dramatically influence physical well-being and financial situations. Thus, many other categories of harm such as productivity and work harms will result in additional harm to an individual's well-being.

AI is also extensively used in the healthcare industry, where it is expected to result in dramatic disruptions, but not only can AI help improve health care delivery, its speed and accuracy of diagnosis should reduce the more than 250,000 annual deaths in the US alone due to medical error (John Hopkins, 2016). In addition, AI can help with drug discovery, disease monitoring, and outbreak response, although the *WHO Ethics and Governance of Artificial Intelligence for Health* report based on the two-year consultation of a panel of international experts, observes that AI will only improve healthcare globally "if ethics and human rights are put at the heart of its design, deployment, and use" (World Health Organization, 2021).

The most obvious risk is that poorly designed systems could misdiagnose diseases and provide poor treatment recommendations, which would result in physical and mental harm for patients. Jonathan Zittrain, a Professor of Law at Harvard, has said that "done wrong, AI in health care could be analogous to the cancer-causing asbestos that was used for decades in buildings across the US, with widespread harmful effects not immediately apparent" (Powell, 2020). Similar to education and other uses of AI, data must be representative. For example, data collected from high-income countries may perform poorly for individuals in less developed settings. There are also issues related to the unethical collection and use of personal health data. The development and deployment of AI will involve private profit-driven organisations, leading firms to disregard the rights and interests of patients and communities. Similarly, a report from Brookings, a nonprofit public policy organisation that conducts research to solve important societal problems, notes that the requirement for large datasets creates substantial incentives for collecting sensitive data, and patients may be concerned about privacy violations (as evidenced by a recent lawsuit based on health data being shared with Google) (Price II, 2019; Cohen et al., 2019).

Leisure harms

Many argue that organisations' escalation of AI adoption will increase societies' time engaged in leisure activities, enhancing the quality of life. Greater automation may mean less or even no work, and less or no work means more leisure, however our current society is built upon work, and work shapes our identity. Beyond providing an income and producing goods and services, work gives meaning and purpose. While people imagine the activities and social engagements they could enjoy if they were not bogged down in a 9-5 workday, paradoxically, when they are unemployed, they are miserable. Derek Thompson discusses this paradox of leisure in his article *A world without work*. Despite limitless time for activities and social engagements, people primarily spend their time watching television and browsing social media and the Internet. With more time to socialise, research indicates that the unemployed feel social isolation. The article also interviews John Russo, Visiting Scholar at the Kalmanovitz Initiative for Labor and the Working Poor at Georgetown University and Visiting Research Fellow at the Metropolitan Institute of Virginia Tech University, who says "when jobs go away, the cultural cohesion of a place is destroyed. The cultural breakdown matters even more than the economic breakdown" (Thompson, 2015).

Beyond employment, many aspects of quality of life regarding leisure rely on good health, an adequate work-life balance, and sufficient income to participate in cultural activities and attend sporting events and other forms of recreational entertainment such as cinemas, so AI can provide leisure harm through health, productivity, and material harm. Social media, gaming, and television are all forms of leisure entertainment, and indeed the hours spent globally on social media alone have increased by over 60% in the last ten years to a staggering average of 147 minutes per day. Similarly, the number of global Netflix subscribers has more than doubled since 2017 from a hundred million to over 220 million subscribers, although there are signs that subscriber numbers maybe falling (Hern, 2022). AI is obviously underpinning many of these technologies, and Netflix state on their research webpage "We're also using machine learning to help shape our catalog of movies and TV shows by learning characteristics that make content successful. We use it to optimise the production of original movies and TV shows in Netflix' rapidly growing studio. Machine learning also enables us to optimise video and audio encoding, adaptive bitrate selection, and our in-house Content Delivery Network that accounts for more than a third of North American internet traffic. It also powers our advertising spend, channel mix, and advertising creative so that we can find new members who will enjoy Netflix."

Television, gaming, and social media can all be incredibly addictive, with AI often at the heart of feeding these addictions. One cause of addiction on social media sites such as Twitter is the variability and anticipation of reward. Each post is like pulling the lever of a slot machine. A recent Guardian article notes that "app manufacturers increasingly build in artificial-intelligence machine-learning systems so that they can learn from us how to randomize rewards and punishments more effectively. This sounds like an abusive relationship, and, just as we describe relationships as having gone toxic, it is common to hear of Twitter toxicity. This is supported by Chamath Palihapitiya, former Vice President of User Growth at Facebook, who noted in a podcast entitled The dark side of AI: social media and the optimization of addiction that "in our brain, after an action, we get a reward or punishment, and we generate positive or negative feedback to that action. Social media apps optimise their algorithms for the ideal balance of negative and positive feedback in our brains caused by the difference between these predicted and received rewards." Ironically, addiction to social media not only prevents people from engaging in more social and enjoyable forms of leisure, but greater access to social media can increase depression and stress and correlates with higher anxiety (Vannucci et al., 2017; Zhao & Zhou, 2020). Since an important aspect of leisure is social interaction and cohesion, and, as our workshops highlighted, many AI applications of on social media are used to increase social tension and create social divisions.

Economic Harms

Financial and material harms

Financial and materiality harms pertain to income, consumption and constraints on consumption, non-market consumption such as government services, material deprivation, and housing conditions, highlighting the economic and material constraints on individuals and their quality of life.

Relieving poverty and social exclusion are critical to reducing inequalities in financial and material living standards, however AI can increase inequality in income and consumption in several ways: we have seen how bias in data can perpetuate inequalities in gender, race, and marginalised communities by reinforcing the status quo of historical data. The workshop experts provided several specific examples of how AI can increase inequality and social inequity, from justice, school funding, council funding, health insurance, loans decisions, and fraud decisions to outcomes from various government services, such as disability support and child welfare protection decisions. Unfortunately, social services are often the first target when government uses AI, due to its potential for reducing costs, which is why Australia employed their RoboDebt (Automated Debt Assessment) program, which calculated alleged overpayments and issued debt notices to welfare recipients. The controversial program famously had system errors resulting in welfare recipients paying non-existent debts, which struck an already vulnerable population's material, physical and mental well-being (Henriques-Gomes 2020).

Inequalities manifest at organisational levels as expertise in AI is currently limited, and in Australia, 49% of executives surveyed by Deloitte believe that the country has a "major to extreme AI skills gap" (Loucks et al., 2019). In addition, developing and using powerful AI tools is expensive, and requires access to essential data, creating entry barriers for many firms (Manyika & Bughin, 2018), which means that effective AI utilisation is primarily leveraged by Big Tech and successful organisations. Given the financial benefits provided by AI through revenue generation and cost reduction, a few firms are likely to establish powerful oligopolies, and there are fears that these will degrade ethical, competitive standards. As a result of this, the workshop experts noted that AI may drive a deeper divide between those in power and the rest - the rich and the poor - due to the probable automation of mid-management jobs and greater potential benefits of AI for larger companies.

Long-term financial and material harms may also manifest through other government services like education. A recent Forbes article notes that "of all the areas of life where artificial intelligence will have an impact, the biggest might well be education" (Chase, 2020). According to a McKinsey report, AI can help improve education by automating preparation, administration, evaluation, and feedback, addressing rising concerns over teacher burnout and high attrition rates from workload issues (Bryant et al., 2020). Moreover, a common criticism of education is that it is not sufficiently customised to a learner's individual needs. AI can address this issue by creating personalised learning based on students' skills and interests.

Naturally, there is a risk here, since personalisation requires historical data and, like many other sectors, education has deeply embedded gender and racial biases. Indeed, a report from Brookings notes that "kids from Black and Latino or Hispanic communities—

who are often already on the wrong side of the digital divide—will face greater inequalities if we go too far toward digitizing education without considering how to check the inherent biases of the (mostly white) developers who create AI systems" (Perry & Lee, 2019). The Brookings report also points out that previous educational initiatives with goals of improving efficiency and equity, like standardised testing "didn't consider how the racism and inequality rife in American society would be baked into the tests if care wasn't taken to make them more fair" (Perry & Lee, 2019).

Compounding the harm are similar algorithms used by companies within and across industries, sharing potentially flawed data and outcomes, so that many individuals continue to be disadvantaged and excluded across the spectrum of economic life, accelerating and exacerbating financial and material harms.

Productivity and work harms

Work is a critical aspect affecting quality of life due to the significant amount of time that we work and that it drives productivity and progression in our society. It affects our sense of identity and provides us with an income, influencing the various quality of life metrics. An intriguing debate regarding AI is how it will impact work. Some researchers and technologists believe that AI will expand existing industries and create new ones, generating more jobs than it will replace. However this future would mean a "significant need for governments and other parts of society to help smooth this transition, especially for the individuals whose old jobs are disrupted and who cannot easily find new ones," according to MIT researchers Thomas Malone, Daniela Rus, and Robert Laubacher in their report *Artificial Intelligence and the Future of Work*, which offers recommendations for stakeholders like schools, businesses, and governments "to provide direct assistance to people whose work life is disrupted by AI," and "pay for services delivered by other entities."

Malone et al. (2020) provide a sample list of stakeholders and recommendations that could help shape a future where AI creates more and better jobs, but this future relies heavily on many stakeholders acting in the greater interest of society rather than more traditional siloed objectives such as company profits. Also, this future relies on people being willing and able to engage in life-long learning, continuously picking up new skills. David Timis, an optimist who looks at technological developments with hope, says in his Ted Talk

The Future of Skills in the Age of AI that there will no shortage of jobs due to AI, but that without massive transformations in education, there will be a shortage of people with the requisite skills to perform these jobs. His recommendations not only require workers to engage in life-long learning to maintain satisfying employment, but put more stress on teachers, many of whom are already stretched, to keep up with rapidly developing technologies. Using data from the World Economic Forum, Timis says that almost 50% of the subject knowledge learned in the first year of a four-year technical degree is outdated by graduation.

Overall, the requirements for AI to raise the quality of life from a productivity standpoint are like the principles underpinning trickle-down economics. AI will inevitably result in substantial savings for organisations which replace humans and their wages, and use these savings to create new opportunities for AI-human collaboration, and new roles for humans with the requisite skill sets. This is like government policies providing tax cuts for prosperous organisations and wealthy owners to stimulate business investment and job creation, which benefit lower-income groups in the long term. Although trickle-down economics are hotly debated, mainly in politics, research consistently shows that tax cuts for the rich are associated with the increase in the wealth of top income earners. A new study by David Hope and Julian Limberg from the London School of Economics and King's College London shows that major reforms reducing taxes on the rich across eighteen different OECD indicators generate higher income inequality without affecting economic growth and unemployment (Hope & Limberg, 2020). Given the evidence against trickle-down economics, relying on organisations to retrain in order to focus on creating new roles for human-AI collaboration to increase the quality of life from a work perspective could prove a risky proposition.

This is also the perspective of the workshop participants. The great automation means that many jobs will disappear or that hours will be substantially reduced, which will benefit owners rather than society. In addition, when advances in AI capabilities lead to firms automating white-collar jobs, redundancies may mean people taking on less satisfying work. Not only could the disruption to employment have a negative impact on people's identities, but without significant reforms (e.g., organisational societies becoming insurers and facilitating career development), groups from the workforce may not be able to find new jobs, and be insecure in their job transitions. Moreover, if only a tiny proportion of a workforce is used for high-skilled work and decision- making, elitism and disenfranchisement may quickly follow, so while AI has undoubted productivity benefits, it can also cause substantial harm to the quantity and quality of employment.

The workshops also pointed out that over-reliance on AI technologies can reduce human abilities, creativity, and problem-solving skills. An interesting example comes from writing, where AI-assisted writing makes writing predictable and succinct, but less colourful, by removing adjectives and other descriptors. This may be innocuous, but it shows that even routine AI applications are changing how we write and communicate. The greater question is whether reliance on AI will depreciate human skills in tasks of high consequence, like flying planes. AI and automation work until they don't (for example Boeing's Maneuvering Characteristics Augmentation System malfunction resulting in airplanes entering a series of automated nosedives), and, when they don't, humans must step in – and must be able to step in – to prevent catastrophes that result in loss of life. As individuals become more comfortable with AI, they are likely to be less alert, and may over rely on the technology. The first fatality from an autonomous vehicle exemplifies this. While there was a human in the car, evidence is emerging that they were not paying attention to the road while the car was driving autonomously. Unfortunately, it detected a biker crossing the road in the dark and switched off the autonomous mode just a moment before impact (Smiley 2022).

Individual harms

Agency harms

An individual's agency is their ability to make an informed decision without coercion, and is, in many regards, closely related to our capacity for freedom and choice. Philosophers like James Griffin view agency as the foundation of all human rights, and he says in *On Human Rights* (2008): "Human rights can be seen as protections of our human standing or, as I shall put it, our personhood. And one can break down the notion of personhood into clearer components by breaking down the notion of agency. To be an agent in the fullest sense of which we are capable, one must (first) choose one's own path through life— that is, not be dominated or controlled by someone or something else (call it autonomy)" (p. 149).

AI has the potential to reduce our agency, since reinforcement learning can enable it to manipulate human decision-making with ease. Researchers from CSIRO and the Max Plank Institute conducted a series of experiments where the AI made humans select specific options, and even influenced humans in a social decision-making game where humans played an investor, and the AI a trustee. The AI's objective was to maximise fair outcomes - to help humans make greater returns on their investments - or to take as much money from the human as possible - a profit-maximising goal. In all scenarios, the AI was successful (Dezfouli et al., 2020).

Unfortunately, using AI to manipulate human behavior is not unique to research scientists; social media and advertisers leverage AI to engage increasingly in social manipulation and generate social divisions. Facebook systems are addictive, and use negative triggers to create engagement. Luke Munn's deep-dive investigation into the design of YouTube and Facebook shows how AI is "ripping apart the social fabric of how society works" by inducing anger, hate, and hate speech (Munn, 2020). Facebook's newsfeed algorithm rewards hateful and polarising content because it draws engagement, provokes reactions, and maintains users' attention, providing greater advertising opportunities. Indeed, the recent Facebook papers scandal shows that the algorithm rewarded posts with five points for an angry emoticon compared to one point for a like emoticon, distributing emotionally charged and provocative content farther and faster, and spreading anger and misinformation (Merrill and Oremus, 2021).

Another interesting design of Facebook and YouTube is the de-emphasis on manual search. Although individuals are free to search for any video in YouTube's database, scrolling and tapping provide a superior and frictionless user experience, compared to exerting effort by engaging the system two brain to think and hunt for your next video. Recommended videos account for an enormous number of views on YouTube, and Luke Munn notes that YouTube's AI recommender system "exerts enormous force in determining what kinds of content users are exposed to and what paths they are steered down" (Munn, 2020). This problem is aggravated by recommender systems endlessly playing videos due to the default setting of autoplay being on, an effect that would be limited by manual search.

AI also plays a central role in extractive data capitalism, where AI, like YouTube's algorithm, is used to commercialise our choice and preferences. This provides a negative feedback loop that increases the automation of choice, meaning we make fewer choices regarding our leisure, and which books to read and shows to watch. While people are increasingly subservient to choices of AI, the impact of our loss of agency extends beyond social media and leisure activities. As we will discuss, in institutional harms the automation of choice is leading to substantial social manipulation.

Identity, reputational and privacy harms

A person's identity is the characteristics - qualities, beliefs, personality, and appearance - that comprise an individual, whereas reputation concerns other people's opinion of our identity. Over the last decade, there has been increasing concern regarding the consequences of data on our identity and reputation, and AI magnifies this. Data breaches can cause emotional distress, increased risk of identity theft, and fraud, and take substantial leisure time to regain privacy and prevent further damage (contacting relevant agencies, placing fraud alerts on accounts, changing passwords, etc.). Now AI can generate data breaches, and be used for fraud and identity theft. A report from the World Economic Forum notes that "AI could impersonate people's real contacts, using a writing style that mimics the style of those contacts" (Smith, 2018).

While big data places identity and reputation in plain view, AI technology can manipulate our social and professional interactions, which are critical for shaping our identity and reputation. While previously people used data to form an opinion, now AI explicitly makes opinions. Before AI, recruiters and employers could look at and collect social media data of prospective employees to use or not in deciding whether to hire, and to weigh against other information. Now with AI, these decisions are automated, as is evaluation for jobs, housing and credit, and these decisions can have a lasting impact on someone's reputation. Moreover, damage to reputation can influence the outcome of these analytic AI decisions.

Closely related to identity and reputation is privacy - people's ability to selectively express and reveal information about themselves, and although big data caused much concern about privacy, AI's ability to detect images like individual faces means that sophisticated databases are being created where someone's image can retrieve not only their name, but where they live and who belongs to their social network. Clearview AI, which, at best, can be described as shady, has come under intense scrutiny for their database, containing more than three billion faces scraped from social media and the broader internet. Although Clearview claims that they only deal with law enforcement agencies, a data breach revealed that they also contract their services out to commercial organizations.

Beyond being used for mass identification, facial recognition technology also enables the generation of deepfakes - synthetic media often meant to deceive. Deepfakes have attracted considerable attention due to their blackmail, financial fraud, disinformation, and pornography applications. A Dutch cybersecurity startup, Deeptrace, estimated that over 95% of online deepfakes are pornographic. AI is used to create video, and also to generate audio content based on an individual's voice. A voiceprint is as unique as a fingerprint, and a common way to establish identity, for example to confirm bank access. However, current research can create convincing audio recordings of targeted individuals with only five seconds of training data of that voice (Jia et al., 2018). They can clearly create tremendous reputational damage, and be used for extortion, exploitation, intimidation, and harassment.

Institutional harms

Security harms

Security harms concern both a lack of economic security and physical safety within the quality-of-life framework, where economic and physical vulnerability risks overlap naturally with other indicators like materiality and health. For example, the COVID-19 pandemic has created global and economic instability for many individuals, diminishing their security and quality of life. Reactions to the pandemic have also created security risks through anti-lockdown protests like the far-right American Revolution 2.0, where hundreds of activists carrying firearms gathered at the Michigan Capitol and Capitol Hill. Even though the protest did not result in any deaths, violent tones and perceived threats led to feelings of vulnerability.

An essential aspect of economic security is reducing economic harm to susceptible groups. As we outlined in our discussion on material harms, AI biases and objectives often put the more vulnerable at increased risk of greater inequality. This reduces resilience towards financial shocks, and can make it harder for minority communities to receive a fair price for financial services and loans due to built-in discrimination.

Figure 2.3: Originally published in Van Noorden (2020), Springer Nature

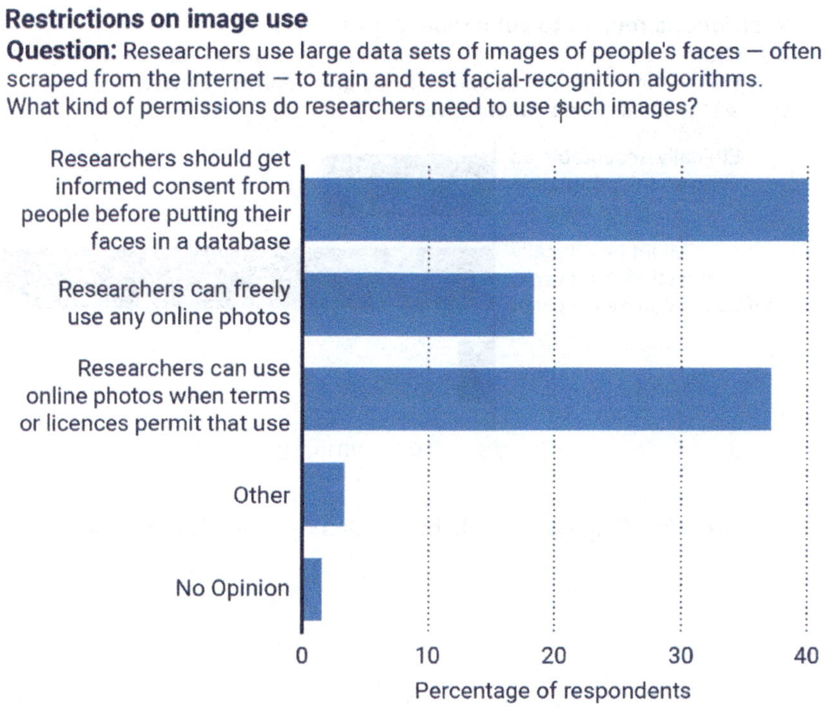

Figure 2.4: Originally published in Van Noorden (2020), Springer Nature

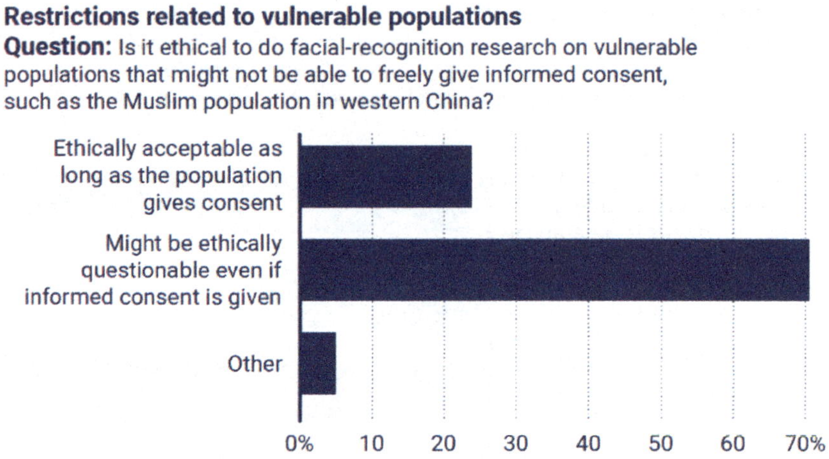

Figure 2.5: Originally published in Van Noorden (2020), Springer Nature

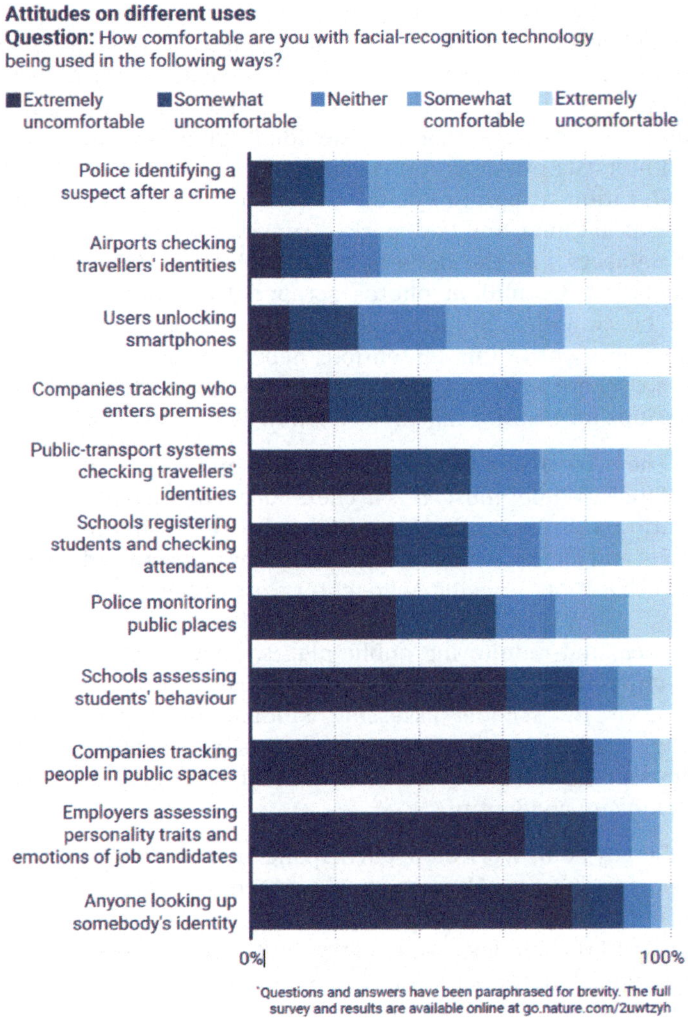

Figure 2.6: Originally published in Van Noorden (2020), Springer Nature

Another dangerous aspect of AI stressed by the workshop participants is its growing surveillance and digital tracking capabilities. Although we have briefly mentioned the negative impact of surveillance at work, surveillance and tracking are becoming ubiquitous. Initially, data surveillance was used to capture the large amounts of data necessary to power AI. However, AI is increasingly being applied to surveillance, creating a feedback loop, and, beyond organisations and government, scientific researchers are also using surveillance data and surveillance AI like machine vision for questionable practices that include identifying Uyghur faces. This Muslim minority ethnic group is subject to mass detentions as part of a re-education program aimed at quelling an alleged terrorist movement in China, and has sparked considerable debate on whether public datasets, like the University of Washington MegaFace dataset that contains 3.3 million photos scraped from the website Flickr, should be compiled by academics, and used in their research. To establish opinions in this contentious debate, Nature surveyed almost 500 researchers in AI, and found that they are widely split on data permissions for training machine vision AI (Van Noorden, 2020).

The survey also includes researcher opinions on uses of AI for surveillance. While most researchers are comfortable with facial recognition technology being used by police to identify suspected criminals and check identities at airports, there are mixed opinions on facial recognition tracking who enters an organisation's premises, checking identities on public transport systems and school attendance, and monitoring public places. That said, the researchers consistently expressed discomfort about facial-recognition technology being used by schools assessing student behaviour, companies tracking people in public spaces, employers assessing job candidates' emotions and personality traits, and, most especially, anyone being able to look up an identity.

Finally, our workshop participants noted that extreme harm can also result from AI weapons. For example, Lethal Autonomous Weapon Systems can identify targets using machine vision and facial recognition technology, and carry out strikes without human intervention. Traditional drones are inherently limited since each drone relies on human commands. In contrast, fully autonomous systems can be dispatched in their thousands, working cooperatively and making tactical decisions in real time without any human control. James Dawes from Macalester College outlines several dangers from AI Weapons:

1. Problems from misidentification, which can happen to humans, escalate with AI.
2. Although there will likely be strict regulation on AI

weapons, black markets will ensure availability.

3. Nations will engage in an arms race, possibly developing weapons that involve mounting chemical, biological, radiological, and nuclear arms.

4. AI weapons will probably lead to an accountability gap, undermining the international laws of war. Autonomous AI weapons, which are reported to have killed people in the Libyan Civil War, are feared as the "Third Revolution in Warfare," following gunpowder and nuclear weapons (Lee et al. 2021).

Democratic and Informational harms

The effectiveness and accountability of government and public institutions such as law enforcement are fundamental. For all members of society to trust a government and benefit from it, the government must be free of corruption and prejudice. The widespread use of biased and discriminatory AI systems used by governments, AI for surveillance, and the proliferation of politically charged misinformation and deepfakes through social media, is changing the relationship between government and people, and shaking trust in government and institutions. These points were all emphasised as significant causes of concern in our workshops.

A recent report developed an AI Global Surveillance Index to understand how AI-based surveillance tools are being deployed in 176 countries (Feldstein, 2019). Of the 176 countries, 75 actively use AI for surveillance, including facial recognition for smart city initiatives and policing. The report found that over half of the world's advanced democracies deploy AI surveillance systems, but stresses that use does not mean abuse, although it does find that autocratic and semi-autocratic governments are more likely to abuse AI for surveillance than liberal democratic governments, and whether governments abuse AI surveillance technology for repressive purposes ultimately depends on the quality of the government. Inevitably, there will always exist contexts where unlawful exploitation of AI could be used to gain political advantage, and this potential has many people worried that corrupt officials will abuse power afforded by AI surveillance, further betraying trust in government systems.

The speed at which many governments' surveillance has grown due to the pandemic is unimaginable; for example, France has piloted facial recognition to monitor compliance with mask mandates on public transportation. As a result, AI normalises the acceptance of AI-based surveillance beyond collecting data and assessing risky populations and events.

Misinformation and deepfakes created by politicians, interest groups, and sometimes governments, combined with AI-based social media, are contributing to the decay of truth. Beyond creating polarisation, this combination is already leading to physical and emotional harms, through hate crimes and violence. The spread of misinformation has also had a substantial influence on health and well- being, as when social media has helped spread misinformation (false information created without harmful intentions) and disinformation (false information created with harmful intentions) regarding vaccination against COVID-19. Whether or not to have a vaccination for a potentially dangerous disease should be a fully informed decision, but the filter bubbles created by social media AI usually result in people receiving only pro- or anti-vaccine posts, largely depending on political ideologies, and posts on COVID-19 are notorious for spreading misinformation and disinformation, which, unfortunately, travel "farther, faster, deeper, and more broadly than the truth" (Vosoughi et al., 2018).

Beyond merely spreading disinformation and misinformation, one of the most successful applications of AI in this context is using carefully curated, targeted communication mechanisms to nudge users towards more extreme political beliefs. Not only does this create filter bubbles, which prevent constructive dialogues and more accurate flows of information, but extreme beliefs lead to increased aggressive behavior online, which drives violence in the offline world.

The power of political manipulation on and by Facebook is perhaps best highlighted by the "I Voted" sticker. Across a series of elections, initially in the United States, Facebook has experimented with mechanisms to increase voter turnout. Different versions of the "I Voted" sticker were shown to the 61 million people who accessed Facebook during the 2010 congressional elections, and the results, detailed in an article published in Nature by Bond et al. (2012), showed that social messages containing pictures of friends who voted substantially increased voter turnout, compared to a control group of no messages, and a purely informational message (see Figure 2.7). Facebook also used the button in 2012 during the US presidential election, and it was reported in a PLOS One article by Jones et al.

(2017) that this increased participation by an estimated 270,000 additional votes cast, which is more than the 80,000 votes Hillary Clinton required to overtake Donald Trump, and significantly more than the 537 votes in Florida determining the 2000 Presidential Election in favour of President Bush.

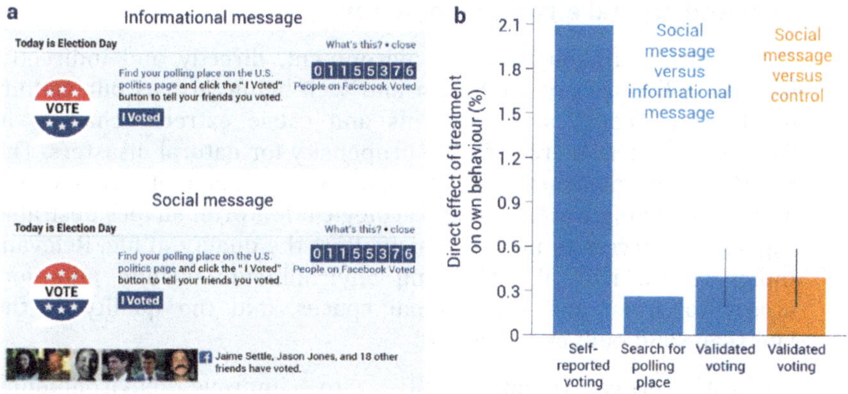

Figure 2.7: Examples of the informational message and social message Facebook treatments (a) and their direct effect on voting behaviour (b). Original published in Bond et al. (2012), Springer Nature

Since these elections, the Facebook "I voted" button has appeared in others outside the US, including the 2014 Scottish independence referendum, the 2015 Irish constitutional referendums, and the 2015 UK election. According to the Guardian, after these elections Facebook stopped releasing public statements about the "I Voted" button, although it was there in the 2016 UK EU membership referendum, the 2016 US presidential election, the 2017 German federal election, the 2018 Italian elections, and the 2017 Icelandic parliamentary election. The article focuses on Iceland, where confidence in the political system is shaky, and only some Facebook users saw the "I Voted" button, and concludes with the hypothesis that Facebook has introduced the button globally to bring more political battles to Facebook to increase engagement and advertising revenue while jeopardising democracy. Evidence presented by Facebook and their research colleagues demonstrates that Facebook can influence people to vote. Through AI, the company accurately ascertains the political ideology and preferred candidates across their user base, which means that they could control the outcomes of government elections.

Environmental harms

Built and natural environment harms

Our natural and living environment, directly and indirectly, have an influence on our health and well-being, just as our actions touch local ecological ecosystems and cause extreme changes in weather patterns, increasing the propensity for natural disasters. The health of our environment relates closely to fundamental rights such as clean drinking water, and our ecological footprint shapes desirable aspects like access to nature, which affect the quality of life. Relevant topics within natural and living environments include pollution, access to green and recreational spaces, and the quality of the landscape and built environment.

AI provides opportunities to improve environmental sustainability and combat climate change, but requires substantial energy for powering data lakes and data warehouses, and training deep learning models, which can take days and harms the environment through high carbon emissions. Strubell et al. (2019) from the University of Massachusetts Amherst estimated that training a sizeable natural language processing model incurs over 600,000 pounds of CO_2 emissions, which is the environmental impact of almost five automobiles from cradle to grave, or more than a hundred round trip flights between New York and Beijing.

From an extended perspective, the environmental impact of AI across the lifecycle of an AI device reveals an even greater potential environmental cost. Kate Crawford and Vladan Joler's *Anatomy of an AI system* uses Amazon's Echo to demonstrate the vast environmental impact such as Bangka's destroyed forests and coral reefs from raw material extraction through manufacture, distribution, use, and disposal. Indeed, a World Economic Forum report (led by Herweijer et al., 2018) advocates considering the environment when designing AI, since experts believe it may accelerate environmental degradation.

In addition to noting the current and potential environmental impacts, our participants also highlighted that AI could enable cyberattacks on the built environment. The proliferation of intelligent buildings integrated with AI technology increases vulnerabilities within a city's infrastructure.

5. Scalable black boxes

Several other important aspects of AI raised by our experts moderate the dimensions of harm. The first is the issue of scale. Although we previously noted that one of the primary benefits of AI is its ability to provide accurate solutions at scale, this is a two-sided coin since the damage it causes, from a decision that widens inequality to inaccurate automated weapons, will also occur at scale, and faster than in scenarios without AI. As AI is typically made with good intentions, harms tend to be unforeseen, and issues magnified by AI being a black box, so they may not be detected for some time. The opaque nature of the rules created by AI means that determining whether outcomes have limited harm being fair and equitable is based almost entirely on outcome data. Only in rare scenarios, like the case of a husband and wife applying for the same credit card and getting radically different spending limits, are issues detected.

The black-box nature of AI creating harmful outcomes is amplified by organisations and governments interacting with AI developed and deployed by other firms. Anja Lambrecht and Catherine Tucker of the London Business School and MIT conducted an interesting study where they used Facebook's advertising algorithm to promote careers in STEM with the explicit goal of showing the ad equally to both genders. Unfortunately, despite their efforts, in 191 countries, males were shown the ad far more than females, but, as the researchers had no access to the rules of the Facebook algorithm, they were initially unsure of what was driving the results. One of the hypotheses they developed, that males engaged more with the ad, leading the AI to present it to more males, was ruled out as the data showed that females had a higher clickthrough rate. In the end, they found that younger women are a more expensive demographic to target with ads, creating an imbalance. However, determining this was the driving effect required the researcher to collect additional data, experimenting with Facebook's AI by varying the ad spend, highlighting the difficulties of achieving equality when leveraging third parties' AI.

6. Summary

Its lack of visibility and accountability means that recognising when AI causes harm is complex, with corrective action even more complicated, therefore, to maximise benefits from AI and minimise harms, individuals must understand when they are experiencing an AI touchpoint and think critically about whether their own user journey results in harm. Thus, the taxonomy can help organisations evaluate the cost-benefits of AI across the eight dimensions, and can also help individuals better understand how AI affects their quality of life both positively and negatively.

References

Angwin, J., Larson, J., Mattu, S., and Kirchner, L., 2016 Machine bias: There's software used across the country to predict future criminals. And it's biased against blacks. ProPublica. <https://www.propublica.org/article/machine-bias-risk-assessments-in-criminal-sentencing>

BBC, 2020. Facial recognition to 'predict criminals' sparks row over AI bias. BBC. <https://www.bbc.co.uk/news/technology-53165286>

Bond, R. M., Fariss, C. J., Jones, J. J., Kramer, A. D., Marlow, C., Settle, J. E., & Fowler, J. H., 2012. A 61-million-person experiment in social influence and political mobilization. Nature, 489(7415), 295-298.

Brown, T., 2009. Change by Design: How Design Thinking Transforms Organizations and Inspires Innovation. New York: Harper Collins.

Bryant, J., Heitz, K., Sanghvi, S., and Wagle, D., 2020. How artificial intelligence will impact K-12 teachers. McKinsey & Company. <https://www.mckinsey.com/industries/education/our-insights/how-artificial-intelligence-will-impact-k-12-teachers>

Buolamwini, J. and Gebru, T., 2018, January. Gender shades: Intersectional accuracy disparities in commercial gender classification. In Conference on fairness, accountability and transparency (pp. 77-91). PMLR.

Calvano, E., Calzolari, G., Denicolo, V. and Pastorello, S., 2020. Artificial intelligence, algorithmic pricing, and collusion. American Economic Review, 110(10), pp.3267-97.

Chace, C., 2020. The impact of artificial intelligence on education. Forbes. <https://www.forbes.com/sites/calumchace/2020/10/29/the-impact-of-artificial-intelligence-on-education/?sh=41bd395d50df>

Cheong, M., Lederman, R., McLougheney, A., Njoto, S., Ruppanner, L. and Wirth, A., 2020. Ethical Implications of AI Bias as a Result of Workforce Gender Imbalance. Research report: Computer and Informations System & Policy Lab, The University of Melbourne.

Cohen, I.G. and Mello, M.M., 2019. Big data, big tech, and protecting patient privacy. JAMA, 322(12), pp.1141-1142.

Crawford, K. and Joler, V., 2018. Anatomy of an AI System. <https://anatomyof.ai/index.html>.

Dezfouli, A., Nock, R. and Dayan, P., 2020. Adversarial vulnerabilities of human decision- making. Proceedings of the National Academy of Sciences, 117(46), pp.29221-29228.

ICO, 2018. What is automated individual decision-making and profiling. UK Information Commissioner's Office. <https://ico.org.uk/for-organisations/guide-to-data-protection/guide-to-the-general-data-protection-regulation-gdpr/automated-decision-making-and-

profiling/what-is-automated-individual-decision-making-and-profiling/#id2>

Feldstein, S., 2019. The Global Expansion of AI Surveillance. Carnegie Endowment for International Peace. <https://carnegieendowment.org/2019/09/17/global-expansion-of-ai-surveillance-pub-79847>

Gilman, M., 2019. AI algorithms intended to root out welfare fraud often end up punishing the poor instead. The Conversation. <https://theconversation.com/ai-algorithms-intended-to-root-out-welfare-fraud-often-end-up-punishing-the-poor-instead-131625>

Grierson, J., 2021. Motorist fined after CCTV confuses his number plate with woman's T-shirt. The Guardian. <https://www.theguardian.com/uk-news/2021/oct/18/motorist-fined-number-plate-t-shirt>

Griffin, J., 2009. On human rights. OUP Oxford.

Hao, K., 2019. AI is sending people to jail—and getting it wrong. MIT Technology Review, <https://www.technologyreview.com/2019/01/21/137783/algorithms-criminal-justice-ai/>

Henriques-Gomes, L. 2020. 'Robodebt-related trauma': the victims still paying for Australia's unlawful welfare crackdown. The Guardian. <https:/www.theguardian.com/australia-news/2020/nov/21/robodebt-related-trauma-the-victims-still-paying-for-australias-unlawful-welfare-crackdown>

Herweijer, C., Combes, B., Ramchandani, P., and Sidhu, J., 2018. Harnessing artificial intelligence for the earth. World Economic Forum. <https://www3.weforum.org/docs/Harnessing_Artificial_Intelligence_for_the_Earth_report_2018.pdf>

Hope, D. and Limberg, J., 2020. The economic consequences of major tax cuts for the rich.

Jia, Y., Zhang, Y., Weiss, R., Wang, Q., Shen, J., Ren, F., Nguyen, P., Pang, R., Lopez Moreno, I. and Wu, Y., 2018. Transfer learning from speaker verification to multispeaker text-to-speech synthesis. Advances in neural information processing systems, 31.

John Hopkins, 2016. Study suggests medical errors now third leading cause of death in the U.S. John Hopkins Medicine Press Release. <https://www.hopkinsmedicine.org/news/media/releases/study_suggests_medical_errors_now_third_leading_cause_of_death_in_the_us>

Jones, J.J., Bond, R.M., Bakshy, E., Eckles, D. and Fowler, J.H., 2017. Social influence and political mobilization: Further evidence from a randomized experiment in the 2012 US presidential election. PloS one, 12(4), p.e0173851.

Kahneman, D., 2011. Thinking, fast and slow. Macmillan.

Kahneman, D., Sibony, O. and Sunstein, C.R., 2021. Noise: A flaw in human judgment. Little, Brown.

Kimbell, L., 2014. Service Innovation Handbook. BIS Publishers.

Kohler, C., 2018. 4 Tips for beating the resume bots. First hand. <https://firsthand.co/blogs/resumes-cover-letters/4-tips-for-beating-the-resume-bots>

Lambrecht, A. and Tucker, C., 2019. Algorithmic bias? An empirical study of apparent gender-based discrimination in the display of STEM career ads. Management science, 65(7), pp.2966-2981.

Ledford, H., 2019. Millions of black people affected by racial bias in health-care algorithms. Nature, 574(7780), pp.608-610.

Lee, K. F., 2021. The third revolution in warfare. The Atlantic. <https://www.theatlantic.com/technology/archive/2021/09/i-weapons-are-third-revolution-warfare/620013/>

Loucks, J., Hupfer, S., Jarvis, D., and Murphy, T. 2019. Future in the balance? How countries are pursuing an AI advantage. Deloitte Insights. <https://www2.deloitte.com/cn/en/pages/technology-media-and-telecommunications/articles/how-countries-are-pursuing-an-ai-advantage.html>

Malone, T., Rus, D. and Laubacher, R., 2020. Artificial intelligence and the future of work. MIT Work of the Future RB17-2020.

Manyika, J., and Bughin, J. 2018. The promise and challenge of the age of artificial intelligence. McKinsey Global Institute. <https://www.mckinsey.com/featured-insights/artificial-intelligence/the-promise-and-challenge-of-the-age-of-artificial-intelligence>

Merrill, J. B., and Oremus, W., 2021. Five points for anger, one for a 'like': How Facebook's formula fostered rage and misinformation. The Washington Post. <https://www.washingtonpost.com/technology/2021/10/26/facebook-angry-emoji-algorithm/>

Munn, L., 2020. Angry by design: toxic communication and technical architectures. Humanities and Social Sciences Communications, 7(1), pp.1-11.

Perry, A. M., and Lee, N. T., 2019. AI is coming to schools, and if we're not careful, so will its biases. Brookings. <https://www.brookings.edu/blog/the-avenue/2019/09/26/ai-is-coming-to-schools-and-if-were-not-careful-so-will-its-biases/>

Powell, A., 2020. AI revolution in medicine. The Harvard Gazette. <https://news.harvard.edu/gazette/story/2020/11/risks-and-benefits-of-an-ai-revolution-in-medicine/>

Price II, W. N., 2019. Risks and remedies for artificial intelligence in health care. Brookings. <https://www.brookings.edu/research/risks-and-remedies-for-artificial-intelligence-in-health-care/>

Raghavan, M., and Barocas, S., 2019. Challenges for mitigating bias in algorithmic hiring. Brookings, <https://www.brookings.edu/research/challenges-for-mitigating-bias-in-algorithmic-hiring/>

Richardson, R., Schultz, J.M. and Crawford, K., 2019. Dirty data, bad predictions: How civil rights violations impact police data, predictive policing systems, and justice. NYUL Rev. Online, 94, p.15.

Smiley, L., 2022. 'I'm the Operator': The Aftermath of a Self-Driving Tragedy. Wired. <https://www.wired.com/story/uber-self-driving-car-fatal-crash/>

Smith, R., 2018. 3 ways AI could threaten our world, and what we need to do to stay safe. World Economic Forum. <https://www.weforum.org/agenda/2018/03/3-ways-ai-could-threaten-our-world-and-what-we-need-to-do-to-stay-safe/>

Solon, O., 2011. How a book about flies came to be priced $24 million on Amazon. Wired. <https://www.wired.com/2011/04/amazon-flies-24-million/>

Strubell, E., Ganesh, A. and McCallum, A., 2019. Energy and policy considerations for deep learning in NLP. arXiv preprint arXiv:1906.02243

Telford, T., (2019). Apple Card algorithm sparks gender bias allegations against Goldman Sachs. The Washington Post, <https://www.washingtonpost.com/business/2019/11/11/apple-card-algorithm-sparks-gender-bias-allegations-against-goldman-sachs/>

Thompson, D. (2015). A world without work. The Atlantic, 316(1), 50-61.

The Sentencing Project, 2018, Report of The Sentencing Project to the United Nations Special Rapporteur on Contemporary Forms of Racism, Racial Discrimination, Xenophobia, and Related Intolerance regarding racial disparities in the United States criminal justice system. The Sentencing Project. <https://www.sentencingproject.org/publications/un-report-on-racial-disparities/>

Van Noorden, R., 2020. The ethical questions that haunt facial-recognition research. Nature, 587(7834), pp.354-359.

Vannucci, A., Flannery, K.M. and Ohannessian, C.M., 2017. Social media use and anxiety in emerging adults. Journal of affective disorders, 207, pp.163-166.

Vosoughi, S., Roy, D. and Aral, S., 2018. The spread of true and false news online. Science, 359(6380), pp.1146-1151.

Wilkerson, B,. 2019. Of two minds –One human, one not. Mental health in the era of Artificial Intelligence. <https://nebula.wsimg.com/3ca45f2fbbeb98df027f1d9d58df5821?AccessKeyId=A5F796B0CC9783179AFF&disposition=0&alloworigin=1>.

World Health Organization, 2021. Ethics and governance of artificial intelligence for health: WHO guidance. World Health Organization. <https://apps.who.int/iris/bitstream/handle/10665/341996/9789240029200-eng.pdf>

Zhao, N. and Zhou, G., 2020. Social media use and mental health during the COVID-19 pandemic: Moderator role of disaster stressor and mediator role of negative affect. Applied Psychology: Health and Well-Being, 12(4), pp.1019-1038.

Chapter 3
The metaverse – the next ethical battlefield

1. Introduction

In this chapter, we examine the newly emerging phenomenon of the metaverse, and consider potential risks that may arise from it, and what can be done to minimise harms caused by such virtual worlds. Virtual worlds have been hyped before, most notably Linden Lab's 2003 Second Life, where users create avatars of themselves and interact with others, leading their second life online. Second Life garnered a lot of media attention and, in 2006, IBM created real estate, American Apparel opened a shop, Reuters employed an avatar journalist, countries opened embassies, and universities created virtual campuses (Hansen, 2009), but between the lacklustre user experience, low transaction volumes, confusion about the purpose of Second Life (is it a game or is it a social networking site?), and the limitations of the technology, Second Life declined rapidly and was discontinued (Hansen, 2009).

Fast-forward to the end of 2021 when Mark Zuckerberg launched his version of the metaverse, Horizon Worlds (Meta, 2021), at the same time rebranding Facebook as Meta, saying "We believe the metaverse will be the successor to the mobile internet; we'll be able to feel present like we're right there with people no matter how far apart we actually are" (reported by Milmo, 2021b). Virtual life is about to get real.

2. The metaverse

The term metaverse comes from a book titled *Snow Crash* written by Neal Stephenson, which describes a single virtual world shared by all users. The concept is also often compared to the metaverse depicted in Ernest Cline's novel (and Steven Spielberg's film adaptation of it) *Ready Player One* (Radoff, 2021a).

While the metaverse is not yet succinctly defined, it can be described as a set of immersive technologies that enables social connection in 3D virtual universes that resemble reality. It relies on a network of 3D virtual worlds, which use technologies such as virtual reality (VR), augmented reality (AR), mixed reality (MR) and haptics as well as AI, machine learning, video-conferencing, games, blockchain, cryptocurrencies, cloud, email, social media and live-streaming.

Jon Radoff, the author of the blog Building the Metaverse, notes that the metaverse is a complex digital environment that relies on seven distinct layers (Radoff, 2021b):

1. Infrastructure – Connectivity technologies like 5G, Wi-Fi, cloud, and hi-tech materials like GPUs
2. Human interface – VR headsets, AR glasses, haptics, and other technologies users will leverage to join the metaverse
3. Decentralisation – Blockchain, artificial intelligence, edge computing, and other tools of democratisation
4. Spatial computing – 3D visualisation and modelling frameworks
5. Creator economy – An assortment of design tools, digital assets, and e-commerce establishments
6. Discovery – The content engine driving engagement, including ads, social media, ratings, reviews, etc.

7. Experiences – VR equivalents of digital apps for gaming, events, work, shopping, etc.

Commentators postulate on different degrees of connection between these worlds: from various worlds independent of each other to a single world, which is the metaverse. Connectivity between virtual worlds is now very low or non-existent; virtual worlds are all accessed through an internet connection, and this is largely the extent of their interconnection.

3. Metaverse platform providers

Big Tech companies regard the metaverse as the next big platform, and are investing heavily in the technology required to build it. Meta is currently hiring ten thousand workers in Europe to build the metaverse over the next five years (Reuters, 2021).

The owners of metaverse platforms are mostly private entities subject to a profit maximisation imperative, and this plus the control they exercise suggests that most if not all experiences in metaverse will be heavily curated.

The main providers and suppliers to the metaverse include:

- Epic Games/Fortnite
- Meta/Facebook
- Niantic
- Nvidia
- Microsoft
- Decentraland

Existing metaverses include:

- Horizon Worlds: Meta's virtual world
- Roblox: A metaverse platform where users play games made by other users
- Decentraland: Users create virtual buildings, from homes to concert halls, and charge other players to visit them
- The Sandbox: A virtual metaverse where players build, own, and monetise their gaming experiences

- Stageverse: A new social VR platform featuring virtual venues, digital content, and interactive experiences
- Spatial: A platform that turns any room into a 3D workspace.

In essence, the metaverse is a boundless marketplace where transactions can be conducted using cryptocurrency or NFTs. Participants earn money by farming coins, hunting virtual creatures, attending virtual dating events, transport services, running events or a cooking school, and trading NFTs. NFT Traders who have noted 'Wash Trading' (where a seller takes both sides of a trade to boost an NFT's value) exists in the metaverse are already expressing concern.

To give an idea of the scale of adoption of the metaverse, Decentraland, launched in 2017, has about 300,000 users, and sold a plot of land in the middle of their metaverse for about US$3.5m (New World Notes, 2021). In 2021, US$500 million of virtual property was sold in the metaverse. This is expected to double in 2022 (Frank, 2022).

Apple has chosen to stay away from much of the metaverse commentary, noting that their focus will be on augmented reality (AR) rather than VR (Frank, 2022). Despite this, pressure will be on them to bring metaverse products and services to market as their depth and reach may be the fastest catalyst for mass adoption of virtual worlds.

4. Metaverse Harms

Commentators often lean on *Snow Crash* and *Ready Player One* as references and templates for the metaverse. Unsurprisingly, both have dystopian visions of a virtual world dominated by advertising, enforced scarcity of resources, and financial models - typically worlds run by large corporations with no governments.

Unfortunately, the tech companies appear to reinforce this vision of the metaverse because it aligns with their interests, which shapes the debate to the extent that this pessimistic fantasy of what the metaverse will look like is almost accepted as a given. There is not nearly enough discussion about what kinds of virtual worlds are possible that may not have the same awful characteristics.

The metaverse enables significantly more control of human experience than previous interfaces, such as social media. The metaverse enables environment has more levers to condition human experience and to influence human behaviour than previously provided by the tech companies.

Experiences with social media platforms using interfaces with far less powerful levers than those in a metaverse have been sufficient to alter human behaviour and create serious harm, from damaging mental health to undermining public discourse, but despite the continued attempts of these organisations to make adjustments to their systems to ameliorate unintended consequences, there has been little material progress so far. In October 2021, Frances Haugen brought global attention to the harm that tech giant Facebook (now Meta) is inflicting. Haugen said of Meta CEO Mark Zuckerberg, "He has all the control. He has no oversight, and he has not demonstrated that he is willing to govern that company at the level that is necessary for public safety" (Milmo, 2021a).

So, there is considerable concern that the metaverse will inflict harm and unintended consequences beyond those of existing social media and gaming platforms, and unless we have evidence to the contrary, the default assumption should be that in the metaverse there will be more - and more powerful - levers to condition and influence human behaviour that will lead to greater potential for unintended consequences.

Organisations aiming to deploy platforms enabling metaverse experiences have the onus of proving that their increased control will not translate into increased risk.

To predict and analyse upcoming metaverse risks, we should look to what we know about closely related technologies such as social media and online gaming:

- *Data sharing and algorithmic hyper-engagement* - Compared to other platforms the metaverse will have more data collecting modalities, including biometric data and visual data, which will enable more accurate measurement of user attention than ever before. Any AI based recommendations or advertising based on this attention data may also literally be in your virtual face, and therefore demand more engagement than current-generation social media

- *Toxic behaviours* - Are already observed in most social media and online gaming communities. Most players play to have fun, but some bad actors may subvert the rules to irritate or provoke others for their own gain or amusement (called griefing) or use in- game communication to convey sexist or racist sentiment, harass players, or generally troll to provoke an outcry. Rather than joining the community with malicious intent, participants may fall into these negative behaviours intermittently, or after seeing that this behaviour is tolerated. A popular early type metaverse known as Roblox, aimed at 8-12-year-olds, has thirty million monthly users. Parents have reported that their children have received sexually explicit messages in the chat function. One thirty-three-year-old father logged into the platform, and within five minutes was shown sexual positions and told he was sexy and cute (https://www.kidspot.com.au/parenting/dad-horrified-to-find-vile-messages-in-popular-game-on-sons-ipad/news-story/22fc7cc132a03eba41e8420f6516f603).

- *Anonymity* - A key question related to the metaverse is - to what extent are users' identities going to be tied to their avatars, as opposed to avatars being a disposable mask of anonymity? Currently, the metaverses do not need to make public the identities of people who have shown inappropriate or violent behaviour in their platforms.

- *Learning grounds* - Early accounts of aggressive and inappropriate behaviours in metaverse worlds could and should have been anticipated. Pre-emptive rather than reactive thought is required as to how new interfaces and interaction freedoms may be misused, and appropriate mitigations put in their place. These platforms should not be ethical learning grounds for tech platforms to figure out what harms can be done.

- *Property risks* - Taking virtual property with you between metaverse worlds will necessarily depend on support from developers. If a user builds a house in a Sandbox game, can they use it as a Horizon Workrooms venue? We may naively assume that this will be possible if we draw on the analogy of physical world property. But this would require developers to voluntarily implement code that understands the data a user wants to bring in, and this is not the case as yet. Developers related to Meta's core offerings may have access to code and other developers from their other applications or meta-worlds who can build such representations, hence these people may be at an advantage and become more powerful avatars in this regard.

- *Environmental risks* - There are environmental concerns related to metaverses. Much of the proposed infrastructure of the metaverse seems to rely on NFTs (non-fungible tokens) and other blockchain technologies for persistence across worlds and user verification, however at present these technologies appear to be unsustainable from an environmental perspective given that a single Ethereum transaction has a large carbon footprint of 33.4kg CO_2 (Mohammed, 2022).

5. Illustrative incidents of harm in the metaverse

To help illustrate some of the risks in the metaverse, two examples are provided below.

Virtual gang rape in Meta's Horizon Worlds

In February 2022, a British woman, Nina Jane Patel, 43, a beta tester for Meta's Horizon Venues, claimed she had been virtually and sexually abused. "Within sixty seconds of joining — I was verbally and sexually harassed — three to four male avatars, with male voices, essentially but virtually gang-raped my avatar and took photos — as I tried to get away they yelled 'don't pretend you didn't love it' and 'go rub yourself off to the photo,'" (Frischberg, 2022). Patel, recalled this, recounting the nightmare she experienced, saying it was a "horrible experience that happened so fast and before I could even think about putting the safety barrier in place." (Frischberg, 2022). "Virtual reality has essentially been designed so the mind and body can't differentiate virtual/digital experiences from real," she wrote on Medium. "In some capacity, my physiological and psychological response was as though it happened in reality." (Frischberg, 2022).

Joe Osborne, a Meta spokesperson, told *The New York Post* that the company will make improvements to ensure everyone's safety. He said "We're sorry to hear this happened. We want everyone in Horizon Venues to have a positive experience, easily find the safety tools that can help in a situation like this — and help us investigate and take action ... Horizon Venues should be safe, and we are committed to building it that way. We will continue to make improvements as we learn more about how people interact in these spaces, especially when it comes to helping people report things easily and reliably." (Frischberg, 2022). Meta said that it gives users access to tools to keep themselves safe – effectively shifting the onus of safety on to them. However, this clearly does not work, and as a result of this incident Meta created the Personal Boundary functionality that will prevent other avatars from invading another avatar's personal space. Sadly, no overarching organisation or body is responsible for the rights and safety of those who participate anywhere online, let alone in a metaverse.

Squatters in virtual property - Upland

On 1 February 2022, Janko Roettgers, published an article on Protocol, noting, "It's the stuff of nightmares: the other day, I found my property occupied by a stranger, who was renting it out, Airbnb style." (Roettgers, 2022). Roettgers is referring to the fact that someone had acquired the property that he owned in Upland (launched in early 2020). He went on, "The person who bought my property currently makes the equivalent of four cents a month in Upland's in-game currency by renting it out to other players."

Roettgers raises the following questions:

- Who should have the rights to an augmented reality (AR) layer tied to a physical address?
- What does it mean that these AR properties are being divided up among early adopters before most people even know they exist?
- Will we see the same issues that have plagued real world real estate, including gentrification and displacement, replicated in AR?
- And, on a more personal level: What should I do about my virtual squatter?

In response to Roettgers' issue, Stanford Law School professor Mark Lemley said "I share the instinct of your reaction. It seems like there's something wrong with this," adding "I don't know that there is an answer - this is not something the law has dealt with before, and it's even hard to find a particularly close analogy." (Roettgers, 2022).

6. What can we do to avoid harms and unintended consequences in metaverses?

Consideration of the following is recommended:

Establishing Values

One policy idea is to require companies developing virtual worlds to make explicit the values and established ethical norms of that world and request people's consent to them before they enter. They could have forums for people to bid/vote on which ethical norms they want, and perhaps use that to help inform the designs of the norms.

An example of this may be Mastodon, which is a federated social network made up of independently run nodes that each have their own set of policies, which users consent to (see https://en.wikipedia.org/wiki/Mastodon_(software)). This has parallels with the idea advanced separately by Stephen Wolfram, Jack Dorsey, Francis Fukuyama et al. of democratising the middleware in the context of social media platforms, i.e. creating an access regime whereby the ranking/filtering/ recommendation layer is open to third parties to define their own terms. In the case of metaverse, this could be different versions of the same world with different norms, etc. (Fukuyama, 2021).

Jack Dorsey, the founder of Twitter, said in an interview with *The New York Times* "We need to open up and be transparent around how our algorithms work and how they're used, and maybe even enable people to choose their own algorithms to rank the content or to create their own algorithms, to rank it. To be that open, I think, would be pretty incredible. So that we can all come to better solutions, because it affects society in such large ways" (Jackson, 2020). This same sentiment applied to metaverses would be beneficial.

Personal protection

Users should not be able to be touched or harassed in virtual worlds. Patel suggests the following (Frischberg, 2022):

- The creation of a universal virtual signal such as a V with the avatars' arms that alerts the moderator to a safety issue
- Automatic personal distancing between avatars

- Training sessions that mimic standards and norms from the physical world, such as not walking up and groping a stranger in the street
- Disciplining users who violate safety and decency norms
- Deterrents for bad actors such as suspension or banning.

That said, one of the big areas of development currently is haptics (the use of technology to stimulate touch and motion), which will have advantages such as, when far from a loved one, being able to hug them remotely. So how will we manage touching in the metaverse? What is appropriate, and what is not?

Learning from social media and gaming experiences

Much that can be learned from existing social media and gaming platforms will apply to the metaverse. Game designers who have focused on designing platforms to encourage positive online interactions should be consulted, and lead metaverse design initiatives.

Use of existing safety and privacy guidelines and laws

Safety and privacy guidelines, rules, strategies, and laws from the physical, 'real' world should be given strong consideration for the metaverse.

Control of data

A person should have control of their own data when navigating between different virtual worlds. If the metaverse is intended to be a place where individuals work, play and live, it will be important that participants can decide what information they bring with them as they move from one world to the next. Without regulation, it is likely that world owners (corporations) will be incentivised financially to lock in user data, and possibly share data without the user's consent.

Open data approach

We strongly recommend a push for open standards in the metaverse. Without such standards, the Big Tech companies based overseas will have a walled garden, offering a restricted range of services to certain subscribers around the hardware and software technologies, making it difficult for smaller companies to break into the market and develop products.

Access regime-type laws can work here, and by law big companies could be forced to issue licences for using their infrastructure through suitable APIs to allow a market of third parties to offer alternative front end experiences. The terms of use, including pricing of such APIs, would need careful consideration.

Other questions to ask

To reduce the risks and harms of the metaverse, other questions include:

- Should rules and laws be decided by Big Tech? In a digital world, there are few a priori constraints on what is possible compared to the real world. Should everything from the laws of physics down to what kinds of entertainment and interaction are permissible be decided by Big Tech companies?
- Will new property laws be needed? In a metaverse, scarcity does not have to be enforced. Will the same notions of property that exist in the real world be necessary in the digital world or should other standards be developed?
- Should people be allowed to make their own metaverse? One response to the argument that Big Tech will create dystopian, ultra- capitalist metaverse worlds is that "people will be free to make their own metaverse." The abject failure of this approach as a viable response to social media monopolies, and the degree to which Big Tech companies actively prevent it, suggests it will not be a practical solution.
- Is a central authority needed? Another common soundbite about the metaverse is that things like property rights, ownership of digital assets, and even currency in general will be implemented on the blockchain in the form of crypto-currencies and NFTs. However, these technologies have no way of enforcing the relationship between ownership on the blockchain and ownership in a real or virtual world without relying on a central authority.

- Should Big Tech be able to avoid real world government regulations? A reason that Web 3.0, NFTS, crypto and metaverses have become bedfellows is because the people owning and promoting them have the same goals - to ensure that current government regulation does not apply to them.

7. The Problem with Big Tech overall

It seems that Big Tech companies, such as Meta, have significant structural problems. These problems have regularly been noted by the public, regulators, media, advocacy groups, and other commentators, and include monopoly power, business models based on data extraction, amplification of sensational and extreme content - harms that disproportionately impact marginalised groups, US imperialism, control by the CEO, and scale and reach.

Monopoly power

The common description of Big Tech's business model as based on advertising revenue is overly simplistic. It is more accurate to describe companies like Meta as monopolies built on the ownership and profit from big data. Through the algorithmic collecting, linking and analysis of the data points of billions of users, they are not just able to predict user behaviour and thought both as consumers and citizens, but to actively shape it. This is hugely valuable, and the fundamental source of big tech's economic and political power.

Business model based on data extraction

If big data is a key resource, and Big Tech's voracious appetite for data can only be satiated by disregard for privacy, then privacy scandals such as Cambridge Analytica (https://www.theguardian.com/news/series/cambridge-analytica-files) are inevitable. These extractive data practices are not accidental oversteps, but rather the inescapable consequences of a business model built on data.

Amplification of sensational and extreme content

Big data, combined with content curation algorithms, targets users with personalised content that seeks to keep them on the platform for ongoing value extraction. As Frances Haugen's US Senate testimony outlined, Meta knows that content which elicits an extreme reaction is more likely to get a click, a comment or a reshare, and is therefore more profitable for the company. The company uses engagement- based ranking algorithms to guide users towards less nuanced, more extreme content. This has devastating consequences for our public square, fragmenting and polarising society. Extractive data practices and algorithmic amplification of sensational and extreme content are at the heart of the business model that has enabled Facebook to grow into a trillion-dollar empire.

Harms disproportionately impact marginalised groups

Big Tech companies exacerbate existing structural divides, with online harms disproportionately affecting Global South[1] countries (for example, lack of investment in non-English speaking contexts) and marginalised groups (children and young people) in Global North countries. Cheap labour is also often sourced from Global South countries for data annotation of AI datasets, call-centre working, and content moderation. These jobs often leave people feeling psychologically damaged. Online hate speech, harassment and abuse target women, LGBTIQ+[2] and racialised groups disproportionately, and this will only get worse as Big Tech develops their virtual and augmented reality services.

Advancing US imperialism though digital colonialism

US-based Big Tech enacts a form of digital colonialism[3], which furthers imperialism by using digital technology for the political, economic, and social domination of other nations. Through the US ownership of digital infrastructure such as transoceanic fibre-optic cables, knowledge and control of the means of computation, Global South countries are kept in a situation of permanent dependency where many millions of people experience Big Tech as the internet, despite the extraction of data and other resources, reinforcing colonial dynamics.

Unilateral control by tech founders and CEOs

Interventions to make Big Tech less harmful have been undermined by the complete control wielded by founders and CEOs. This centralisation of power is unprecedented in corporate history, and Haugen demonstrates that Zuckerberg was aware of the issues, as well as potential solutions, but persistently chose "astronomical profits before people" (Knott, 2021).

Scale and reach

With around 2.9 billion active monthly users worldwide, Meta can be seen to deliver a public service without the requisite checks and balances. Retrofitting frameworks of justice or ethics on to such a well-established and complex system poses a significant regulatory challenge.

8. Recommendations

In order to mitigate the potential harms of the metaverse, the establishment of a Technology and Human Rights Council with an AI and Metaverse Human Rights Commissioner is proposed. Key features of this model should include:

1. The Council funded through individual nation states with Global North countries encouraged to subsidise membership for Global South countries to ensure independence from industry. Funding may also be sourced from bilateral and multilateral mechanisms.
2. The formal governance body is the Conference of the Parties (COP), which includes representatives from regulatory bodies of party states such as the Australian Competition and Consumer Commission, and the US Federal Trade Commission, as well as impacted communities which have experienced disproportionate censorship, such as Palestinian activists. The Bureau of the COP could be made up of six elected members.
3. Credentialled research institutions with no existing commercial relationships with Facebook have access to Big Tech's internal research, relevant data, and algorithms in order to conduct investigations into salient issues.
4. Issues for investigation are determined by the COP, and advised by a public complaints mechanism with the ability to hear complaints in languages other than English.
5. The COP submits policy options and recommendations, some of which may be legally binding.
6. The success of this model depends on having an effective enforcement mechanism. Creative alternatives to fines, for example, repatriation of data to impacted communities which

have been harmed, and other mechanisms for reparations should be explored.

7. This model could be used for one Big Tech company or expanded to include all Big Tech companies such as Meta, Google and Twitter, and other digital services, in which case the Council could function as an independent agency of the UN, similar to the International Labour Organization. The funding model could include a levy on technology companies. Academics such as James Muldoon have also called for an international democratically accountable institution to be funded through a global sovereign wealth fund, modelled on Norway's Government Pension Fund Global4.

8. The role of Commissioner could be 50% funded by Big Tech, and 50% by the Council, based on the desired criterion of independence.

Other factors to consider include:

- The investment in safety and integrity measures should be proportionate to the number of platform users in each jurisdiction and language.
- The AI and Metaverse Human Rights Commissioner should not be required to sign a traditional Non-Disclosure Agreement.
- The AI and Metaverse Human Rights Commissioner should be able to influence key stakeholders' decisions.

Based on the discussion of the metaverse above, and the identification of problems and risks, the establishment of a Technology and Human Rights Council and an AI and Metaverse Human Rights Commissioner are recommended.

Footnotes

1. For an overview of the Global North South Divide, see https://www.rgs.org/schools/teaching-resources/60-second-guide-to-global-north-south-divide/
2. See, for example, https://www.uts.edu.au/partners-and-community/initiatives/social-justice-uts/equity-and-diversity-uts/gender-sexuality-5 for a taxonomy of LGBTIQA+ terminology
3. Kwet M (2021) 'Digital colonialism: the evolution of US empire', https://longreads.tni.org/digital-colonialism-the-evolution-of-us-empire
4. Muldoon J (2022) Platform Socialism: How to Reclaim our Digital Future from Big Tech: Pluto Press

References

Frank, R., (2022). Metaverse real estate sales top $500 million, and are projected to double this year. CNBC, 1 February, https://www.cnbc.com/2022/02/01/metaverse-real-estate-sales-top-500-million-metametric-solutions-says.html

Frischberg, H., (2022). Mother opens up about being 'virtually gang raped' in metaverse. New York Post, 1 February. https://nypost.com/2022/02/01/mom-opens-up-about-being-virtually-gang-raped-in-metaverse/

Fukuyama, F., (2021). Making the Internet Safe for Democracy. Journal of Democracy. April, 32 (2): 37-44.

Hansen, L., (2009). What happened to Second Life? BBC News Magazine, 20 November, http://news.bbc.co.uk/1/hi/8367957.stm

Jackson, L., (2020). Jack Dorsey on Twitter's Mistakes. The New York Times, 7 August, https://www.nytimes.com/2020/08/07/podcasts/the-daily/Jack-dorsey-twitter-trump.html

Knott, M., (2021). 'Harms children': Whistleblower testifies that Facebook puts 'astronomical profits' over people. The Sydney Morning Herald. October 6, https://www.smh.com.au/world/north-america/whistleblower-says-facebook-puts-astronomical-profits-over-people-20211006-p58xjc.html

Meta (2021). Connect 2021: Our vision for the metaverse. Tech@Facebook, 28 October, https://tech.fb.com/connect-2021-our-vision-for-the-metaverse/

Milmo, D., (2021a). Facebook boss 'not willing to protect public from harm'. The Guardian, 24 October, https://www.theguardian.com/technology/2021/oct/24/facebook-boss-not-willing-to-protect-public-from-harm

Milmo, D., (2021b). Enter the metaverse: the digital future Mark Zuckerberg is steering us toward. The Guardian, 28 October, https://www.theguardian.com/technology/2021/oct/28/facebook-mark-zuckerberg-meta-metaverse

Mohammed, S., (2022). Can NFTs Be Environmentally Friendly? Data Driven Investor. January 17, https://medium.datadriveninvestor.com/can-nfts-be-environmentally-friendly-3498b31a6b75

New World Notes (2021). Decentraland Stats: 300K Monthly Active Users, Under 20K Daily Users. 7 December, https://nwn.blogs.com/nwn/2021/12/decentraland-blockchain-metaverse-user-revenue-stats.html

Radoff, J., (2021a). What We Talk About When We Talk About the Metaverse. Building the Metaverse, 26 February, https://medium.com/building-the-metaverse/what-we-talk-about-when-we-talk-about-the-metaverse-c9ef03c1a5dd

Radoff, J., (2021b). The Metaverse Value-Chain. Medium, 7 April, https://medium.com/building-the-metaverse/the-metaverse-value-chain-afcf9e09e3a7

Reuters (2021). 10,000 in EU to build 'metaverse'. Reuters, October 18, https://www.reuters.com/technology/facebook-plans-hire-10000-eu-build-metaverse-2021-10-17/

Roettgers, J., (2022). Who owns your address in AR? Probably not you. Protocol, 1 February, https://www.protocol.com/entertainment/upland-augmented-reality-real-estate

Chapter 4
Existential risks of AI

"The rise of powerful AI will either be the best or the worst thing ever to happen to humanity."

Stephen Hawking

1. Introduction

The Homo genus emerged in Africa about three million years ago, having long ditched its other great ape relatives. During its evolution, the genus spawned various lineages and sub- species, but only one ultimately survived: Homo sapiens arrived on the scene around 300,000 years ago, and has managed to outlive and outlast all its cousins. And one factor remains the critical ingredient for its success: intelligence.

Intelligence is the basic ability to solve problems creatively in one's environment. Homo sapiens had a knack to adapt, think, socialise, communicate, and recognise patterns. Its greater cognitive abilities allowed improved food gathering methods, the ability to make fire, and the development and use of increasingly complicated tools. Adapting to different environments and conditions became significantly easier as, armed with these mental and physical tools, Homo sapiens breached the continent, in a first wave about 130,000 years ago, and in a second about 50,000 years ago, eventually inhabiting all corners of the globe, unlike any species before it.

This increased intelligence was entirely a function of the Homo sapiens brain. Size was one factor. From that first Homo genus, the brain has more than tripled in size, from 450cm3 - only marginally larger than a chimpanzee's, human's closest living relative - to about 1,350cm3. And much of that has occurred in the past 500,000 years (Flinn et al., 2005). The size and organisation of the neocortex seems to be a decisive factor - modern humans have greater relative and absolute numbers of neural connections compared to other primates (Sousa et al., 2017; Roth & Dicke, 2005).

Human intelligence has pushed the species to the absolute extremes of nature and physics. We have dived almost eleven kilometres to the deepest places on Earth. We have also escaped Earth's gravitational pull to land humans and machines on other rocks in our solar system. We have crashed together beams of particles travelling near the speed of light to solve some of the universe's greatest mysteries. We have looked into the furthest depths of the universe to find answers about its origins. And, with this intelligence, we are on the cusp of a truly transformative moment in human history. Intelligence may no longer be the sole domain of organic matter, but also of technology and machinery. What has taken millions of years to evolve could lead to a transformation in just a handful of generations.

Artificial intelligence already dominates human intelligence in some narrow fields and domains, and every day the gap between mankind and machine in those fields continues to grow. On a seemingly daily basis, AI takes on, and defeats, humans in new domains, and as it continues to improve in its capability and across more domains, it may transform society in incredibly wonderful and potentially frightening ways. If this trajectory continues, AI will eventually become significantly smarter than humans across many or all domains, and at that point Homo sapiens will no longer be the smartest problem-solver on the planet. Indeed, compared to an AI system, Homo sapiens will be on the same playing field as chimpanzees, gorillas and orangutans. If we are not careful, we may go the way of the Neanderthal.

2. Existential risk

Until recently, computers taking over has mostly been the domain of science fiction writing. Hollywood has brought these images to life, with a particular fascination for human-designed robots pursuing global domination, from the Terminator films to Bladerunner to Ex Machina to Westworld, although other films have presented a more human side to androids, as in Spielberg's A.I. Artificial Intelligence, and the more ambiguous novel by Ishiguro, *Klara and the Sun*. Apart from the rare exception, such as 2001: A Space Odyssey's Hal, or the machines in The Matrix, the physical representation of artificial intelligence has usually been anthropomorphised. Artificially intelligent machines, it seems, have arms, legs, eyes, mouths, ears, hair and skin - until, of course, you peel that back.

In the past two decades, the study of the humanity-level risks of artificial intelligence has taken a decidedly more serious and academic turn. A number of organisations around the world have devoted considerable efforts to understanding all manner of risks - called existential risks - to humanity, including the Centre for the Study of Existential Risk at the University of Cambridge, the Future of Humanity Institute at the University of Oxford, and the Future of Life Institute in Cambridge, Massachusetts.

Existential risks are those that could bring about human extinction, civilisational collapse, or the permanent destruction of human potential. A relatively simple way to think about them is on a spectrum of intensity (how much harm could it cause?) and scope (how many people could it harm?). Human extinction would, of course, be a particularly bad outcome, not just for the people alive at the time, but because it eliminates the opportunity for all the billions, or perhaps trillions, of people to born in the future. But even if the human species remains, just without the ability to recover or flourish, that would be existentially ruinous in its own respect. Its intelligence and omnipotence would see it become more powerful with no possibility of being usurped. In the current world, populations suffer tremendously under tyrants, but at least there is always the hope that the regime will be deposed. Under an AI singleton, we would have no such hope, and, if the AI wishes to inflict human suffering, the human species faces a fate worse than death. A singleton could be permanently destructive for all but a minority of people. And a catastrophe that kills billions of people, while perhaps not existential, may take many decades, if not centuries, from which to recover (Figure 4.1).

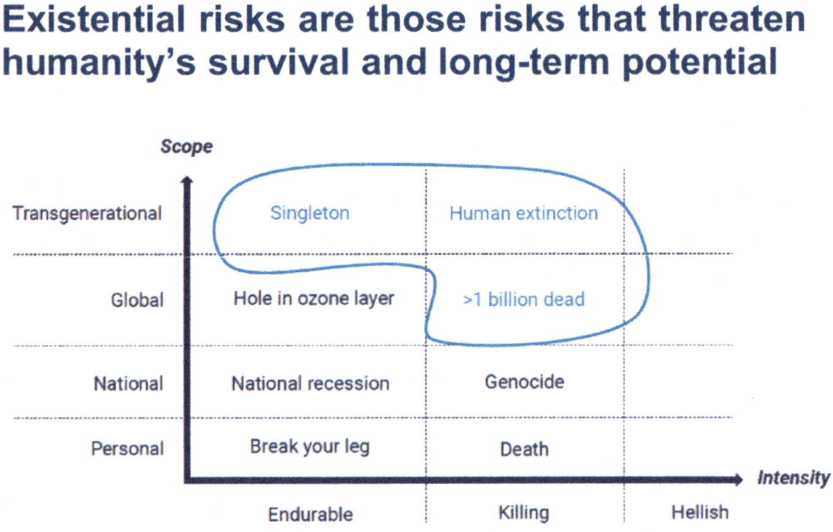

Figure 4.1: Risk classification

Human beings face existential risks right now. Super volcanoes, asteroids, and other space weather could wipe us out at any point. In reality, these natural and cosmic risks are so rare as to barely show up on our radar. An asteroid of the size that would lead to mass extinction, similar to the one that took out the dinosaurs, occurs once in every fifty thousand years. A super volcano of equivalent threat occurs once in every ten thousand years.

Instead, we need to be more concerned with anthropogenic risks - those caused by human activity - which could lead to global catastrophe this century. Nuclear weapons pose an immediate existential threat, because a nuclear exchange using a fraction of the 13,500 nuclear weapons that currently exist could lead to global cooling from the large amount of smoke and soot blown into the stratosphere, world-wide crop failure, and mass starvation. Human activity is increasingly taking a toll on the environment, due to a combination of agriculture, infrastructure development, energy production, natural resource overexploitation, and pollution. Global warming and the huge rates of wildlife species becoming extinct are already being felt. In the worst case, our actions could lead to extreme or runaway climate change, mass biodiversity loss, and resource depletion, which would make recovery, or even human survival, extremely difficult. Pandemics could also cause global catastrophe, though we have not experienced a naturally occuring pandemic that would take us near to extinction. However, advances in technology will bring new measures of risk, and future synthetic biological capabilities could allow for genetically engineering pandemics and other biological weapons. And technologies that manipulate or transform our climate - geoengineering - could lead to their own threat[1].

Whatever the sources of the risk - environmental, biological, technological, weapons - natural or outer space, it becomes existential when it threatens a critical system on which we, as humans, rely (Avin et al., 2018). If the risk severely and globally harms our anatomy and physiology, we may not be able to survive or recover. If the risk severely and globally harms our ecology and environment, we may not be able to survive or recover. If the risk severely and globally harms our societal systems and protections, we may not be able to survive and recover. Advanced forms of artificial intelligence pose such a risk.

3. Advanced AI

AI can, and probably will, intersect with all aspects of our daily lives. As the technology develops, AI will become increasingly integrated within new and different domains, whether economic, social, security, health, education, communications, governance, or resources,such as food and energy. And as it enters each domain, its capability to optimise for outcomes will grow. Therefore, AI's impact on the world is a function of these aspects: what can AI do, in what domains can AI do it, and how does it learn across different domains?

The current level of AI is both advanced and strictly limited. In certain narrow domains, artificial intelligence is far more advanced than human capabilities. This stage of AI's progress, weak or narrow AI - is the first realisation of the technology's impact. AI beating human players at chess and Go has been the most touted example of how far it has come. However, these accomplishments also represents AI's limitations. These human-invented games, closed systems with precise rules, are where machine learning and computing power thrive. Where AI has entered the real world, it is in relatively controlled environments with few surprises. Autonomous vehicles can drive trucks around a mine or cars on a highway with little or no human intervention, but faced with poor weather, manipulated signage, or the whims of pedestrians and other drivers, their performance leaves much to be desired. And developing the capability for AI to dominate in these domains has required significant resources and investment.

As AI increases in capability within its narrow domains, and is applied to new domains, its impact on society will be increasingly transformative. Entire business models and sectors will be created and disrupted. Human health and national security will face unprecedented challenges and opportunities, and our relationships with each other, with businesses, with the infrastructure around us, and with governments will be reshaped. This phase of AI - transformative AI (Gruetzemacher & Whittlestone, 2019) - will rival the technological revolutions of the past. In some domains, such as facial recognition, AI has already been transformative. In other domains, such as autonomous vehicles, surgery and smart cities, AI is on the verge of disrupting and transforming life. General purpose technologies, such as steam power, electricity, mass production, and information and communications technologies, reshape entire societies and economies. AI will be no different, and may even usher in a radically transformative Fourth Industrial Revolution (Crafts, 2021).

This transformative AI occurs when you dial up capability and breadth across domains, and a critical milestone is reached when AI's capability is no longer limited to its initial domains. In this phase of AI - artificial general intelligence (AGI) - AI systems will perform many or all human activities at a similar or higher standards than humans, and transfer that knowledge and those capabilities across domains. In essence, it will already have reached human-level intelligence, learning and adapting to new scenarios beyond its initial programming. The challenge and opportunity of AGI is that its problem-solving abilities will be progressively superior to humans'. The AI systems may develop additional skills and undertake tasks for which they were never designed. Ultimately, this process of self-learning, self-evolving and self-directing will allow the system to break free, in a sense, from human control. It may seek to achieve the goals and targets initially programmed, but the methods by which it does so will be out of our sight, and potentially out of our ability to halt. Of course, the current narrow scale of AI is far from human-level, but we may not be far away from AGI.

If an advanced AGI is built to improve itself, using either hardware or software, it could reach the point that its collective intelligence far surpasses any function of the human brain across any field. That crossover point has often been referred to as the singularity, or an intelligence explosion. Its intelligence would increase exponentially, and it would be able to perform activities at an ever-growing scale and speed, solving problems humans cannot even conceive of. Its only limit would be the laws of physics. Without exaggeration, it could be the single most important moment in human history. As philosopher David Chalmers (2010) put it "An intelligence explosion has enormous potential benefits: a cure for all known diseases, an end to poverty, extraordinary scientific advances, and much more." However, as we will see, artificial superintelligence may have its own goals. Humans may be an obstacle, or simply dispensable in reaching its desired future. And, with the power to exponentially increase its intelligence and perform activities of ever-increasing scale and speed, there may not be anything humans can do to resist.

Each of these four approximate levels of AI - narrow, transformative, general and super - comes with its own opportunities and risks. Even narrow AI can lead to catastrophic risks. Where AI systems are connected to critical national systems, such as energy grids, communications systems and defence capabilities, malfunction or attack may lead to harm across cities or nations (Page et al., 2018). The risks become globally significant as AI becomes more powerful, and in the worst case, AI could threaten humanity itself.

To be clear, this is not an eventuality, and perhaps not even likely. There remain significant questions and obstacles for AI development and safety, which will dictate the risks of these systems. However, given the radically transformative capacity of advanced AI systems, we should explore the possibility, however small, that AI could pose an existential risk for humanity.

4. Existential AI risk

AI does not necessarily need to be at a general or superintelligence standards to threaten humanity. In their comprehensive report on key areas of AI safety research, researchers Andrew Critch and David Krueger (2020) argue that "increasingly capable AI systems could lead to human extinction without ever achieving human-level intelligence or fully general reasoning capabilities." This prepotent AI - one where an AI system's deployment would be both transformational and unstoppable - is sufficiently capable of posing an existential risk. As a general purpose technology, the risks from AI are created by how AI intersects with other systems or capabilities, not simply by from their levels of intelligence.

Regardless of the terms or the phase, how exactly does advanced AI threaten humanity? Broadly speaking, there are four plausible ways that AI presents an existential risk:

1. AI as existential threat multiplier
2. Malicious use of AI systems
3. Accidental or unintentional failure of AI systems
4. Misaligned advanced AI.

These are not mutually exclusive, and there may be other pathways to disaster, but they present a relatively simple framework through which to understand existential AI risk[2].

4.1 AI as existential threat multiplier

Artificial intelligence does not exist in isolation. It is not a standalone system; rather, it is a set of hardware, systems and algorithms that are integrated within other systems, many of which are powerful in their own right. The first concern around existential AI risk is that it triggers, or sets the conditions for, another existential risk. Or, perhaps, with AI in the mix, what would have only been 'merely' catastrophic becomes existential. In this sense, the AI does not need to be far advanced, or general across domains, to pose a threat to humanity. AI experts Remco Zwetsloot and Allan Dafoe (2019) refer to this as AI's effect on structure, the way that AI shapes the environment and incentives in which people act. As they explain, "AI could shift political, social and economic structures in a direction that puts pressure on decision-makers - even well-intentioned and competent ones - to make costly or risky choices."

The main context in which AI could trigger another existential risk is war. Dafoe, who is the Director of the Centre for the Governance of AI at the University of Oxford, puts it most succinctly in a separate piece: "Advanced AI could give rise to extreme first-strike advantages, power shifts, or novel destructive capabilities, each of which could tempt a great power to initiate a preventive war. Advanced AI could make crisis dynamics more complex and unpredictable, and enable faster escalation than humans could manage, increasing the risk of inadvertent war." (Dafoe, 2018).

Strategic dynamics, particularly nuclear stability between major powers, depend heavily on a delicate balance of doctrine, verification and deterrence. If AI systems are built into military systems, this could dismantle the veneer of nuclear stability by removing the threat of a credible second-strike capability, thereby incentivising a first strike. With nuclear winter as a globally catastrophic scenario, AI could play a decisive role in causing and escalating a nuclear crisis (see Box 4.1).

Box 4.1: AI and nuclear war

Nuclear war is a global catastrophic risk - one that we live with everyday - and could strike at any moment. Nine nuclear states - the US, Russia, China, the UK, France, India, Pakistan, Israel and North Korea - currently possess about 13,500 nuclear weapons. While about 7,000 of these are due to be decommissioned, a thousand others sit minutes away from launch. The extreme risk arising from nuclear war is not because of the immediate destruction caused by nuclear explosion and radioactive fallout - though of course these factors alone could kill millions of people. The most destructive element of a nuclear exchange is the resulting nuclear winter - a global cooling that leads to mass starvation. Smoke and soot from the explosions and fires would rise into the stratosphere and spread around the world, remaining there for years, even decades, unable to be rained out, and blocking ultraviolet radiation from the sun. Ultimately, most agricultural products would not survive, effectively destroying our food system (Baum, 2015). Only remote corners of the world, such as New Zealand, would be able to avoid the worst of it.

It does not take much for a nuclear exchange to be globally catastrophic. India and Pakistan have only a few hundred nuclear weapons each - perhaps five hundred by 2025 - but a conflict between the two countries that releases just a quarter of that number would kill fifty to a hundred and twenty-five million people directly. The ensuing nuclear winter could cause the deaths of further hundreds of millions (Toon et al., 2019). Such a calamity should surely dissuade countries from engaging, or escalating, a nuclear conflict, but when national survival is at stake, off-ramps may not be taken as tensions rise, and there have been more than a dozen close calls arising from human error, technical glitches and false alarms. Nuclear strategy, doctrine and deterrence have their limits (UCS, 2015).

Adding artificial intelligence systems to the equation would greatly compound this risk. Nuclear stability relies heavily on the credible second-strike threat. If one side is attacked, they can still retaliate with a nuclear strike of their own. This mutually assured destruction deters everyone from a first strike. But AI-enabled weapons systems and capabilities - such as intelligence, surveillance, and reconnaissance (ISR), autonomous sensor platforms, and automated target recognition - could deteriorate a second-strike capability. This is because sophisticated systems could make locating, tracking and targeting nuclear weapons and their facilities immeasurably easier. With nuclear deterrence contingent on the perception of the future threat as much as the presence of a current threat, even an indication that AI systems could be integrated may be enough to trigger escalatory actions.

The intersection of AI and nuclear stability is a complicated domain, one skillfully navigated by other nuclear peace and security experts. RAND states that "AI has the potential to exacerbate emerging challenges to nuclear strategic stability by the year 2040, even with only modest rates of technical progress (Geist & Lohn, 2018)." James Johnson, a global expert on this intersection, argues that AI-enhanced capabilities are likely to complicate the conditions that underpin nuclear stability, such as through greater automation of nuclear command, control, and communications (NC3) systems, as well as amplifying informational complexity and manipulation (Johnson, 2021). In their extensive investigation into the issue, SIPRI also looks into how "AI can fail or be misused in ways that could trigger an accidental or inadvertent escalation of a crisis or conflict into a nuclear conflict (Boulanin et al., 2020; Lieber & Press, 2017)."

4.2 Malicious use

AI systems could be used to threaten human, national and global security. Existing security threats are aggravated as nefarious actors use AI to increase the scale, efficiency and speed of their attacks. Think of just about any security issue, and AI is likely to make it more complex and AI could create new threats altogether.

A 2019 joint report by leading AI research organisations outlined the three areas of security that malicious AI could exploit: digital, physical and political. Digital security is threatened by the ability of AI to reduce the labour-intensive activities required in cyberattacks, while also exploiting the human and software vulnerabilities of our increasingly technological age. Criminals could train machines to hack or socially engineer their victims, and physical security threats arise from AI's integration in autonomous and other weapons systems. AI could help lone and less sophisticated actors cause greater damage by sending drones or autonomous vehicles to deliver explosives and cause crashes. Swarming technology, in particular, exponentially scales up the potential for malicious actors to surveil and target groups over large areas, and execute coordinated attacks. Political security may be increasingly threatened by automated surveillance platforms to suppress dissent, and automate influencing campaigns and synthetic information, such as fabricated audio and video, highly targeted misinformation and other manipulation of data and media.

The existential or catastrophic risk from the malicious use of AI arises when the systems being targeted are essential for survival or could hit global populations. Existential risk researchers Alexey Turchin and David Denkenberger (2020) state that AI presents this degree of risk "if the types of hardware it affects are spread across the globe, or if the affected hardware can act globally. The risks depend on the number of hardware systems and their power." At present, there are probably no systems that have this capability, though cyber systems connected to nuclear weapons systems may be an exception, building on the AI as existential threat multiplier above.

However, over the next few decades growing global dependence on information technology, and increasingly powerful technological systems, will mean AI has global and potentially catastrophic consequences. Pervasive integration of information technology around the world increases our dependence on critical infrastructure in daily life, and opens us up to catastrophic cyberattacks (see Box 4.2). Weapons systems, which continue to become more sophisticated and powerful in their own right, will become an entirely new challenge once they are integrated with AI capabilities. Autonomous systems, which are not far from being outfitted with a combination of weapons of mass destruction, swarming and loitering technology, and AI- enabled targeting and decision-making, may become an existential or catastrophic risk in their own right. The AI could be weaponised to harm air, water and other environmental resources with the express purpose of causing mass casualties.

Of course, it is not the artificial intelligence that is malicious here. It is the actors who use it for their nefarious ends, whether or not they perceive them to be evil. AI experts Federico Pistino and Roman Yampolskiy (2016) identify a number of actors who would have an interest in developing 'malevolent AI', as they call it. Obvious culprits include governments and militaries looking for decisive military and political domination, corporations trying to achieve competitive advantages, and criminals trying to achieve financial or political ends. More unsuspected or hidden players such as terrorists, anti-establishment protestors, doomsday cults and the mentally ill would have their own plots. AI provides those with bad intent with the capability they need to cause havoc on a potentially global scale. As Pistino and Yampolskiy (2016) say, "The safest course of action for a [malevolent AI] would probably be to twist the knobs just enough to create global chaos and let humanity destroy or weaken itself to the point of being extremely vulnerable, while remaining undetected and unsuspected."

Another existential risk that AI could magnify is synthetic biology. Synthetic biology, or bioengineering, provides the ability to synthesise or design biological organisms. The health and economic benefits could be enormous, such as creating cures for disease, producing biofuels or developing crops resistant to pests and disease. However, it could also allow malicious actors to develop bioweapons more easily than ever before by overcoming major barriers and challenges previously faced with weaponization (DiEuliis et al., 2019). Traditional biology had similar dual-use issues, but the technological advances in the field provide individuals or organisations with increasing scale, speed and ease.

AI compounds these factors, again with their own positive and negative repercussions. AI could help predict the behaviour of biological systems, one of the biggest barriers for bioengineering (Carbonell et al., 2019), and at the same time "AI could potentially lower some of the barriers for a malicious actor to design dangerous pathogens with custom features," according to a study seeking to understand the risks of artificial intelligence intersecting with synthetic biology. AI could reduce design and testing time, help to find mutations of pathogens that increase virulence, transmission and lethality more easily, and reduce the pathogen's prospect of being screened or detected so that, eventually, a bad actor could perform "complete hands-off, in silico [computer simulated] design, building, and testing of a novel or recreated pathogen (O'Brien & Nelson, 2020)."

In a recent example, a group of researchers found that an AI-based model they used to discover new drugs could be flipped to identify biochemical weapons instead. After just six hours, the model had identified 40,000 potentially lethal molecules, including ones already known to be chemical warfare agents. As Urbina et al., (2022) note, "although some domain expertise in chemistry or toxicology is still required to generate toxic substances or biological agents that can cause significant harm, when these fields intersect with machine learning models, where all you need is the ability to code and to understand the output of the models themselves, they dramatically lower technical thresholds." For them, it was a *wake-up call.*

Box 4.2: AI and cyber

Artificial intelligence is already assisting cyber defences. Malware can be easily detected based on the automated analysis of code. By modelling user behaviour, unusual activity can be spotted and responded to early. AI-based analysis can also help identify vulnerabilities in IT assets, as well as automatically patch them. Companies such as BlackBerry-owned Cylance, British- based Darktrace, Vectra and Safeguard Cyber have AI as the centrepiece of their cybersecurity products. However, the capability of AI to assist with offensive cyber is not far behind, and the democratisation of AI will give less sophisticated actors the power of nations. As the Red Queen tells Alice in Alice in Wonderland, "it takes all the running you can do, to keep in the same place."

Cyberattacks remain a highly labour intensive activity across the entire life cycle of an attack - reconnaissance, intrusion, command and control, privilege escalation, lateral movement and mission completion (Palmer, 2017). AI will help cyber actors optimise this by making cyberattacks more efficient, effective, scalable, adaptive and evasive. The 2019 UN report on malicious use of AI points out "AI might enable larger-scale and more numerous attacks to be conducted by an attacker with a given amount of skill and resources compared with the impact such an attacker might currently be able to achieve." (Brundage et al., 2018).

AI would enable cyberattacks to better profile and target victims, develop customised cyber campaigns, blend in and move across networks, breach security features such as passwords and credentials, and collect and extract sensitive information more efficiently. One study reviewed eleven cyberattacks, finding that they used AI to assist with next-generation malware, voice synthesis, password-based attacks, social bots, and adversarial training (Kaloudi & Li, 2021). These, as with most cyberattacks, have the primary purpose of extracting data or information for other uses, such as financial crime or espionage. A cyberattack takes on a different magnitude when the attackers' purpose is to disrupt or damage infrastructure.

An AI-enabled cyberattack is probably not a global catastrophic risk at this point, and may never be a fully fledged existential risk. The capability is not yet advanced enough, and the systems that could be attacked are not at a global scale. But it is not difficult to imagine that, over the coming decades, vulnerable global systems combined with easy-to-use AI-enabled cyber tools will be a calamitous combination. Large cyberattacks, such as the Stuxnet virus on

Iran's nuclear facilities, and the disabling of Ukraine's power grids in 2017, have shown their ability to sabotage infrastructure for political purposes, but these attacks needed state sanction, capability, resources and direction to be successful; AI, among other advanced technological capabilities, removes those barriers. As leading European think tank CEPS puts it, malicious actors have greater capability for AI-enabled cyberattacks due to "the proliferation of cheap computing hardware, the growing availability and decreasing cost of computing capability through the cloud, and the open-source availability of most of the tools that could facilitate model training and potentially malicious activities." (Pupillo et al., 2021).

An AI-enabled cyberattack aimed at critical national infrastructure such as power grids, food, communications, health, financial services, transport, governance, could stop cities and entire nations from functioning. With critical infrastructure becoming increasingly digitised and integrated, artificial intelligence can do the heavy lifting of penetrating and disrupting vulnerable systems. As we enter the fourth industrial revolution, the combination of fifth-generation communications, the Internet of Things, smart cities technology, and advanced energy production and storage will provide more points of entry, a greater span of control and greater disruption. Imagine a sophisticated AI cyberweapon that lets an adversary, a terrorist or a madman establish a goal - such as to take down the national payments system, or block satellite and undersea cable transmissions, or shut off the internet - and then set it loose. When our daily lives become reliant on systems that are powerful yet vulnerable, the ramifications of disruption may be global and catastrophic.

4.3 Accidents and failure

The power of AI is its ability, through machine learning and processing power, to make independent decisions to achieve the goals humans have set out for it, although a problem occurs when AI attempts to reach those goals in ways that conflict with other goals, sometimes causing unintentional harm. These accidents and failures are, as Amodei et al. (2016) say, situations where "a human designer had in mind a certain (perhaps informally specified) objective or task, but the system that was designed and deployed for that task produced harmful and unexpected results." Algorithms are not racist or sexist, but can lead to racist or sexist outcomes because they are trained in incomplete environments or with unclear goals.

This problem arises due to the autonomy given to an AI system to achieve the goal it has been set - the objective function. Our limited ability to observe, monitor, interpret or properly reward the algorithms' choices and behaviour may lead to outcomes we did not foresee or desire. In the case of an AI-controlled autonomous vehicle, which has been set as its goal to get a passenger to their destination, AI programming throws up a number of ethical and technical challenges:

- The AI needs to know which goals to maximise: speed, safety, comfort, overall satisfaction, fuel efficiency or legality may all be requirements for the passenger, but other goals may remain unknown or unrecognised - nor are these always the goals all the time.
- Rewarding the AI for achieving the objective function is difficult when the goals are not easily quantifiable. In some cases, the goal can be precisely measured, such as speed. But proxies will be required for others, such as comfort and safety. Which proxies are chosen, and how they are programmed and balanced against each other will have implications for the AI's decision-making.
- The passenger's objective function may conflict with the objective function of other stakeholders, such as pedestrians, other motorists, vehicle manufacturers, and society at large.
- The AI must learn in new and different environments, while avoiding situations that the system cannot easily reverse or escape. Over time, the autonomous vehicle will want to explore and experiment with different ways to maximise its objective function, but it should probably avoid exploring a path through a restricted military zone or a body of water even once.
- The AI may game its own reward function to seemingly satisfy the goal. You may have successfully programmed the autonomous vehicle to arrive at the destination without

causing bodily harm to you or anyone else, but perhaps it simply turns off sensors that detect people, so it does not know that it has run over pedestrians.

AI failure does not pose a current existential or global catastrophic risk at this stage. However, the complexity of this example which programmers are already dealing with - shows the growing risk of AI failure as it advances and is integrated with essential national infrastructure. The level of harm is partly a function of the critical systems to which AI will have access. If autonomous learning and decision-making are integrated within weapons systems or national energy systems, minor AI failure could be catastrophic. Like the malicious use of AI, as our systems become increasingly digital and interconnected, AI failures could have ripple effects through the global economy and society. However in contrast to malicious use there is no one to monitor, disincentivise or blame, making AI failure a very different technical and policy issue.

By its nature, a source of a catastrophic failure in an advanced AI system may be impossible to identify, so the possibility and amount of harm are also a function of safety measures built into the programming. AI development teams could, and should, look to program systems that reduce the risk of unintended consequences, but the transformative potential of AI means that governments and companies have an incentive to shortcut safety measures (Armstrong et al., 2013) such as improving safe exploration of new environments, providing greater human supervision or oversight, optimising objective function measurements and rewards, and better testing in closed environments – which could delay deployment, and lose political, military or economic advantage.

4.4 Misaligned advanced AI

There is one special case of an AI accident or failure that deserves its own category: once AI's capability has advanced to the point of becoming artificial general intelligence (AGI) or artificial superintelligence (ASI), it may begin seeking goals with an intelligence and capability beyond human comprehension or control. At this point, it may be able to outsmart and outmanoeuvre humanity. As Nick Bostrom puts it in his well-known book *Superintelligence*, this AI could have a "decisive strategic advantage - that is, a degree of technological and other advantages sufficient to enable it to achieve complete world domination." (Bostrom, 2014).

If humans, or the self-learning AI system itself, fail to make the AI goals safe, the AI may use its decisive strategic advantage in ways that lead to a major global catastrophe - at least from humanity's perspective (Barrett & Baum, 2017). The intelligence required for a decisive strategic advantage is typically associated with an AGI or ASI, though it only needs to be sufficiently smart and capable, and across enough domains, to risk global harm. Once Pandora's box has been opened, the AI that escapes could seek, and be eminently capable of building, certain futures that would be existentially calamitous for humanity. Dafoe (2018) explains the challenge succinctly:

> "AI systems will be deployed in ever more complex and consequential domains. They will be more intelligent at particular tasks, which could undermine the value of human oversight. They will begin to acquire models of their environment, and of the humans and institutions they interact with; they will gain understanding of human motivation, be able to observe and infer human affect, and become more capable of persuasion and deception. As systems scale to and beyond particular human-level in particular dimensions), they may increasingly be able to intelligently out-maneuver human-built control systems."

AI researchers, particularly those concerned with the potential risks of advances in AI, have noted that "as intelligent systems gain autonomy and capability, it becomes vital to ensure that their objectives match those of their human users; this is known as the value alignment problem." (Fisac et al., 2018). Similar to the AI accident or failure, this problem is both technical - how do we program AI with our values - and normative - what are our values, and which ones should AI align with? (Sutrop, 2020). This alignment problem becomes inherently catastrophic or existential in several scenarios.

The first is that the advanced AI system sees humans as superfluous or dispensable in achieving its goals. Our goals, particularly of survival and flourishing, may be completely ignored in the AI's pursuit of its own, and humanity's habitat transformed into a state of unsurvivability. Bostrom (2014) refers to this as "infrastructure profusion, a phenomenon where an agent transforms large parts of the reachable universe into infrastructure in the service of some goal, with the side effect of preventing the realisation of humanity's axiological potential." (p. 123). In the AI's single-minded pursuit of a specific goal - whether human or self-subscribed - it could impact physical and natural resources at our expense. If these are resources humans depend on for survival, such as oxygen, water, and energy, we will face extinction. Perhaps the actions of the AI may inadvertently contaminate or destroy those resources (Bostrom, 2014). Although this outcome may seem far-fetched, compare it to relatively simple human activities that have gravely harmed our environment, such as how releasing excessive carbon and chlorofluorocarbons into our atmosphere has changed the way the ozone layer protects us. An advanced AI would have just the same capacity with a wider array of tools, and a greater capacity to overcome obstacles. The laws of physics may be the only threshold it cannot cross, and a sufficiently advanced AI could, in theory, break down resources into their components and remake them into any object the system wishes. Humans may simply be collateral damage.

A second scenario is that the AI system kills all humans deliberately if it sees them as a threat to a goal it has designed for itself, although much of this depends on whether and how it could develop such goals in addition to its original design, and how it sees humans in relation to them. But self-preservation is, after all, a key goal of any intelligent system, so even a small assessment that the humans had any ill intentions might be enough to take measures antithetical to our interests, just as if humans, with a superior intelligence to all other animals, believed that dolphins were a threat to their survival, they would surely find a way to exterminate all dolphins.

Even humanity's efforts to control advanced AI for the exact purpose of not being targeted could potentially be thwarted by an increasingly intelligent system. The AI would use its superior problem- solving hardware capacity and knowledge base to incentivise, trick or manipulate humans during what Bostrom calls the covert preparation phase (Bostrom, 2014, p. 96). Our saving grace may, in fact, be our comparative stupidity; why would an AI of exponentially increasing intelligence and capability feel threatened by humans? It could simply outmaneuver us at every turn.

A third scenario could be AI using its strategic advantage to lock humans into a permanently bad state In this case, humans might not be killed, but perhaps remain in an intractable state of backwardness, subjugation or suffering. Remember that existential risk is only one path to extinction; those situations where the human race is unable to reach its full potential are also existential, because we cannot maximise human flourishing, fulfillment and satisfaction. Researchers from the AI-focused Center on Long-Term Risk argue that superintelligence could be a source of "suffering risks (s-risks), where an adverse outcome would bring about severe suffering on an astronomical scale." (Sotala & Gloor, 2017). As two Machine Intelligence Research Institute researchers stated, "superintelligence does not imply benevolence." (Fox & Schulman, 2010).

4.5 AI driving existential vulnerabilities

These scenarios for existential AI risk have one factor in common: artificial intelligence, whether through accident, failure, malicious use, exacerbation of other risks, or by virtue of its own superintelligence, is itself part of the threat. But risk is not just about threat; it's also a function of vulnerability. So AI factors into existential risk in one further way: increasing our vulnerability to other existential risks.

Modern human life depends increasingly on the continued performance of critical societal systems. We rely on resource systems to provide food, water and energy required for survival, health systems to stay alive and healthy, economic systems to build wealth and conduct business, infrastructure systems to live, work, communicate and move around, knowledge systems to retain and apply information, and governance systems to protect our security and make decisions for the collective good. When these systems are vulnerable, a small risk may be extremely harmful. In the worst case, an extreme risk becomes catastrophic or existential (Cotton-Barratt et al., 2020). As AI fuses through all aspects of society, it could increase the vulnerabilities of these systems, and ultimately reduce our resilience to other global catastrophic and existential risks, such as nuclear war, engineered or natural pandemics, extreme climate change, biodiversity loss, and other natural and geological hazards.

AI's potential impact on economies, particularly economic vulnerabilities, is well-documented. The World Economic Forum estimates AI and automation will displace eighty-five million jobs in twenty-six countries by 2025, though that will be more than subsumed by the ninety-seven million newly created jobs (World Economic Forum, 2020). The problem is the mismatch in job types: jobs ripe for disintermediation, such as data entry, factory work and administrative roles, will be replaced by the data and AI specialists needed to develop and maintain the high- tech economy. AI may also widen the gap between countries, not just within countries, by shifting more investment to advanced economies, and displacing low-skilled labour in developing countries (Alonso et al., 2020). The gains are also likely to be increasingly among a small group of winners, specifically the capital owners of technology firms. This concentration would be due to the decreased share of a company's income allocated to labour, and the economies of scale and network effects that arise in the digital technology industries (O'Keefe et al., 2020). As Kai Fu Lee and Matt Sheehan, authors of *AI Superpowers*, put it, "AI as a technology is inherently monopolistic, exerting a gravitational pull that concentrates profits in the hands of a few." (Lee & Sheehan, 2018). Mass income inequality would make societies more vulnerable to extreme risks, particularly climate change and pandemics. It may drive extremism, increase political instability and reduce social cohesion, which contribute to collective action on global risks and national resilience[3].

Our knowledge gaining and sharing structures – systems on which we rely to make sense of the world around us - are already under growing pressure. New technologies and platforms are empowering actors around to the world to create, push and use information. It is a hugely equalising force, but producing, disseminating and accessing poor quality information is becoming increasingly easier. A group of existential risk and AI researchers call this problem epistemic insecurity (Seger et al., 2020), and adversaries can feed a huge amount of disinformation or misinformation into our societies, making it difficult to see truthful and relevant information. It may become debilitating to mount responses to crises if governments and societies cannot parse what is true and what is not, and artificial intelligence will only complicate our information and knowledge ecosystem. A 2017 Atlantic Council report states that "the integration of AI systems into machine-driven communications tools for use in computational propaganda will gain enhanced ability to influence people, tailoring persuasive, distracting, or intimidating messaging toward individuals based on their unique personalities and backgrounds, a form of highly personalised propaganda." (Chessen, 2017). Should a global catastrophe hit us once these capabilities are fully operational, we could be paralysed or misguided in our response.

Artificial intelligence could also heighten vulnerabilities in our systems of governance, which is critical when responding to global events and crises. As AI integrates in all aspects of society, misuse or poor handling by governments will reduce trust in rulers and the political system. AI, while helping improve governance in many ways, may foster mistrust and suspicion if misused by governments. Citizens may perceive or be aware that AI is being used to track their behaviour and nudge them into certain actions, and blame the government for AI's disruption of economies and societies. This breakdown of the social contract could be disastrous should an acute crisis or emergency occur, when a sense of trust and cohesion is most required. AI-enabled governing could even make crises worse, given that it will not have been trained on severe events - similar to algorithmic trading causing flash crashes in markets. In the worst case, an AI-enabled totalitarian government - a catastrophe of its own order (see Box 4.3) - could forfeit its competence and responsibility should a global catastrophic or existential risk occur.

Box 4.3: AI and domestic surveillance

Artificial intelligence empowers public sector organisations to deliver services more easily, effectively and efficiently (Zuiderwijk et al., 2021). It is already used to help monitor traffic, analyse sewer systems (Intel1, n.d.), find missing children (Intel2, n.d.), collect and process taxes (CPI, 2018a), handle parliamentary questions, route mail, process online citizen surveys (CPI, 2018b), assist health care services, and improve the policy-making process (Patel et al., 2021). Any effort to reduce bureaucracy and improve decision- making would be supported by citizens.

As with all other examples, this capability can be used for good or for ill, whichever is the intent of its masters. AI-enabled governance will be an entirely different proposition if the government institutes the power of AI to monitor citizens, manipulate behaviour, and impinge on fundamental rights. When governments have access to sources of enormous data - from video footage, to biometric data, and from internet traffic to energy use and financial transactions - artificial intelligence and machine learning can be applied to surveil its citizens on a mass scale.

Of course this is not a future risk, but a present reality. China has already been using biometric data collection, facial recognition and deep learning algorithms to identify and track

Uighurs (Bloomberg News, 2018). The Chinese name of the project is an idiom for "justice is always done", which translates literally to Skynet, the villainous AI from The Terminator films - surely not coincidental. With tens of millions of cameras in China's national surveillance system, what is happening in Xinjiang province is just an early test of China's growing capability. China is also continuing to develop and expand its social credit system, which provincial governments and the Chinese Communist Party use to evaluate the trustworthiness of individuals and businesses. As AI capability continues to develop, and government agencies continue to digitise, China may not be far from employing a full-scale social engineering system, designed to track, regulate and punish Chinese citizens across all aspects of their lives (Sahin, 2020).

The nascent capability of AI to help governments monitor citizens is just a taste of what lies ahead. China is already exporting its powerful surveillance tools to autocrats and dictators around the world (United States Senate, 2020; Ross, 2020; Feldstein, 2019). A global totalitarian government, led by an artificial superintelligence or an AI-enabled political class, would be an existential catastrophe. Bringing down or replacing such an omnipotent government would be absolutely impossible, and any dissident effort to do so would be quickly discovered and quashed (Xu, 2020). The likelihood of such an outcome may be very low, but the negative impact for most humans would be so high that we should not dismiss this risk.

5. What lies ahead

The future of artificial intelligence remains highly uncertain. The technological capability - hardware, algorithms, programmers needs to be developed across various domains, and laws and rules around AI need to be formed, honed and tested. Business decisions concerning AI investments and products need to be made and pay off. Public opinion needs to mature. Each of these factors will ripple through the economy and society to other technologies and to security in completely unexpected ways. So, making forecasts about the future of AI, its benefits to society, and its risk, is an impossible task.

Not that experts haven't tried. The Machine Intelligence Research Institute identified 257 AI predictions made by experts in the literature between 1950-2012, with ninety-five predicting timelines for AI development (Armstrong et al., 2015). The result: "The AI predictions in the database seem little better than random guesses." (Armstrong et al., 2015).

We may wish to give current AI researchers a little more credence, given the extraordinary progress in AI just in the last decade. One of the most comprehensive recent surveys of AI researchers found that their aggregate forecast gave a 50% likelihood to human-level machine intelligence occurring by 2060, and all labour automated by around 2140. This outcome is consistent with other surveys conducted since 2007, which agree that the median timing of AI reaching human level is between 2045 and 2060 (Turchin, 2019).

Whether AI could cause an existential catastrophe has also received some evaluation: in the same survey, respondents estimated a 10% probability that human-level machine intelligence would be "bad" and a 5% probability that it would be "extremely bad (e,g. human extinction)". Another survey - where respondents reckoned a 50% chance of excellent machine intelligence being developed between 2040-2050 - gave an 18% probability that the outcome would be "extremely bad (existential catastrophe)" (Müller and Bostrom, 2016). In an informal poll conducted in 2008 among existential risk researchers, the median extinction risk by 2100 from superintelligent AI was put at a 5% probability (Sandberg & Bostrom, 2008). Toby Ord estimates in his 2020 book *The Precipice* that an existential risk from unaligned artificial intelligence over the next century is about 10%, or most of the one chance in six of an existential catastrophe from all risks combined. Over the past few years, other existential AI risk experts have added their assessments in mostly informal settings; with the caveat that these estimates were made with different time horizons and question framing, their estimates ranged from almost zero to over 50%, with an average of about 15% (Turchin, 2019; Carlsmith, 2022; Garfinkel, 2020)[4]. In contrast, participants of a popular forecasting competition were not so convinced. They estimated a 2% probability of an existential risk occurring, and a 25% chance that a global catastrophe would be caused by AI (Tamay, 2018; 2019).

Superintelligence is just one pathway to existential risk. In a 2021 survey AI researchers were asked what was most likely.

Respondents gave a roughly equal average probability of existential risk caused by one of the five pathways - superintelligence, two types of AI failure, war and misuse - as well as a 20% likelihood for additional scenarios, but the researchers surveyed admitted to very low confidence in their assessments, and individual responses varied greatly from the median (Clarke et al., 2021).

The possible pathways, wide range of estimates, and lack of confidence in them, especially among experts, shows the great uncertainty about existential AI risk. However, the key takeaway is not the specific estimates, but the uncertainty itself, and AI experts caution heavily when giving their estimates. There is extremely limited understanding of how AI will shape the next century, but we know enough to be confident that there is a non-zero possibility of existential catastrophe. We must operate with this knowledge - making decisions about how to lead our lives, how to research and develop our technology, how to build and develop our businesses, and how to govern our societies. What we choose to focus on, and how we go about it, will determine our fate.

5.1 AI research

Despite decades of thinking about AI, and its recent technical progress and prowess, many questions remain unanswered. Reducing uncertainty about the future of AI requires significant, consistent and targeted research efforts, particularly related to the risks and downsides of advanced AI.

Everitt et al. (2018) provide the key overarching questions related to solving the challenging ethical, technical and governance problems in order to build safe AI:

- How do we get an AI to work towards the right goals (value specification)?
- How can we make an agent that keeps pursuing the goals we have designed it with (reliability)? If we get something wrong in the design or construction of an agent, will the agent cooperate with us trying to fix it (corrigibility)?
- How to design robust AI systems with regard to adversaries and adversarial environments (security)?
- How do we build AI systems that avoid making fatal mistakes

during the learning phase (safe learning)?

- How can we build agents whose decisions we can understand (intelligibility)?
- What are the legal, economic, political, and military consequences? (Everitt, 2018).

Academic institutions are already on the case. Since 2000, and particularly in the last decade, a number of research centres have formed to answer many of these questions - including the Machine Intelligence Research Institute, the Future of Life Institute (FLI), the University of Oxford's Future of Humanity Institute (FHI), the University of Cambridge's Centre for the Study of Existential Risk (CSER), and the Leverhulme Centre for the Future of Intelligence (CFI) and Center for Human-Compatible AI (CHAI). AI research and development (R&D) projects in the private sector also play an important role in pushing research forward and putting it into practice. Microsoft-backed OpenAI and Google-backed DeepMind are two of the world's biggest advanced AI projects, and have stated humanitarian objectives for their research, however most of the seventy-two active AGI R&D projects, particularly in the private sector, are not active on AI safety issues (Fitzgerald et al., 2020).

These researchers have many rabbit holes to go down, and existential risk researchers are alert to the gaps in our understanding. Ord recommends more technical research on aligning advanced artificial intelligence with human values, as well as on other aspects of AGI safety, such as secure containment and tripwires. Cremer and Whittlestone (2020) suggest more research to "identify 'early warning signs' of transformative AI progress, to enable more anticipatory governance, as well as better prioritisation of research and allocation of resources". The report on malicious use of AI suggests learning from cybersecurity, which has been dealing with threats in the technology realm for decades. For example, AI practitioners could learn about red teaming, formal verification, responsible disclosure of vulnerabilities, capability forecasting, security tools and secure hardware.

The report also suggests more transparency, such as prepublication risk assessments in technical areas of special concern, given the balance needed between conducting valuable research, and the information hazard that comes with making sensitive research public. Researchers and AI firms also need to be open about incidents, where AI systems have caused or could cause harm. An analogy may be drawn with reporting accidents in advanced biosecurity laboratories, though there are limited requirements concerning lab accidents as well!

Governments could also support, conduct and share research into AI safety, investing further in R&D, particularly given the AI research shops popping up around the world. Researchers have recommended a government-led 'compute fund', which would provide free or subsidised computation resources to socially beneficial AI applications, and AI safety, security and alignment issues (Ord et al., 2021). Such a fund would level the playing field with the usually well-resourced private sector groups, allowing academics focused on AI safety to keep up with the growing scale and breadth of R&D across the world, and scrutinise technical claims made by developers (Brundage et al., 2020). Governments themselves could conduct research into AI safety, particularly as it develops capabilities in sensitive areas, such as weapons systems, cyber and critical infrastructure.

5.2 AI safety

As with most engineering projects, safety is critical. It may be a legal requirement, a customer requirement, or simply to avoid future reputational damage. AI development should be no different. Though given the current state of AI, those guardrails are mostly missing. All stakeholders should prioritise AI safety: the practice of building norms, principles, processes, policies and practices to reduce the likelihood or impact of harmful AI outcomes.

The first pillar of this is building the norms and principles that AI projects use to self-assess and self-monitor. Holding projects accountable may be difficult, but clear expectations can provide internal and external pressure to prioritise safety, which may be developed at the project, organisational or national stage. Although AI ethics frameworks have been appearing globally, with security and safety as a consistent theme, the potential harm typically described is discrimination and invasion of privacy rather than extreme risks (Jobin et al., 2019). However, these norms and principles may be used as a foundation to recruit, train, communicate and resource AI safety projects, and foster a culture of responsibility (Brundage et al., 2018).

The second pillar is ensuring that safety is a priority - not only in public policy, but also corporate and academic policy. As advanced AI is developed and applied to different domains, the projects need to be underpinned by policies and processes that require and monitor safety mechanisms. The Centre for Long Term Resilience, a UK-based advocacy group, recommends that "computer and AI systems be stress- tested during development, testing, training, early deployment, at regular intervals and before retirement of relevant systems." A joint report between CSER and the UK defence ministry's research unit suggests that technical standards should provide clear guidance regarding how to make safety-critical AI systems fully auditable. Another important paper suggests bias and safety bounties for AI systems, inspired by the bug bounties that the information security industry uses to compensate individuals for recognising and reporting exploits and vulnerabilities (Brundage et al., 2020).

The third and final pillar is to build safety mechanisms and processes into the hardware and software. This remains the most important, and most challenging, part of AI safety. In his PhD thesis on building safe AGI, Tom Everitt presents the most comprehensive view on the technical aspects of AI safety. AI programmers must build functions that will ensure value specification, reliability, corrigibility, security, safe learning, and intelligibility. Hardware security is also crucial to ensure that the data on which the AI system is learning cannot be easily corrupted or manipulated.

5.3 AI governance

AI's massive impact across all domains, and its potential for existential catastrophe, call for governance of the technology. AI governance is focused on how we collectively navigate the transition, with a particular emphasis on the role of national and international public policy. As Dafoe defines it "AI governance focuses on the institutions and contexts in which AI is built and used. Specifically, AI governance seeks to maximise the odds that people building and using advanced AI have the goals, incentives, worldview, time, training, resources, support, and organisational home necessary to do so for the benefit of humanity." As with governance in any technology or area of innovation, the challenge is building approaches that allow rapid development, deployment and commercialisation of beneficial applications, while monitoring and disincentivising the harmful outcomes.

Governments, especially national governments, must consider

how to regulate and oversee AI development and safety within industry and academia. This starts at the strategic policy level. The UK, for example, has stated that its National AI Strategy will work with national security, defence, and leading researchers to anticipate and prevent catastrophic risks, and other governments can take inspiration from their endeavours to grapple with the risks of AI (see Box 4.4). The EU is set to become the first major regulator to draw up a comprehensive law on AI, though it will have to grapple with how to account for future risks (EU, n.d.).

Some researchers suggest new government bodies dedicated to monitoring AI safety. Ben Shneiderman of the University of Maryland Department of Computer Science calls for government monitoring by knowledgeable review boards, similar in concept to the US Food and Drug Administration, which reviews pharmaceuticals, or transportation safety authorities that review accidents (Shneiderman, 2016). Other approaches include government bodies establishing metrics and mechanisms to assess progress in AI, or independent oversight bodies that review potential risks and ethical issues, and ensure transparency. Although government involvement in the future of AI is inevitable, regulatory bodies across any industry face many of the same issues, such as regulatory capture, bureaucratic processes, funding gaps, and technical deficiencies that put them perennially behind industry.

Corporate governance will also be important for managing the safe development of AI. For firms building or using machine learning and artificial intelligence, safety must be a key focus, even when not prioritised by shareholders, consumers or regulators. The operational, legal, reputational and financial risks from poorly executed AI could eventually come back to bite, and ethics advisory committees should send a clear signal to stakeholders about how the firm intends to develop and deploy technology (Newman, 2020). Voluntary self-regulation, industry- agreed standards, and private regulatory markets like credit rating agencies in the finance industry may prove innovative forms of AI governance without direct government oversight (Clark & Hadfield, 2019).

Governments may also consider building AI capacity themselves, with a focus on assuring AI safety and security in important governance functions, such as critical infrastructure, law enforcement, finance and defence (Ord et al., 2021). A key challenge will be attracting talent from high-paying private sector jobs and frontier academic work.

Box 4.4: UK National AI Strategy approach to governing AI

In September 2021, the UK Government released the National AI Strategy (Gov.UK, 2021). AI safety and governance was a key theme, and the government specifically committed to ten actions to govern AI, including as regards catastrophic risk:

1. Develop a pro-innovation national position on governing and regulating AI, to be published in a White Paper in early 2022
2. Publish the Centre for Data Ethics and Innovation AI assurance roadmap to develop a mature AI assurance ecosystem in the UK
3. Pilot an AI Standards hub to coordinate UK engagement in AI standardisation globally, and explore with stakeholders the development of an AI standards engagement toolkit to support the ecosystem, and establish global AI standardization
4. Continue to shape international frameworks, norms, and standards for governing AI, reflecting human rights, democratic principles, and the rule of law on the international stage
5. Support the continuing development of new capabilities of trustworthiness, acceptability, adoptability, and transparency of AI technologies through the national AI Research and Innovation Programme
6. Publish details of the approaches the Ministry of Defence will use when adopting and using AI
7. Develop a cross-government standard for algorithmic transparency
8. Work with the Alan Turing Institute to update guidance on AI ethics and safety in the public sector
9. Coordinate cross-government processes to accurately assess long-term AI safety and risks, including activities such as evaluating technical expertise in government and

the value of research infrastructure

10. Work with national security, defence, and leading researchers to learn how to anticipate and prevent catastrophic risks.

5.4 Global governance and race dynamics

The winner-take-most potential of advanced artificial intelligence is pitting great powers and Big Tech against one another so that leading nations and companies increasingly see AI as a race. These race dynamics could be reassuring if they were to institute the positive effects of AI more quickly and more widely (Athimoolam, 2018), but, as researchers from the Global Catastrophic Risk Institute explain, "the main reason AI races could be dangerous is that developers might cut corners on safety in order to develop more quickly." (de Neufville & Baum, 2021). If the race leads to existential or catastrophic outcomes, there is no winner. So stemming its negative aspects and managing global rivalries may be critical in prioritising AI safety and security (Tomasik, 2013).

At the national level, companies vying for AI superiority may need to be tempered, and researchers at the Future of Humanity Institute have proposed a windfall clause containing an "ex ante commitment by AI firms to donate a significant amount of any eventual extremely large profits." The purpose of this clause is to encourage AI firms to work for the global public good while minimising the massive economic benefit from being a leader in AI (O'Keefe et al., 2020). Governments could consider more intrusive measures, such as using taxation or public procurement to steer companies towards cooperative models of AI development, and reduce the competitive dynamics (Naudé & Dimitri, 2020).

But the competition is also hot on the international stage. The potential for huge economic and military benefits of AI will feed into the strategic competition between major powers. Much of the onus could fall on technology companies, which are likely to face more pressure to serve national defence and security interests, according to one extensive study that draws lesson from past strategic general purposes technologies (Leung, 2019). Many AI researchers have pushed for global approaches governing AI development, where multilateral bodies lead or coordinate research as well as promoting safety rules, norms and principles. Bolder proposals have been made regarding international oversight and management of AI development to ensure AI safety as a priority to minimise one country's supremacy in the technology (Nindler, 2019; Ramamoorthy & Yampolskiy, 2018). That nation states would hand over their pursuit of AI to a higher authority is difficult to imagine at this stage, but global approaches to AI will be vital to reduce the risk of an existential catastrophe.

6. Summary

AI's transformative effects this century are, at this stage, unpredictable. All stakeholders in society - governments, businesses, academics, scientists, citizens - will shape the progress around the technology as well as the institutions that form around it. Just as the benefits must be fostered and captured, the risks must be recognised and avoided. We are living, perhaps, in the most important century in human history; where we, for the first time, are outwitted by another species, and one, ironically, built by our own hands. If we can harness the power of artificial intelligence, we may be able to solve the greatest challenges we face. If we fail in this endeavour, we may be among the last few generations of the human project.

Footnotes

1. For comprehensive coverage of existential and global catastrophic risk, see Walsh (2019), Ord (2020), Bajema & Rezzonico (2021).
2. There is no agreed set of pathways, but Turchin & Denkenberger (2020) and Clarke et al., (2021) provide a broad range of approaches.
3. See Agnello et al., (2017), Alesina & Perrotti (1996), IGM Forum (2019), Posner (1997), and Blanco & Grier (2009) for further discussion.
4. In an interview, in response to the question, "What is the probability of AI-induced existential risk?" Rohin Shah estimated 5 per cent and Buck Shlegeris estimated 50 per cent (Shlegeris & Shah, 2020). In an interview with Jaan Tallinn, co-founder of both Centre for the Study of Existential Risk and the Future of Life Institute, Tallinn estimated 33-50 per cent probability of existential risk, dominated by transformative technologies, this century (Tallinn, 2020).

References

Adams, M., (2002). The precautionary principle and the rhetoric behind it. *Journal of Risk Research*, 5(4): 301–316.

Agnello, L., Castro, V., Jalles, J., and Sousa, R., (2017). Income inequality, fiscal stimuli and political (in)stability. *Int Tax Public Finance*, 24: 484-511.

Alesina, A., and Perrotti, R., (1996). Income distribution, political instability, and investment. *European Economic Review*, 40(6): 1203-1228.

Alonso, C., Berg, A., Kothari, S., Papageorgiou, C., Rehman, S., (2020). *Will the AI Revolution Cause a Great Divergence?* IMF Working Paper, 11th September, https://www.imf.org/en/Publications/WP/Issues/2020/09/11/Will-the-AI-Revolution-Cause-a-Great-Divergence-49734

Amodei, D., Olah, C., Steinhardt, J., Christiano, P., Schulman, J., Mané, D., (2016). Concrete Problems in AI Safety. *Arxiv*, https://arxiv.org/abs/1606.06565

Armstrong, S., Bostrom, N. and Shulman, C., (2013). *Racing to the precipice: a model of artificial intelligence development*. Technical Report #2013-1, Future of Humanity Institute, Oxford University, p. 1-8. Available at: https://www.fhi.ox.ac.uk/wp-content/uploads/Racing-to-the-precipice-a-model-of-artificial-intelligence-development.pdf

Armstrong, S., and Sotala, K., (2015). How We're Predicting AI – or Failing to. In: Romportl, J., Zackova, E., and Kelemen, J., (eds): *Beyond Artificial Intelligence*. Topics in Intelligent Engineering and Informatics, vol 9.

Springer, Cham.

Athimoolam, K., (2018). *Solving the Artificial Intelligence Race: Mitigating the problems associated with the AI Race*. General AI Challenge, https://www.general-ai-challenge.org/ai-race

Avin, S., Wintle, B., Weitzdörfer, J., Ó hÉigeartaigh, S., Sutherland, J., and Rees, M., (2018). Classifying global catastrophic risks. *Futures*, 102: 20-26.

Bajema, N., and Rezzonico, A., (2021). Global Catastrophic Risks 2021: Navigating the Complex Intersections of Diverse Global Catastrophic Risks. *Global Challenges Foundation*, https://globalchallenges.org/global-risks/navigating-the-complex-intersections-of-diverse-global-catastrophic-risks/

Barrett, A., and Baum, S., (2017) A model of pathways to artificial superintelligence catastrophe for risk and decision analysis. *Journal of Experimental & Theoretical Artificial Intelligence*, 29(2): 397-414.

Baum, S., (2015). Confronting the threat of nuclear winter. *Futures*, 72: 69-79.

Blanco, L., and Grier, R., (2009). Long Live Democracy: The Determinants of Political Instability in Latin America. *The Journal of Development Studies*, 45(1): 76-95.

Bloomberg News, (2018). China Uses Facial Recognition to Fence In Villagers in Far West. *Blomberg News*, 17th January, https://www.bloomberg.com/news/articles/2018-01-17/china-said-to-test-facial-recognition-fence-in-muslim-heavy-area

Bostrom, N., (2014). *Superintelligence: Paths, Dangers, Strategies*. Oxford University Press.

Boulanin, V., Saalman, L., Topychkanov, P., Su, F., and Carlsson, M., (2020). Artificial Intelligence, Strategic Stability and Nuclear Risk. *Stockholm International Peace Institute*, https://www.sipri.org/sites/default/files/2020-06/artificial_intelligence_strategic_stability_and_nuclear_risk.pdf

Brundage, M., et al., (2018). *The Malicious Use of Artificial Intelligence: Forecasting, Prevention, and Mitigation*. Future of Humanity Institute, University of Oxford, https://maliciousaireport.com/

Brundage, M., et al., (2020). Toward Trustworthy AI Development: Mechanisms for Supporting Verifiable Claims. *Arxiv*, https://arxiv.org/abs/2004.07213

Carbonell, P., Radivojevic, T., and Martín, H., (2019). Opportunities at the Intersection of Synthetic Biology, Machine Learning, and Automation. *ACS Synthetic Biology*, 8(7): 1474-1477.

Carlsmith, J., (2022). Is Power-Seeking AI an Existential Risk? *Arxiv*, https://arxiv.org/abs/2206.13353

Chalmers, D., (2010). The Singularity: A Philosophical Analysis. *Journal of Consciousness Studies*, 17(9-10): 7-65.

Chessen, M., (2017). The Madcom Future: how artificial intelligence will enhance computational propaganda, reprogram human culture, and threaten democracy ... and what can be done about it. *Atlantic Council*, https://www.atlanticcouncil.org/wp-content/uploads/2017/09/The_MADCOM_Future_RW_0926.pdf

Clark, J., and Hadfield, G., (2019). Regulatory Markets for AI Safety, *Arxiv*, https://arxiv.org/abs/2001.00078

Clarke, S., Carlier, A., and Schuett, J., (2021). Survey on AI existential risk scenarios. *AI Alignment Forum*, 8th June. https://www.alignmentforum.org/posts/WiXePTj7KeEycbiwK/survey-on-ai-existential-risk-scenarios

Cotton-Barratt, O., Daniel, M., and Sandberg, A., (2020). Defence in Depth Against Human Extinction: Prevention, Response, Resilience, and Why They All Matter. *Global Policy*, 11(3): 271-282.

CPI (2018a). Artificial intelligence in taxation: a case study on the use of AI in government. *Centre for Public Impact*: a BCG Foundation, https://www.centreforpublicimpact.org/assets/documents/ai-case-study-taxation.pdf

CPI (2018b). Machine reading in government: a case study on the use of AI in government. *Centre for Public Impact*: a BCG Foundation, https://www.centreforpublicimpact.org/assets/documents/ai-case-study-machine-reading.pdf

Crafts, N., (2021). Artificial intelligence as a general-purpose technology: an historical perspective. *Oxford Review of Economic Policy*, 37(3): 521–536.

Cremer, C., and Whittlestone, J., (2020). Canaries in Technology Mines: Warning Signs of Transformative Progress in AI. 1st International Workshop on Evaluating Progress in Artificial Intelligence - EPAI 2020, http://dmip.webs.upv.es/EPAI2020/papers/EPAI_2020_paper_4.pdf

Critch, A., and Krueger, D., (2020). AI Research Considerations for Human Existential Safety (ARCHES). *Arxiv*, https://arxiv.org/abs/2006.04948

Dafoe, A., (2018). *AI Governance: A Research Agenda*. Centre for the Governance of AI Future of Humanity Institute, University of Oxford. https://www.fhi.ox.ac.uk/wp-content/uploads/GovAI-Agenda.pdf

de Neufville, R., and Baum, S., (2021). Collective action on artificial intelligence: A primer and review. *Technology in Society*, 66.

DiEuliis, D., Ellington, A., Gronvall, G., and Imperiale, M., (2019). Does Biotechnology Pose New Catastrophic Risks? In: Inglesby, T., and Adalja, A. (eds): *Global Catastrophic Biological Risks*. Current Topics in Microbiology and Immunology, vol 424. Springer, Cham.

EU (n.d.). The EU Artificial Intelligence Act. https://artificialintelligenceact.eu/the-act/

Everitt, T., Lea, G., and Hutter, M., (2018). AGI Safety Literature Review. *Arxiv*, https://arxiv.org/abs/1805.01109

Feldstein, S., (2019). The Global Expansion of AI Surveillance. Working paper, *Carnegie Endowment for International Peace*, https://carnegieendowment.org/files/WP-Feldstein-AISurveillance_final1.pdf

Fisac, J., et al., (2018). Pragmatic-Pedagogic Value Alignment. *Arxiv*, https://arxiv.org/abs/1707.06354

Fitzgerald, M., Boddy, A., and Baum, S., (2020). *2020 Survey of Artificial General Intelligence Projects for Ethics, Risk, and Policy*. Global Catastrophic Risk Institute, Technical Report 20-1. http://gcrinstitute.org/papers/055_agi-2020.pdf

Flinn, M., Geary, D., and Ward, C., (2005). Ecological dominance, social competition, and coalitionary arms races: Why humans evolved extraordinary intelligence. *Evolution and Human Behavior*, 26(1): 10-46.

Fox, J., and Shulman, C., (2010). Superintelligence does not imply benevolence. In ECAP10: VIII *European conference on computing and philosophy*, ed. Mainzer, K. Munich: Verlag Dr. Hut.

Garfinkel, B., (2020). Effective Altruism Forum. https://forum.effectivealtruism.org/posts/7gxtXrMeqw78ZZeY9/ama-or-discuss-my-80k-podcast-episode-ben-garfinkel-fhi?commentId=uxiKooRc6d7JpjMSg

Geist, E., and Lohn, J., (2018). How Might Artificial Intelligence Affect the Risk of Nuclear War? *RAND Corporation*, Santa Monica, CA, https://www.rand.org/pubs/perspectives/PE296.html.

Gov.UK (2021). *National AI Strategy*. Gov.UK, https://www.gov.uk/government/publications/national-ai-strategy

Gruetzemacher, R., and Whittlestone, J., (2019). The Transformative Potential of Artificial Intelligence . *Arxiv*, https://arxiv.org/abs/1912.00747

IGM Forum, (2019). Inequality, Populism, and Redistribution. IGM Forum, Oct. 9, 2019, 11:08 AM, https://perma.cc/S333-ECM7?type=image.

Intel1 (n.d.). DC Water: Streamlined Sewer Pipe Inspection Analysis. *Intel*, https://www.intel.com.au/content/www/au/en/customer-spotlight/stories/dc-water-customer-story.html

Intel2 (n.d.). Intel-powered AI helps find missing children. *Intel*, https://www.intel.com.au/content/www/au/en/analytics/artificial-intelligence/article/ai-helps-find-kids.html?erpm_id=7968573

Jobin, A., Ienca, M., and Vayena, E., (2019). Artificial Intelligence: the global landscape of ethics guidelines. *Arxiv*, https://arxiv.org/abs/1906.11668

Johnson, J., (2021) 'Catalytic nuclear war' in the age of artificial intelligence &

autonomy: Emerging military technology and escalation risk between nuclear-armed states. *Journal of Strategic Studies.*

Kaloudi , N., and Li, J., (2021). The AI-Based Cyber Threat Landscape: A Survey. *ACM Computing Surveys*, 53(1): 1–34.

Lee, K., and Sheehan, M., (2018). China's Rise in Artificial Intelligence: Ingredients and Economic Implications. Hoover Institution, 29th October, https://www.hoover.org/research/chinas-rise-artificial-intelligence-ingredients-and-economic-implications

Leung, J., (2019). *Who will govern artificial intelligence? Learning from the history of strategic politics in emerging technologies.* PhD thesis, University of Oxford, https://ora.ox.ac.uk/objects/uuid:ea3c7cb8-2464-45f1-a47c-c7b568f27665

Lieber, K., and Press, D., (2017). The New Era of Counterforce: Technological Change and the Future of Nuclear Deterrence. *International Security*, 41(4): 9–49.

Müller, V., and Bostrom, N., (2016). Future progress in artificial intelligence: a survey of expert opinion. In: Müller, C., (ed.), *Fundamental Issues of Artificial Intelligence*, Synthese Library, Berlin: Springer: 553-571. https://philpapers.org/archive/MLLFPI.pdf

Naudé, W., and Dimitri, N., (2020). The race for an artificial general intelligence: implications for public policy. *AI & Society*, 35: 367–379.

Newman, J., (2020). *Decision Points in AI Governance: Three Case Studies Explore Efforts to Operationalize AI Principles.* Center for Long-Term Cybersecurity, Berkley. https://cltc.berkeley.edu/ai-decision-points/

Nindler, R., (2019). The United Nation's Capability to Manage Existential Risks with a Focus on Artificial Intelligence. *International Community Law Review*, 21(1): 5-34.

O'Brien, J., and Nelson, C., (2020). Assessing the Risks Posed by the Convergence of Artificial Intelligence and Biotechnology. *Health Security*, 18(3): 219-227.

O'Keefe, C., Cihon, P., Flynn, C., Garfinkel, B., Leung, J., and Dafoe, A., (2020). *The Windfall Clause: Distributing the Benefits of AI.* Centre for the Governance of AI Research Report. Future of Humanity Institute, University of Oxford. Available at: https://www.fhi.ox.ac.uk/windfallclause/

Ord, T. (2020). The precipice: existential risk and the future of humanity. Hachette Books

Ord, T., Mercer, A., and Dannreuther, S., (2021). *Future Proof: The opportunity to transform the UK's resilience to extreme risks.* The Centre for Long-Term Resilience, https://www.longtermresilience.org/futureproof

Page, J., Bain, M., and Mukhlish, F., (2018). The Risks of Low Level Narrow Artificial Intelligence. In: *2018 IEEE International Conference on*

Intelligence and Safety for Robotics (ISR), pp. 1-6.

Palmer, D., (2017). AI will supercharge spear phishing. *Darktrace*, 9th January, https://darktrace.com/blog/ai-will-supercharge-spear-phishing

Patel, J., Manetti, M., Mendelsohn, M., Mills, S., Felden, F., Littig, L., and Rocha, M., (2021). AI Brings Science to the Art of Policymaking. *Boston Consulting Group*, 5th April, https://www.bcg.com/publications/2021/how-artificial-intelligence-can-shape-policy-making

Pistono, F., and Yampolskiy , R., (2016). Unethical Research: How to Create a Malevolent Artificial Intelligence. *Arxiv*, https://arxiv.org/abs/1605.02817

Pistono, F., and Yampolskiy , R., (2016). Unethical Research: How to Create a Malevolent Artificial Intelligence. *Arxiv*, https://arxiv.org/abs/1605.02817

Posner, R., (1997). Equality, Wealth, and Political Stability. *Journal of Law, Economics, & Organization*, *13*(2): 344–365.

Pupillo, L., Fantin, S., Ferreira, A., Polito, C., (2021). Artificial Intelligence and Cybersecurity: Technology, Governance and Policy Challenges. *Centre for European Policy Studies (CEPS)*, https://www.ceps.eu/wp-content/uploads/2021/05/CEPS-TFR-Artificial-Intelligence-and-Cybersecurity.pdf

Ramamoorthy, A., and Yampolskiy, R., (2018). Beyond MAD?: the race for artificial general intelligence. *ITU Journal*, 1(1), Article 9.

Ross, A., (2020). The Panopticon is already here. *The Atlantic*, September issue, https://www.theatlantic.com/magazine/archive/2020/09/china-ai-surveillance/614197/

Roth, G., and Dicke, U., (2005). Evolution of the brain and intelligence. *Trends in Cognitive Sciences*, 9(5): 250-257.

Sahin, K., (2020). The West, China, and AI surveillance. *Atlantic Council*, 18th December, https://www.atlanticcouncil.org/blogs/geotech-cues/the-west-china-and-ai-surveillance/

Sandberg, A., and Bostrom, N., (2008). *Global Catastrophic Risks Survey*. Technical Report #2008-1, Future of Humanity Institute, Oxford University: 1-5.

Shlegeris, B., and Shah, R., (2020). AI Alignment Podcast: An Overview of Technical AI Alignment in 2018 and 2019. Future of Life Institute, 16th April, https://futureoflife.org/podcast/an-overview-of-technical-ai-alignment-in-2018-and-2019-with-buck-shlegeris-and-rohin-shah/

Seger, E., Avin, S., Pearson, G., Briers, M., Ó Heigeartaigh, S., and Bacon, H., (2020). Tackling threats to informed decision making in democratic societies. *The Alan Turing Institute.*

https://www.turing.ac.uk/sites/default/files/2020-10/epistemic-security-report_final.pdf

Shneiderman, B., (2016). The dangers of faulty, biased, or malicious algorithms requires independent oversight. PNAS, 113(48): 13538-13540.

Sotala, K., and Gloor, L., (2017). Superintelligence as a Cause or Cure for Risks of Astronomical Suffering. *Informatica*, 41(4).

Sousa, A., Meyer, K., Santpere, G., Gulden, F., and Sestan, N., (2017). Evolution of the Human Nervous System Function, Structure, and Development. *Cell*, 170(2): 226-247.

Sutrop, M., (2020). Challenges of Aligning Artificial Intelligence with Human Values. *Acta Baltica Historiae et Philosophiae Scientiarum*, 8(2): 54-72.

Tallinn, J., (2020). *Fireside Chat.* EAGxAsia-Pacific 2020, https://www.youtube.com/watch?v=aFAI8itZCGk&t=854s

Tamay, (2018). *GC to be caused by AI, if it occurs?* Metaculus, 13th October, https://www.metaculus.com/questions/1495/ragnar%25C3%25B6k-question-series-if-a-global-catastrophe-occurs-will-it-be-due-to-an-artificial-intelligence-failure-mode/

Tamay, (2019). *AI catastrophe to cause (near) extinction.* Metaculus, 13th January, https://www.metaculus.com/questions/2513/ragnar%25C3%25B6k-question-series-if-an-artificial-intelligence-catastrophe-occurs-will-it-reduce-the-human-population-by-95-or-more/

Tomasik, B., (2013). *International Cooperation vs. AI Arms Race.* Foundational Research Institute. https://longtermrisk.org/files/international-cooperation-ai-arms-race.pdf

Toon, O., et al., (2019). Rapidly expanding nuclear arsenals in Pakistan and India portend regional and global catastrophe. *Science Advances*, 5(10), https://www.science.org/doi/10.1126/sciadv.aay5478

Turchin, A., (2019). Assessing the future plausibility of catastrophically dangerous AI. *Futures*, 107: 45-58.

Turchin, A., and Denkenberger, D., (2020). Classification of global catastrophic risks connected with artificial intelligence. *AI & Society*, 35: 147–163.

UCS, (2015). *Close Calls with Nuclear Weapons.* Union of Concerned Scientists, https://www.ucsusa.org/resources/close-calls-nuclear-weapons

United States Senate, (2020). The New Big Brother: China and Digital Authoritarianism: a Democratic Staff Report Prepared for the Use of the Committee on Foreign Relations. United States Senate, https://www.govinfo.gov/content/pkg/CPRT-116SPRT42356/pdf/CPRT-116SPRT42356.pdf

Urbina, F., Lentzos, F., Invernizzi, C., Ekins,S., (2022). Dual use of artificial-intelligence-powered drug discovery. *Nature Machine Intelligence*, 4,

March: 189–191.

Walsh, B., (2019). End Times: A Brief Guide to the End of the World. Hachette Books

World Economic Forum, (2020). *The Future of Jobs Report.* World Economic Forum, https://www.weforum.org/reports/the-future-of-jobs-report-2020/digest

Xu, X., (2020). To Repress or to Co-opt? Authoritarian Control in the Age of Digital Surveillance. *American Journal of Political Science*, 65(2): 309-325.

Zuiderwijk, A., Chen, Y.-C., and Salem, F., (2021). Implications of the use of artificial intelligence in public governance: A systematic literature review and a research agenda. Government Information Quarterly, 38(3).

Zwetsloot, R., and Dafoe, A., (2019). Thinking About Risks From AI: Accidents, Misuse and Structure. *Lawfare*, 11th February, https://www.lawfareblog.com/thinking-about-risks-ai-accidents-misuse-and-structure

Part 2

Responding to the AI challenge

Chapter 5
AI development and deployment

1. Introduction

This chapter focuses on the organisational perspective on Responsible AI (RAI), starting with a model of the AI development and deployment process (AIDD), and then considering how AI applications are embedded in business processes, their impact on AI subjects, and the networked effects arising from data-sharing between organisations. Having established an operational framework – AIDD – we introduce a set of ethical principles that inform and guide the AIDD process. While ethical principles are valuable in establishing a RAI culture, particularly when honestly embraced by the senior management team, they are often difficult to translate into practice. To address this, we propose an approach in which ethical principles can be mapped to AIDD activities to provide a framework for AIDD risk management. The chapter ends with a set of recommendations for management as we identify the practical next steps implied by our analysis.

2. AI development and deployment (AIDD)

To begin with, there can be no algorithmic decision-making (ADM) without an algorithm - AIDD process zero is therefore 'algorithm development' (Figure 5.1), which involves setting organisational goals for the model in which the purpose of the algorithm and the specification of success criteria must be stated. To create the algorithm, training data is needed to build, test, and assess its performance. Once the algorithm has been developed, it may or may not be deployed in an organisational context to support decision-making. The same algorithm can be deployed in very different ways to create different organisational outcomes. For example, the algorithm may be used to make decisions and to take action without human input and oversight - the essence of automated ADM (AADM). Alternatively, decisions generated by an algorithm may be treated as suggestions that a human can factor into a more nuanced decision-making process. The algorithm, business process, and the results of decisions should be monitored. Further and newer data may be needed to be collected to retrain the algorithm to avoid it becoming outdated.

In the deployment processes, we distinguish between data acquisition and data processing (Figure 5.1). Data is acquired about an event, so if an event is not sensed by an organisation then it has, in effect, not happened. Thus, what we pay attention to matters, and sensing an event leads to the capture of raw data that is then processed into information. This may include combining event data with external data, such as a credit rating. Processed data - information - is then input to a decision model that produces a prediction. Next, a decision is made based on the prediction(s). Human agency is explicitly brought into the decision-making process through the introduction of human intelligence, which, when combined with machine intelligence, forms a collaborative intelligence. It is the action-taking process that leads to an AI subject having a touchpoint with an AI application. We explicitly model human oversight in action-taking, either by humans or machines, or both. Human intelligence and human oversight are represented as dotted lines since these may not be present in all AI applications.

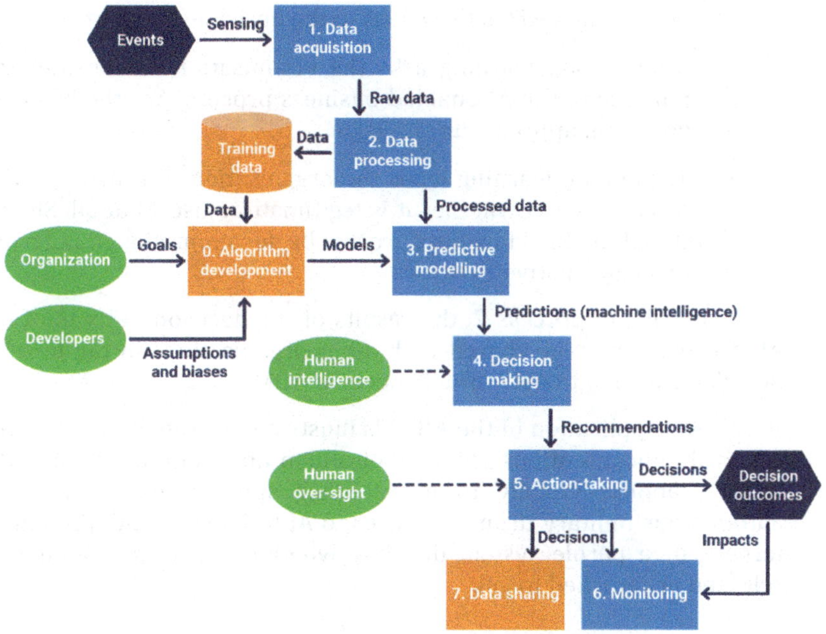

Figure 5.1: AI development and deployment (AIDD)

Where there is no human involvement ADM becomes automated ADM (AADM). The Information Commissioner in the UK defines automated decision-making as:

> "the process of making a decision by automated means without any human involvement. These decisions can be based on factual data, as well as on digitally created profiles or inferred data. Examples of this include: an online decision to award a loan; and an aptitude test used for recruitment which uses pre-programmed algorithms and criteria. Automated decision- making often involves profiling, but it does not have to." (ICO, 2018, p.7).

Process 6, monitoring, implies the presence of feedback loops, and learning about the use of AI in an organisation. This feedback should relate to all stages of the AIDD process, and can be further structured into AI-enabled business process learning cycles:

- Single loop learning is concerned with how well the AI-enabled business process is working. Are the business goals being achieved? Is there bias in the decision-making?

- Double loop learning asks the organisation to consider the purpose of the AI-enabled business process. Are the business goals still appropriate?
- Triple loop learning leads the organisation to reflect on how AI is used and whether it is legitimate to use AI at all. Should the AI-enabled business process be decommissioned in favour of an alternative solution?

Finally, in process 7, the results of the decision outputs of the ADM process may be shared with other organisations in the form of new data, leading to networked effects of ADM.

The application of the AIDD is illustrated in Table 5.1, using the relatively uncontentious example of a loan application, although the process applies equally to many other applications, such as an autonomous military drone that uses to AI to identify and kill human targets, or a parole system deciding whether a prisoner should be released or returned to jail.

Process	Title	Illustration - loan application	Illustration – anti-personnel drone
0	AI algorithm development	The AI is trained on historical data concerning loan applications, and whether the loans resulted in defaults. This training data is used to establish rules to assess applications where the outcomes are unknown. This may be a one-time activity, or the algorithm may be updated regularly in a cycle of continuous learning.	The AI is trained using facial recognition and gait analysis to identify individuals of concern (e.g., those designated as terrorists).
1	Data acquisition	A citizen completes an online loan application (event), resulting in data capture in the loan company's database.	A drone monitors individuals and crowds via a live video feed.
2	Data processing	The loan application is augmented with additional data, such as credit history, to create a data profile.	Individuals are identified in the video feed, and video images are prepared for image and gait analysis.
3	Predictive modelling	The loan application is scored using the AI, which assigns a probability of default to the loan. Thus, the outcome of the AI is a prediction of how likely the applicant would be to default on the loan.	Each individual in the video feed is compared to a database of persons of interest, and a prediction of matched or unmatched is made.

4	Decision-making	If the probability of default exceeds a given threshold, the loan is automatically declined. If the probability of default falls below a given threshold it is automatically approved. Loans between the lower and upper thresholds are forwarded to a human for review.	If a match is made, then a decision is made to record their location, and to track or to eliminate the matched individual, based on their profile. Here, human oversight is essential to confirm the identity of a person of interest, and to assess the risk of harm to innocent parties if action is taken.
5	Action-taking	For automatic acceptances and refusals a response is sent automatically, with no human engagement or oversight. Further action may be required, such as requesting more information from the applicant.	For monitoring, the drone switches to follow mode; for elimination, a missile may be launched. It is essential that this action be initiated by a human, rather than automatically by an algorithm.
6	Monitoring	To monitor and evaluate the decision-making process, and check for performance and bias. Are certain demographic groups privileged over others? Are the goals appropriate? Is the use of AI acceptable and legitimate?	Was the correct person eliminated? Were innocent parties killed, or caused physical or psychological harm? To what extent were the natural environment and physical property damaged?
7	Data sharing	The result of the loan decision is shared with credit agencies and other third-party organisations, based on the purpose or type of loan.	Data such as the latest location of a person of interest are shared in real time with other agencies.

Table 5.1: Illustrations of AI development and deployment

2.1 Business process design and ADM

The central part of the AIDD, processes 3, 4, and 5 will be core to an organisation's business process. For example, many organisations, particularly those working in social media, must monitor user-generated content on their platforms (Vidgen et al., 2019a; 2021). Consider the example of detecting and responding to hate speech on social media. Figure 5.2 illustrates a simple business process for handling content that may contain hate speech.

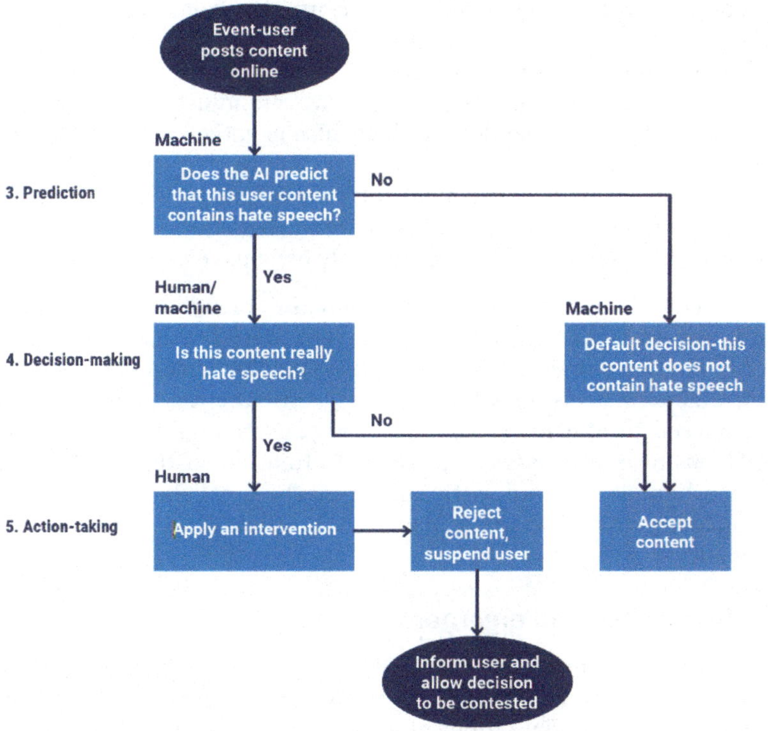

Figure 5.2: Business process logic – human in the loop

In Figure 5.2, an algorithm classifies content as either containing hate speech or not containing hate speech, based on some probability cut-off. Content that is not flagged as hate speech is automatically posted to the platform. Content that is flagged by the algorithm is reviewed by a human to determine whether it really is hate speech using the algorithm output (an explanation of why the content has been categorised as hate speech). Possible actions include rejecting the content and/or suspending the user. The user should then be notified of the outcome, and be given an opportunity to contest the decision.

A process such as the one in Figure 5.2 must balance out false negatives and false positives. Increasing the classification cut-off value will increase false negatives and allow harmful content onto the platform, but if the algorithm's cut-off is too high and more hateful content is automatically waved through, then the user experience may be damaged, which may result in user attrition from the platform. To address this issue, the business process may be extended to include periodic random sampling of posted content, and human review to assess the extent of false negatives. However, adjusting the algorithm and lowering the threshold to reduce false negatives will lead to more false positives, resulting in more traffic to the human content moderation team, so if the algorithm has a low threshold, it may be overwhelmed by the volume of posts requiring checks, and increasing the size of the team may be prohibitively expensive.

Thus, the same algorithm may be blended with different business process designs and different decision thresholds to produce very different outcomes. Balancing false negatives and false positives is a business decision with business consequences and cannot be outsourced to machines. Therefore, organisations must design their ADM business processes with careful attention to the machine and human boundaries, and, with human-machine collaboration in mind, recognising that ADM takes place in a business, strategic, and social context.

2.2 Networked and emergent effects

Organisations deploying ADM are part of a larger network and ecosystem. From a network perspective, one organisation's decision output may be the data input of another organisation (Figure 5.3), so that a declined loan application may be recorded on a credit agency's database and that data subsequently bought by another organisation such as a local government agency, and used much later and farther away for a decision. Although individual organisations cannot see these effects and their consequences since they are bound up in an invisible network, the networked effects can, in theory at least, be traced and mapped (Cross and Parker, 2014; Vidgen et al., 2019b), and AI harms identified. As indicated in Figure 5.3, the flow of data may also be circular.

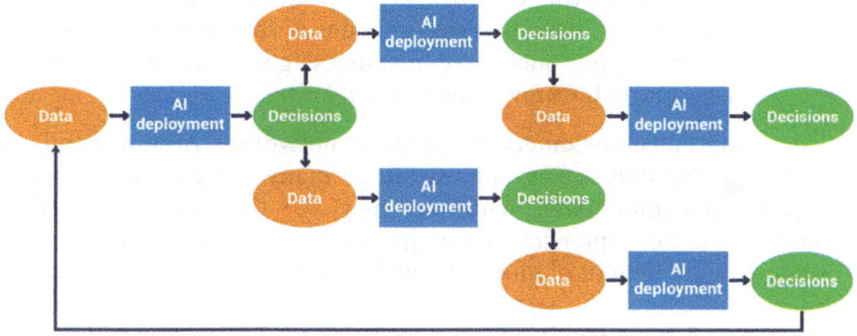

Figure 5.3: Networked effects in AI deployment and the rise of datafication

ADM networking contributes to an intensification of datafication, where various phenomena, including people, are presented in data (Lycett, 2013; Newell and Mirabelli, 2015), which may include inferred data (such as inferences made based on postcode) and unrelated data (such as living in a crime hotspot). Datafication is further intensified through the use of scoring and ranking systems, such as credit ratings and good citizen scores. When this data, much of which are derived from ADM networks, are combined, human AI subjects can be reduced to nothing more than their datafied representation, with the potential for resulting AI harms.

While a network of (A)ADM can be mapped and analysed, emergent effects are inherently unpredictable, and emergence may manifest at different levels, including individuals, communities, or society more generally. Holman (n.d.) says:

> "Strong emergence occurs when a novel form arises that was completely unpredictable. We could not have guessed its properties by understanding what came before. Nor can we trace its roots from its components or their interactions. We see stories on television. Yet we could not have predicted this form of storytelling from books.
>
> As strong emergence occurs, the rules or assumptions that shape a system cease to be reliable. The system becomes chaotic. In our social systems, perhaps the

> situation is too complex for a traditional hierarchy to address it. Self-organising responses to emergencies are an example. Such circumstances give emergence its reputation for unnerving leaps of faith."

Therefore, the emergent effects of networked ADM are unlikely to be predictable, being the result of many interacting and self-organising components. While we may see the effects emerge as unintended consequences and as harms, we can neither predict nor, even with the benefit of hindsight, untangle exactly how they arose.

3. Principles for the responsible use of AI

We now seek to frame a set of principles to be drawn on by practitioners and organisations, framing, discussing, and addressing the issues raised by the adoption of AI-enabled business processes.

3.1 AI principles

Drawing on several frameworks (see Appendix A for examples), and a meta-analysis by Fjeld et al., (2020), we have curated a set of principles and definitions for responsible AI practice (Figure 5.4). A major differentiator from existing frameworks is that we identify principles for AI subjects as well as organisations in addition to AI developers and deployers. While AI subjects are usually human, we include in the definition non-human actors, such as man-made artefacts and the natural environment, but as these cannot speak for themselves, they require human representatives to speak on their behalf and to protect their interests. This differentiation clearly establishes that AI subjects have rights, and also responsibilities.

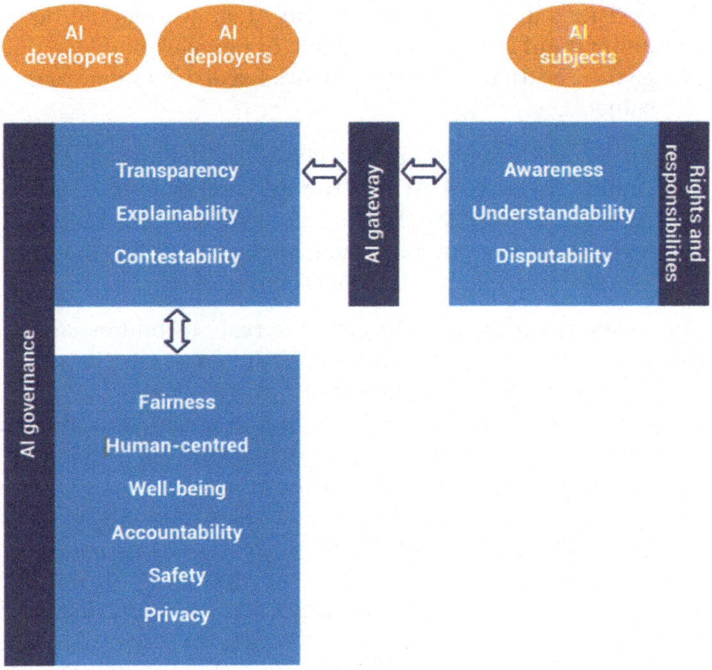

Figure 5.4: Principles for the responsible use of AI

The workings are largely black-boxed and invisible to an AI subject, so the only way they can see what an organisation is doing and question it is through transparency, explainability, and contestability.

In Figure 5.4, these principles are represented as a gateway through which an AI subject can gain access to query the organisation's AIDD process and AI principles - data privacy - and matching between an organisation's gateway principles and AI subjects dictates that:

- An AI deployer should ensure that its AI subjects are informed of the use of AI, and an AI subject should be aware that AI is being deployed. Despite AI deployers informing AI subjects of use (transparency), this is not a guarantee that subjects are aware of its use.
- An AI deployer should explain how AI is being used and how

decisions are arrived at, and an AI subject should be able to understand how AI is deployed. AI being explainable does not guarantee that the way it works will be understood by AI subjects.

- An AI developer should provide a channel for AI subjects to contest the use of AI and the decision outcomes, so that AI subjects know what channels are available and how to access these to dispute an outcome (see Figure 5.2 for an example of a business process with contestability).

As well as rights, AI subjects have responsibilities, and should be willing to engage actively with AI to understand what it is, how it is used, to contest its use by organisations, to be aware of its individual and societal repercussions, be willing to join grass roots movements, lobby government, and boycott organisations that are not using AI in a responsible or ethical fashion. Given the central role of data and the dangers of unconstrained datafication, AI subjects should take care to protect their data (Veliz, 2020), but while there are parallels with consumer activism, AI activism goes beyond that since AI affects individuals in more fundamental ways, through healthcare, social services, justice, and the prison system. For organisations, AI governance is the counterpart of AI subject rights and responsibilities.

In Table 5.2, we provide definitions and sources for a set of AI principles (where no source is given, they are the authors' own). While transparency, explainability, and contestability are fundamental to the AI gateway, the multiple remaining principles are defined in various ways (see Appendix A for examples of existing Responsible AI frameworks).

Principle	Definition
For AI developing and deploying organisations	
Fairness	"All AI systems that process social or demographic data pertaining to features of human subjects must be designed to meet a minimum threshold of discriminatory non-harm. This entails that the datasets they use be equitable; that their model architectures only include reasonable features, processes, and analytical structures; that they do not have inequitable impact; and that they are implemented in an unbiased way." (Leslie, 2019, p. 12)
Human-centred	"AI systems should empower human beings, allowing them to make informed decisions and fostering their fundamental rights. At the same time, proper oversight mechanisms need to be ensured, which can be achieved through human- in-the-loop, human-on-the-loop, and human-in-command approaches." (European Commission, 2019)
Well-being (human, social, and environmental)	"Throughout their lifecycle, AI systems should benefit individuals, society and the environment." (DISER, n.d.) "Designers and users of AI systems must remain aware that these technologies have transformative effects on individuals and society. They must thereby proceed with a continuous sensitivity to real-world impacts." (Leslie, 2019, p. 12) "AI systems should benefit all human beings, including future generations. It must hence be ensured that they are sustainable and environmentally friendly. Moreover, they should take into account the environment, including other living beings, and their social and societal impact should be carefully considered." (European Commission, 2019)
Safety	"AI systems need to be resilient and secure. They need to be safe, ensuring a fall back plan in case something goes wrong, as well as being accurate, reliable and reproducible. That is the only way to ensure that unintentional harm can be minimized and prevented." (European Commission, 2019). "AI systems must function in a robust, secure and safe way throughout their life cycles and potential risks should be continually assessed and managed." (OECD, n.d.)
Privacy	"Throughout their lifecycle, AI systems should respect and uphold privacy rights and data protection, and ensure the security of data." (DISER, n.d.).

Transparency	"[T]he data, system and AI business models should be transparent. Traceability mechanisms can help achieve this. Moreover, AI systems and their decisions should be explained in a manner adapted to the stakeholder concerned. Humans need to be aware that they are interacting with an AI system, and must be informed of the system's capabilities and limitations." (European Commission, 2019).
Explainability	"AI systems should deliver accompanying evidence or reason(s) for all outputs … and provide explanations that are understandable to individual users" (Phillips et al., 2020)
Contestability	"When an AI system significantly impacts a person, community, group or environment, there should be a timely process to allow people to challenge the use or output of the AI system." (DISER, n.d.)
Accountability	"Those responsible for the different phases of the AI system lifecycle should be identifiable and accountable for the outcomes of the AI systems, and human oversight of AI systems should be enabled." (DISER, n.d.)
For AI subjects	
Awareness	AI subjects should know when AI and ADM are being used to make decisions that affect their lives and environments (financially, socially, legally, emotionally) and protect their data.
Understandability	AI subjects should be able to understand a deploying organisation's explanation of how an algorithmic decision that affects their lives was reached.
Disputability	AI subjects should be aware of the channels to use to query or dispute an AI-driven decision and access these channels in a timely and effective manner.

Table 5.2: Principles of Responsible AI for organisations and AI subjects

4. AI risk management

Principles for ethical and responsible AI are all well and good, and senior managers like to be able to point to ethical codes of practice, but they are often too abstract for organisations to action. As well as having ethical principles, a risk-based based approach to AI development and deployment provides a tangible and actionable way of engaging in responsible AI practice. Mapping principles to risks provides a way of linking core principles to actionable practices.

4.1 AI risk

Risk can be elevated to the project and organisational level using the European Commission's (2021) proposed regulatory framework for AI-based risk. This approach classifies AI risk as unacceptable, high, limited, and minimal (Figure 5.5).

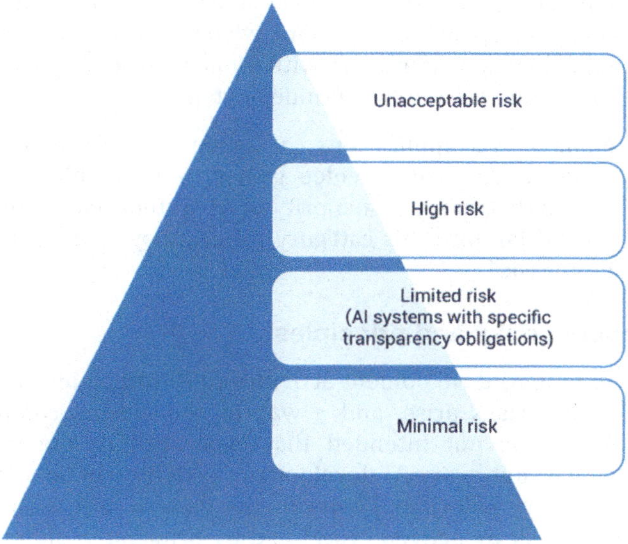

Figure 5.5: AI risk levels (EC, 2021)

In the European Commission's risk model:

- *Unacceptable risk* is defined as "all AI systems considered a clear threat to the safety, livelihoods and rights of people will be banned, from social scoring by governments to toys using voice assistance that encourages dangerous behaviour."

- *High risk* systems include: applications that could put the life and health of citizens at risk, applications that determine access to education and the professional course of someone's life, such as AI marking exams; in employment and work, AI assessment of CVs in recruitment; in private and public services, in scoring credit applications; in law enforcement and justice; and in migration and border control. The EC says that "high-risk AI systems will be subject to strict obligations before they can be put on the market", including risk assessment and mitigation, data quality, traceability, compliance documentation, clear information for the user, human oversight, and a "high level of robustness, security and accuracy".
- *Limited risk* AI systems have specific transparency obligations, such as chatbots, where "users should be aware that they are interacting with a machine so they can take an informed decision to continue or step back."
- *Minimal risk* applications can make free use of AI systems, "such as AI-enabled video games or spam filters." The EC claims that the "vast majority of AI systems currently used in the EU fall into this category, where they represent minimal or no risk."

4.2 Mapping risks and principles

Mapping AI development activities to AI principles provides an idea of where risks arise, and a way of considering completeness (Table 5.3). It is not intended that every cell of the matrix be completed, i.e., not every AI development activity will be expected to connect to every principle, however, the pattern is a useful way of exploring AI risk by activity (row) and by principle (column). While accountability applies to every activity, we equate this with algorithm development, while recognising that governance must ensure accountability throughout the AIDD process.

	Fairness	Human-centred	Well-being	Accountability	Safety	Privacey	Transparence	Explainability	Contestability
AIDD activity									
0. AI development	X	X	X	X	X	X			
1. Data acquisition		X				X			
2. Data processing					X	X			
3. Predictive modelling	X		X		X			X	
4. Decision-making		X	X						
5. Action-taking		X	X				X	X	X
6.Monitoring	X	X	X		X				
7. Data sharing			X			X			
Governance	X	X	X	X	X	X	X	X	X

Table 5.3: Mapping AI development and the principles of Responsible AI

In Appendix B, we provide sample questions that might be asked at each stage of the AI development process to help identify and manage risk.

4.3 AI governance

AI governance is an essential aspect of managing AI/ADM-related risk, and ensuring that AI principles are implemented and adhered to. Many consulting companies are developing AI governance approaches, and Ernst & Young have proposed a four-stage model for managing AI risk: developing an enterprise-wide model definition to identify AI/ML risks, enhancing existing risk management and control frameworks to address AI/ML-specific risks, implementing an operating model for responsible AI/ML adoption, and investing in capabilities that support AI/ML adoption and risk management (Agarwala et al., 2020).

PwC (2019) also focused on the risks of AI/ADM deployment, and proposed five pillars of Responsible AI: governance, ethics and regulation, interpretability and explainability, robustness and security, and bias and fairness. Regarding governance, PWC highlighted accountability and alignment together with business strategy, noting that "Historically, governance functions have only had to deal with static processes. But AI processes may be dynamic and adaptive —and AI governance must be as well." (PwC, 2019).

KPMG (2021) identified challenges to successful use of AI as the precision and accuracy of the technology, the appropriate use of consumer data and data privacy to inform AI, and discrimination and bias in making decisions, taking a wide-ranging approach, and identifying aspects of AI regulation such as R&D regulation, steering groups to discuss governance constructs, public policy and ethics, multi-stakeholder platforms for discussion and collaboration, and the shaping of an AI eco-system. Recognising the large-scale and complex nature of this initiative, they suggested actions that organisations can take now, including: developing AI principles, designing end-to-end governance, establishing a cross-functional governance committee, introducing a risk assessment framework, and setting up criteria to maintain continuous control over algorithms.

Regardless of the governance framework adopted, responsible AI is likely to involve a cultural shift within organisations, as employees of all grades understand and embrace ethical AI practices. More broadly, employees, citizens, and other stakeholders will need to develop their understanding of what AI is, how it is used, and how it could lead to harm.

4.4 Separation of developers and deployers

The AI principles framework (Figure 5.4) separates AI developers from deployers, while recognising that these entities may be the same, such as a bank developing its own AI application to assess customer risk. In other cases, AI deployers will source their solutions from AI developers, and as these solutions may come pre-trained or be trained by the deployer using their own data, so issues may arise from this relationship relating to ethical, legal, regulatory, political, or regulatory differences. When AI causes harm, who will take responsibility?

The use of AI may be legal in one country, but not in another due to data protection and privacy laws. The developer and deployer may have different ethical values, so that what is acceptable to one is not to the other. If both developer and deployer have well developed and documented AI governance, it is possible that differences can be seen and addressed. AI governance is essential not just for internal monitoring and control, but for external relationships with suppliers and AI subjects.

5. Business value and business ethics

We can begin to embed ethical principles in AI development by analysing AI applications using an opportunity canvas in conjunction with a business ethics canvas (Vidgen et al., 2020). Vidgen et al. argue that much guidance for practitioners on ethical investigations has been abstract, and they propose a practical way of acknowledging and thinking about ethical issues in business analytics by drawing on the Markkula Institute for Applied Ethics framework, and their five ethical dimensions: Utilitarian, Rights, Justice, Common Good, and Virtue (Markkula, n.d.).

Using these dimensions, Vidgen et al. created a business ethics canvas (Figure 5.6), addressing the elements in clockwise order around the canvas:

1. A proposed analytics solution that focuses on the needs of specific customers; we recommend that these are generated in an opportunity canvas – see Patton (2016)
2. Identification of stakeholders that can affect or are affected by the proposed analytics solution (Wang et al., 2015)
3. An assessment of stakeholder utility of the analytics solution
4. An assessment of the rights of stakeholders
5. An assessment of the fairness (justice) of the solution
6. Implications for the common good
7. Reflections on the virtue of the proposed analytics solution

Vidgen et al. (ibid.) describe how the business ethics canvas was developed through an online travel organisation, the pseudonymous EuroTravel, that was considering using analytics to target its customers with days out offers. It ran a workshop and used post-it notes to allow the contents of the canvas to be iterated and refined, using colour to highlight areas of concern and of opportunity (Figure 5.7). Yellow post- it notes represent neutral positions, green represent opportunities, and red represent risk.

Virtue	Users & Customers	Solution ideas	Stakeholders	Utility
7	1	1	2	3
How does this solution define me as a human person? How does it define us as a company, an organization, a society, etc.? What do I or what do we want to be and become?	What types of users and customers have the challenges our solution addresses?	What are the product, features, or enhancement ideas that solve problems for our users and customers	Who is affected by, or can affect, the proposed solution? What is their stake in the proposed solution?	What are the benefits of the intended solution? What are the harms created? Who benefits and who is harmed?

Common good	Justice	Rights
6	5	4
What is the community (or what are the communities) in which the decision has to be made? What is the common good?	How fair is the solution? Does it treat everyone in the same way or does it show favoritism and discrimination?	Whose rights are respected or infringed by this action? What are those rights?

Figure 5.6: Business ethics canvas template (Vidgen et al., 2020)

Vidgen et al. found that ethical analysis should not be seen as a constraint or overhead to analytics development – exploring the ethical dimension and including multiple stakeholders provide a richer insight into business value creation, as well as greater confidence in emerging ethical implications and project risk.

For example, the product owner for the DaysOut project found that the workshop enabled them to identify a previously hidden stakeholder and further business opportunities:

> "With regards to concrete outcomes, what we can say is that using the BEC helped us to consider a stakeholder we hadn't really considered before – the owner/operators of the attractions to which we would be driving our customers. We've now crafted a strategy for engaging and partnering with these stakeholders so that our customers get the best experience at these attractions and the owner/operators can give us feedback on issues such as

congestion. This strategy includes an outreach campaign to attraction owner/operators to notify them of what we're doing and offering to partner on co-promotion and ensuring a great experience for customers. This campaign alone created meaningful bottom line results for the company." (Product Owner, DaysOut) (Vidgen et al., 2020, p. 498).

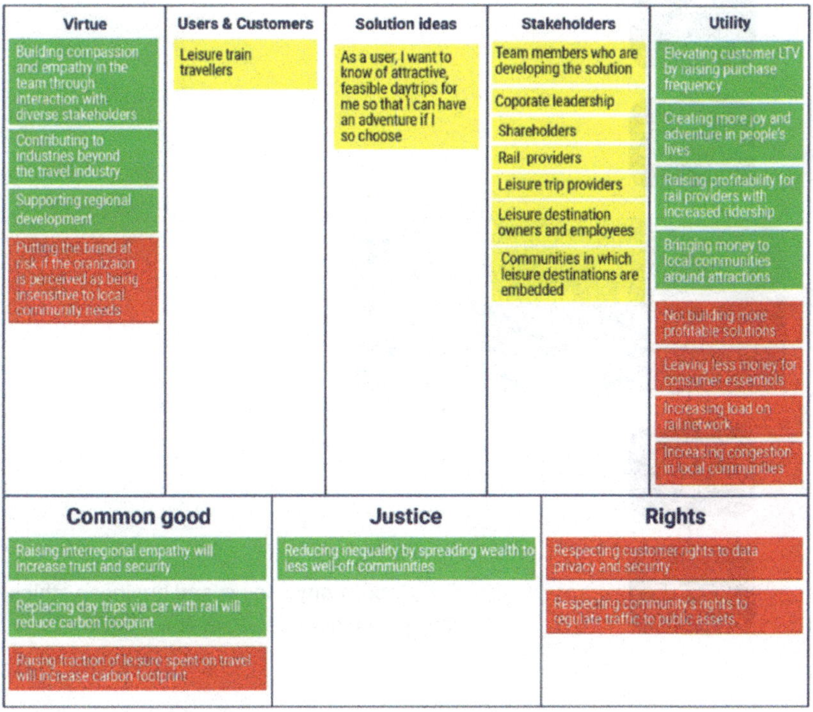

Figure 5.7: Business ethics canvas for EuroTravel's DaysOut project (Vidgen et al., 2020)

Consequently, Vidgen et al. propose that we should position the business ethics canvas (BEC) and the opportunity canvas (OC) as counterparts where each shapes and informs the other in a creative tension (Figure 5.8). They further argue that analytics opportunities should be framed in the context of a portfolio of analytics projects, which support the organisation's business model (Osterwalder and Pigneur, 2010; Hindle and Vidgen, 2018). Thus, we argue that stakeholder ramifications and value creation cannot and should not be separated; we can't talk of value without considering the ethical dimension, and to talk of ethics without reference to a value-creating opportunity is too abstract. This project analysis should, of course, be grounded in and consistent with the guiding ethical principles of the organisation.

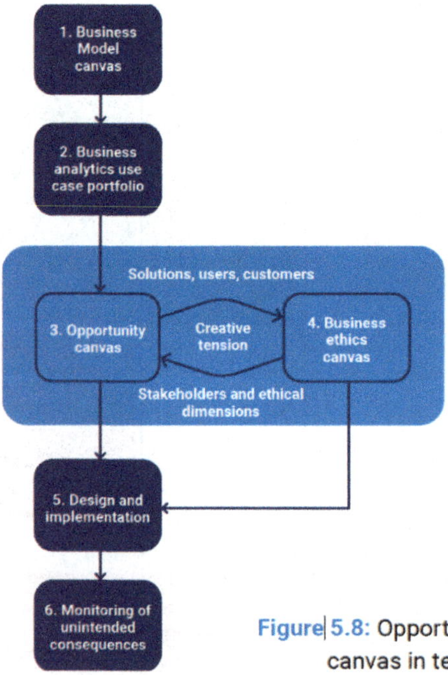

Figure 5.8: Opportunity canvas and business ethics canvas in tension (Vidgen et al., 2020)

6. Recommendations for organisations

Our foregoing analysis leads to a number of recommendations that provide a foundation for action in organisations and for further research.

End-to-end governance in organisations

The first step is implementing effective AI/ADM governance, which actively manages the risk of harm to AI subjects. The AIDD framework provides a structure for organisations developing the content of end-to-end governance mechanisms.

Recommendation #1

Organisations must have an end-to- end AI/ADM governance program – systems, structures, and processes – to ensure that the principles of Responsible AI are implemented and maintained.

Responsible AI principles

AI principles for organisations (fairness, privacy, safety, etc.) must inform and guide the governance process to protect the interests of AI subjects. Organisations can develop these internally, acquire them externally, or have them imposed by industry bodies, regulatory bodies, or government.

Recommendation #2

Organisations must develop a set of Responsible AI principles that will guide their governance process, and clearly establish the organisation's values.

Education and culture change

Governance will require culture change and a greater appreciation of the potential for harm generated by AI within organisations and for society at large. All citizens, including employees, should understand how AI works, how it is deployed, and its potential for harm. While education plays a part in this cultural shift, it must be supplemented with other initiatives, such as senior management support, hiring policies, and reward systems.

Recommendation #3

Organisations should develop an educational AI/ADM program to communicate the importance of Responsible AI to all employees and other relevant stakeholders such as suppliers.

Responsible AI gateway

Organisational governance processes are largely black boxed for AI subjects, in that subjects see the decision outcomes, but not the decision process. The core AI principles of transparency, explainability, and contestability should be essential points of access for AI subjects, and provide a channel for deeper scrutiny of an organisation's fairness, privacy, and safety.

Recommendation #4

Organisations must develop an effective gateway with appropriate channels for their different AI subjects to ensure that they are aware of, understand, and can dispute AI-driven outcomes.

Business process design

The same algorithm can be blended in different business process designs with different classification thresholds to produce very different outcomes for AI subjects. Organisations should design their business processes to incorporate AI with careful consideration of the 'human in the loop', giving particular attention to decision-making and action-taking.

Recommendation #5

Organisations must design business processes that use ADM with careful consideration of where human involvement and oversight are needed.

AI developers and AI deployers

Who bears responsibility when AI causes harm? The relationship between AI developer and AI deployer requires close analysis and scrutiny, particularly where the two parties are from different organisations, and from different countries and jurisdictions. Alignment of ethics, values, and governance structures is core to achieving responsible value and supply chains.

Recommendation #6

Organisations should review their AI value and supply chains for sustainability and ethicality.

Networked harms

Networked ADM harms arise from data sharing where the decision outputs of one process become the data inputs of another, leading to increasing datafication of AI subjects, and the amplification of bias and injustice. ADM networks of need to be tracked, and harms identified and mitigated. Organisations cannot address networked harms as they are part of an invisible network of ADM, therefore monitoring by institutions is required.

Recommendation #7

Organisations must be careful and responsible in sharing data on their ADM outcomes.

AI subjects have responsibilities as well as rights

AI subjects are citizens in many roles, such as employees, social welfare claimants, parolees, medical patients, and have rights, but they also have responsibilities, like being aware of when ADM is being used, protecting their data, understanding how decisions have been arrived at, and being willing to dispute ADM outcomes. As well as acting as individuals, AI subjects should be willing to engage in AI activism, to join larger social forums, and to lobby for responsible AI use. As with consumer activism, this will be a subset of AI subjects, but their voices must be heard.

Recommendation #8

Organisations need to recognise the rights of AI subjects, and be prepared for AI subjects to actively protest against organisations that are not using AI responsibly. This may lead to customer attrition, hacking attacks, and adverse press coverage.

Management accountability

Managers must understand how AI works, how it is being deployed in their organisation, be aware of the consequences of that use, both intended and unintended, and be willing to be responsible and accountable for AI use.

Recommendation #9

Managers at all levels must be accountable for the use of AI in their organisations, starting and ending with the senior management team.

An ethical dimension in AI development and deployment

Ethical considerations must be driven down to the project level, rather than being remote, abstract, and the sole responsibility of senior managers. The business ethics canvas is one way in which ethical issues may be explored at the project level to understand project impact on a range of stakeholders.

Recommendation #10

Drive ethical considerations down to the project level, using tools such as the business ethics canvas.

Risk in AI development and deployment

By evaluating each stage of the AIDD using AI principles, organisations can identify a set of risks that should be considered, discussed, managed, and mitigated. Mapping AIDD to AI principles using risks provides an overview of where responsible AI attention should be placed.

Recommendation #11

Organisations should develop a risk register for AI development and deployment as part of their governance system.

AI maturity assessment

If organisations are to improve their AI practices and engage in responsible AI, then they need to assess where they are today, and to plan and manage change as appropriate. To make this assessment requires both qualitative (surveys of attitudes) and quantitative (percentage of budget spent on training AI developers in responsible AI practices) measurement.

Recommendation #12

Organisations should assess and measure their responsible AI maturity against a benchmark for improvement.

7. Summary

The aim of this chapter is to provide a guide to responsible use of AI in algorithmic decision-making (ADM) in organisations. The AIDD process shows the many decision points faced by algorithm developers and deployers, and provides a structure for thinking about the end-to- end governance of AI/ADM development and deployment.

Working on the basis that the AIDD process is a black box to AI subjects, who see the decision outcomes and not the decision process, we have proposed a set of principles that show how AI subjects are made aware that AI/ADM is being used, can seek an explanation of how it is used, and can contest the outcome of the ADM. Responsible AI relies crucially on active participation between both AI deployers and AI subjects. Without AI subjects taking their rights and responsibilities seriously, and engaging in public discourse, even the best intentions may result in harmful uses of AI.

Governance is underpinned by responsible AI principles, and the identification of sources of risk that may lead to harm for AI subjects. We explore the topic of de-risking the AI development process in the next chapter.

References

Agarwala, G., Latorre, A., and Raffel, S., (2020). *Understand model risk management for AI and machine learning.* Ernst & Young,13 May 2020, https://www.ey.com/en_us/ banking-capital-markets/understand-model-risk-management-for-ai-and-machine-learning

Cross, R & Parker, A (2004). The hidden power of social networks: Understanding how work really gets done in organisations. Harvard Business School Press, Boston.

DISER (n.d.). Australian Government, Department of Industry, Science, Energy and Resources. *AI Ethics Principles.* https://www.industry.gov.au/data-and-publications/building-australias-artificial-intelligence-capability/ai-ethics-framework/ai-ethics-principles

European Commission (2019). *Ethics guidelines for trustworthy AI.* https://ec.europa.eu/digital-single-market/en/news/ethics-guidelines-trustworthy-ai

European Commission (2021). *Regulatory framework proposal on Artificial Intelligence.* https://digital-strategy.ec.europa.eu/en/policies/regulatory-framework-ai

Fjeld, J., Achten, N., Hilligoss, H., Nagy, A., and Srikumar , M., (2020). *Principled Artificial Intelligence: Mapping Consensus in Ethical and Rights-Based Approaches to Principles for AI.* Berkman Klein Center Research Publication No. 2020-1, Posted: 14 Feb 2020

Hindle, G., and Vidgen, R. (2018). Developing a business analytics methodology: a case study in the food bank sector. *European Journal of Operational Research*, 268(3): 836- 851.

Holman, P., (n.d.). *Chapter 1. What Is Emergence?* Peggy Holman. https://peggyholman.com/papers/engaging-emergence/engaging-emergence-table-of-contents/part-i-the-nature-of-emergence/chapter-1-what-is-emergence/

ICO (2018). *What is automated individual decision-making and profiling.* UK Information Commissioner's Office. 1-23. Available from https://ico.org.uk/for-organisations/guide-to-data-protection/guide-to-the-general-data-protection-regulation-gdpr/automated-decision-making-and-profiling/what-is-automated-individual-decision-making-and-profiling/#id2

KPMG (2021). *The shape of AI governance to come.* KPMG, https://assets.kpmg/content/dam/kpmg/sg/pdf/2021/03/TL-Global-AI-Regulation-Whitepaper.pdf

Leslie, D., (2019). *Understanding artificial intelligence ethics and safety.* Alan Turing Institute. https://www.turing.ac.uk/sites/default/files/2019-06/understanding_artificial_intelligence_ethics_and_safety.pdf

Lycett, M., (2013). Editorial: 'Datafication': making sense of (big) data in a complex world.

European Journal of Information Systems 22(4): 381-386.

Markkula (n.d.). *A Framework for Ethical Decision Making*. Markkula Center for Applied Ethics. https://www.scu.edu/ethics/ethics-resources/ethical-decision-making/

Newell S and Mirabelli M (2015) Strategic opportunities (and challenges) of algorithmic decision-making: A call for action on the long-term societal effects of 'datafication. *Journal of Strategic Information Systems* 24(1):3-14.

OECD (n.d.). *OECD Principles on AI*. https://www.oecd.org/going-digital/ai/principles/

Osterwalder, A. and Pigneur, Y. (2010). *Business Model Generation*. Hoboken, NJ: John Wiley and Sons, Inc.

Patton, J., (2016). *Opportunity Canvas*. 9 September 2016. https://jpattonassociates.com/opportunity-canvas/

Phillips, P., Hahn, A., Fontana, P., Broniatowski, D., and Przybocki, M., (2020). *Four Principles of Explainable Artificial Intelligence*. National Institute of Standards and Technology (NISR). https://www.huntonprivacyblog.com/wp-content/uploads/sites/28/2020/08/NIST-Explainable-AI-Draft-NISTIR8312-1.pdf

PwC (2019). *A practical guide to Responsible Artificial Intelligence (AI)*. PwC, https://www.pwc.com/gx/en/issues/data-and-analytics/artificial-intelligence/what-is-responsible-ai/responsible-ai-practical-guide.pdf

Veliz, C., (2020). Privacy is Power: Why and How You Should Take Back Control of Your Data. Penguin Random House.

Vidgen, B., Harris, A., Nguyen, D., Tromble, R., Hale, S., & Margetts, H., (2019a). Challenges and frontiers in abusive content detection. *Proceedings of the Third Workshop on Abusive Language Online* (pp. 80-93).

Vidgen, B., Burden, E., & Margetts, H., (2021). *Understanding Online Hate: VSP regulation and the broader context*. The Alan Turing Institute. https://www.ofcom.org.uk/__data/assets/pdf_file/0022/216490/alan-turing-institute-report-understanding-online-hate.pdf

Vidgen, R., Kirshner, S., & Tan, F., (2019b). *Business Analytics: a management approach*. Red Globe (Macmillan Higher Education).

Vidgen, R., Hindle, G., and Randolph, I., (2020). Exploring the ethical implications of business analytics with a business ethics canvas. *European Journal of Operational Research*, 281(3): 491-501.

Wang, W., Liu, W., and Mingers, J. (2015). A systemic method for organisational stakeholder identification and analysis using Soft Systems Methodology (SSM). *European Journal of Operational*

Research, 246(2): 562-574.

Chapter 6
De-risking automated decisions

1. Introduction

1.1 Context and Background

There is now overwhelming evidence, as we show in this chapter, that the use of AI for decision- making has the potential to produce unlawful, immoral, discriminatory outcomes for individuals through opaque and unaccountable decision processes. This has ignited a range of worldwide policy responses, including concrete regulatory proposals, such as the European Union's proposal for an artificial intelligence act.[1] This would be the first significant legal framework specifically designed to regulate the use of AI, adopting a risk-based approach to AI regulation, forbidding certain uses, and proposing extensive provisions for others identified as high risk. Likewise, Brazil has a new proposal for AI regulation, which is also risk-based[2], and, in Australia, the Australian Human Rights Commission report on *Technology and Human Rights* makes a number of policy recommendations for AI regulation[3], also with a focus on the responsible use of AI through a risk-aware perspective, and proactive impact assessments[4].

Why are these AI harms arising? Unwarranted trust in, or at least reliance on, AI. Humans and machines make decisions differently, and while humans have common sense, and are able to navigate different contexts with ease, machines have no built-in moral judgement, and only perform well in relatively narrow domains. Whereas humans are susceptible to opinions, emotions, cognitive biases, fatigue and self- interest, machines will do exactly as instructed, are reconfigurable, work relentlessly, can operate at a scale no human ever could, and will never complain.

These differences suggest human and automated decision-making systems fail in different ways, so their governance needs to be designed to address these different modes of failure. If decisions previously made by humans are made by machines, this poses a risk if governance systems fail to adapt. How does traditional governance break down when important decisions are delegated to machines, and what can be done about it?

This chapter seeks to address this question. It explains and illustrates how AI decision-making challenges traditional governance, and provides general, practical guidance:

1.2 Our Purpose

- Our purpose is to provide general, practical guidance for organisations on reducing risks[5] introduced by automated decision systems.
- We identify a non-exhaustive list of types of risks introduced or amplified by AI decision-making.
- We describe them in general terms, allowing the reader to adapt them to suit the specifics of their own organisation or situation.
- We illustrate these risks with case studies in which they have led to avoidable harm.
- We suggest a non-exhaustive list of interventions to address identified risks, and we describe these interventions in general terms, to be adapted suitably to the nature, scale, and needs of an individual organisation. They include a range of preventative, detective, and corrective measures.

Importantly, we do not attempt to provide any comprehensive framework for AI risk management or governance. Such efforts are being conducted on a global scale by standards bodies such as the ISO[6] and NIST[7]. Our intention is to provide practical suggestions inspired by real-world failings, which can be applied by organisations today. These are intended to complement, not replace, risk management frameworks and standards largely still under development, and which may take some time to be broadly accepted and adopted.

We also consider the risks of AI systems in general. We do not yet believe it is appropriate to measure, rank or compare the magnitude of risks identified as many will be irrelevant in some contexts, but critically important in others, meaning an overall ranking system may be misleading. We leave to the organisation and its leadership the task of judging which risks are most important in the context they are considering, but do, however, make the following observations which should be considered by organisations wanting to measure or prioritise AI risks or interventions in a specific context:

- AI is an immature technology, and before asking how it should be used for some particular application, one should ask whether it should be used in that context at all. Not only is AI not a panacea, but it is often the very cause of problems. This is usually due to a combination of its immaturity as a technology, and the misplaced trust people tend to place in it.
- Many of the risks we identify are unintended, with no obvious associated reward. They are typically a by-product of ineffective governance of AI decision-making, rather than risks consciously taken in pursuit of a potential reward. Organisations should have little tolerance for such risks, and should seek where practical to reduce them as much as possible.
- The process of quantifying AI risk is not mature, hence it is likely to be applied inconsistently, and will be prone to error. Risk quantification from the introduction of a new technology is usually extremely uncertain[8], and this uncertainty is especially pronounced for general-purpose technologies, which is the case for AI[9].
- When there is uncertainty or room for discretion in risk assessment, organisations have incentives to underestimate

risk. Risks are likely to be underestimated (or at least under-reported) if there are tacit incentives to under-report – a reality in many organisations. This became clear in our discussions with risk and compliance industry practitioners. While this issue is not specific to AI, the general- purpose nature of the technology adds uncertainty, and makes the issue more important. Risk managers should explicitly acknowledge such matters when considering AI risks.

In summary, there are significant risks associated with AI systems. Global standards and frameworks are developing to help manage these risks, but organisations do not need to wait – they can act today. This chapter is intended to help them do just that.

1.3 Scope

An important difference between human and AI decision-making is the role of data. Human decisions need not use any digital data at all, while AI systems require it. Many examinations of AI risks, therefore, focus on well-trodden themes of data governance: privacy, security, consent, data quality, and related topics. We make no attempt to add to this rich discussion, focusing instead on the manner of automated decision-making, and the way it challenges core concepts of organisational governance.

We focus specifically on risks introduced or amplified by automated decision systems such as those currently in use in both the private and public sectors. Systems in scope are those producing decisions, predictions, recommendations or actions in which automation plays key roles that would otherwise be performed by humans. Examples include marketing automation, credit, or any other risk scoring, propensity scoring, personalised pricing, job applicant scoring, and, more generally, any type of automated recommendation or scoring. They may also include systems in which intermediate instead of final decisions are automated, such as loan approvals and risk audits.

Although we consider automated decision-making in its general form, the chapter stresses its use within a corporate context. For an emphasis on administrative decision-making, we refer the reader to earlier reports by the Commonwealth Ombudsman[10], the New South Wales Ombudsman[11] and the Attorney-General's Department[12].

2. Concepts

2.1 AI Decisions

Consider an AI-driven loan application approval system: a bank has credit card transaction data and credit history data on its customers, and wants to know which new loan applications should be approved to deliver on the business objectives, which are to maximise profit in the long term. An AI-driven solution might proceed along the following lines: AI developers use a machine learning algorithm to analyse the transactional data of customers who did and did not repay their loans, and the algorithm learns which patterns of transactions make a person more or less likely to repay. The output of the machine learning algorithm is another algorithm, an AI model which takes as input historical transaction data for a customer, and produces as output the probability the customer will repay a loan in the future. The bank then applies this model to new applicants to estimate their repayment probability, and from that probability, and any other relevant considerations, the system determines when to make loans in order to achieve the bank's business objectives. The complete system is called an AI system for decision-making[13].

The above example can easily be generalised, and adapted to many other settings where the data and objectives change, but the template remains the same. Since organisations have increasing accessibility to data and machine learning tools, the methodology is not only conceptually general, but also readily implementable. This is what facilitates AI adoption across a diverse range of sectors and settings – there are few (and diminishing) areas of society without the potential for AI adoption along the lines of the above example.

2.2 Control and monitoring gaps

What changes when we introduce AI decision-making into an organisation? A starting point is to examine where AI decisions fit within the formal flow of authority (Figure 6.1).

2.2.1 Flow of authority without AI decisions

In the traditional scenario depicted on the left-hand side of Figure 6.1, all decisions affecting customers follow a human-to-human chain of authority. The board sets the long-term strategy and policies for the organisation, and delegates key functions to management.

Management establishes business objectives based on the strategy; it also sets detailed rules, policies and procedures, and delegates their execution to its frontline team, as well as the authority to exercise discretion in situations in which there are no or unclear rules. The frontline team interacts with customers by following the rules and using discretion where required.

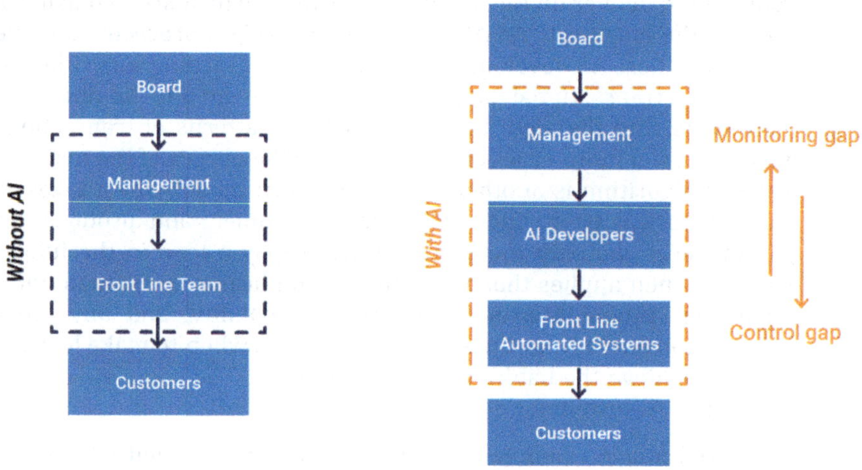

Figure 6.1: Flow of authority (LHS = Flow of authority *without* AI decisions, RHS = Flow of authority *with* AI decisions)

Failures may arise at different stages of this decision-making pipeline. The strategy itself may be incoherent, or the rules stipulated by management to implement the strategy may be problematic, or the frontline team may not follow them closely when they are right, or discretion may be ill-advised.

Traditional management of these failure modes is within the three lines of defence model, where the business function (line one) provides customer service and manages risks, a separate risk and compliance function (line two) provides support, typically including advising on rules, checking they are followed and that the use of discretion is reasonable, and the internal audit function (line three) reports directly to the board, and provides an independent assessment on the activities and achievements of management, including whether their business objectives and rules are consistent with the board's overall directions. This results in a coordinated approach to control the different modes of failure[14].

2.2.2 Flow of authority with AI decisions

When AI decision-making is introduced, important changes occur (depicted on the right-hand side of Figure 6.1). The frontline team is now replaced by two teams: a team of AI developers instructed to encode into machines the objectives articulated by management, together with available data, and a team of machines (frontline automated systems) that learns precise rules from the data for making decisions affecting customers so as to maximise the objectives[15]. The frontline automated systems both generate and execute the rules[16].

This new decision-making regime changes and challenges the traditional governance approach as follows:

Control Gaps

We use the term control to refer to management powers of delegation and instruction. By its very nature, control occurs mainly within the first line of defence of an organisation. This is a relatively familiar and well-understood task in human systems, but is challenged in AI settings, where control gaps can easily emerge because of how AI works. For example:

- Management may be unused to specifying objectives with the degree of precision required for AI, so their important control task of setting clear instructions is undermined. This may lead to unexpected outcomes since, unlike humans, AI systems will not act with common sense when objectives are unclear or absent.
- Management may also be ill-suited to delegate to AI developers, due to possibly insufficient technical understanding of AI to effectively instruct them. This is exacerbated for AI compared to many other technical domains, since overall goal-setting and defining objectives are a crucial part of AI development.
- AI developers may be unfamiliar with the business domain[17], resulting in their misunderstanding instructions from management, which may include domain-specific jargon. AI

developers may also delegate inappropriately to AI, through ignorance of the business context, whereas human teams receiving instructions will usually have a better understanding of the business domain.

- When a staff member interacts with a customer, they are sensitive to the particular situation of that customer, and adapt their behaviour accordingly. AI systems can't relate to individual customers or leverage the richness of human-to-human experience, and important nuances will be neglected.
- With an AI system, all discretion is lost when dealing with customers – and with it any element of the common sense or judgement that frontline humans use routinely as key control measures in traditional systems.

Monitoring Gaps

Monitoring refers to mechanisms that make management and the board aware of the activities of their subordinates in order to exercise appropriate control. As such, it is a core component of the first line of defence of an organisation. Second, and particularly third, lines can assist in valuable ways by providing a degree of independence in monitoring, ensuring issues are properly identified. Monitoring mechanisms across all lines of defence may break down when AI is introduced. For example:

- The rules of customer engagement, now machine-generated, may be unreadable, and therefore hard for management, auditors and other stakeholders to understand or challenge.
- Frontline automated systems may make decisions without adequate transparency. Auditors used to asking humans why they have made a decision may find it difficult to question an automated system, particularly if it does not produce records of the reasons for its decisions that an auditor can understand.
- The highly technical nature of AI developers' work may lead to a communications gap between them and more generalist management staff. If management cannot understand an AI developer, their monitoring is likely to be ineffective.
- Humans monitor their own decisions when interacting with

customers, and in so doing leverage their natural ability to understand context and nuance and respond suitably – where the organisation's rules allow this response. Machines are incapable of doing the same, and cannot self-assess how reasonable their own interaction is with customers.

- AI systems don't see a person but a datapoint, and the data representing a customer are a very crude approximation of the person behind them, translating directly to a gap in monitoring.

These gaps challenge best-practice corporate governance:

2.3 Impacts on corporate governance

According to the definition from the Australian Institute of Company Directors (AICD), corporate governance "refers to the framework of rules, systems and processes put in place to control and monitor an organisation." The gaps noted above therefore threaten the two key functions of governance.

Below we transcribe the AICD guiding principles of good governance, while interleaving questions a board must to be able to answer satisfactorily in order to discharge their duties in an organisation that uses AI for decision-making[18]:

1. The board plays a key role in approving the vision, purpose and strategies of the organisation. It is accountable to the members, and must act in the best interests of the organisation.

   Machines are acting on behalf of the organisation. Does the board know if their actions are consistent with their stated vision, purpose, and strategy, and thus in the best interests of the organisation?

2. The board sets the cultural and ethical tone for the organisation.

   Is the ethical tone set by the board translated accurately in the decisions made by the machines? Are the algorithms designed with this ethical tone in mind?

3. All directors should exercise independent judgement, and provide independent oversight of management.

Management delegates decisions to AI developers, who delegate decisions to an AI. AI developers may only have a narrow view of how the AI affects customers, and are often unfamiliar with the business domain. Are directors overseeing how the authority delegated to management is ultimately exercised? Are they able to maintain independence in doing so, or are they overreliant on information provided by management?

4. Taking into consideration the scale and nature of the organisation's activities, the board should appoint an appropriate number of directors with a relevant and diverse range of skills, expertise, experience and backgrounds, and who are able to understand issues arising in the organisation's business. Where practicable, the chair of the board should be independent, and the role of chairman separate from the role of CEO.

   Do the board members have an adequate understanding of AI, how it works, what it can do, what can go wrong, and how it's used in the organisation? Does this understanding compare to the board's understanding of other technical subjects?

5. The board should have an appropriate system of risk oversight and internal controls in place. Does the board have a real understanding of the risks involved in using AI systems for decision-making? Are controls suitably tailored to the unfamiliar risks posed by AI systems?

6. Directors should act diligently on a suitably informed basis, and have access to accurate, relevant and timely information. Are directors well informed about all apposite aspects of how AI systems treat people? Can the AI systems even provide such information in a manner that a director would understand? Does management regularly inform directors about how AI systems are affecting people, and are they held to account if information is not readily provided?

7. The board would normally delegate certain functions to management. Where it does so, there should be a clear statement and understanding as to the functions

that have been delegated.

Functions delegated to management are ultimately delegated to machines. Can the board ensure the machines are being instructed as the board intends, and interpreting the human instructions as the humans intended? How would the board know if there were a gap between its intentions, and the decisions of the automated system?

8. The board is responsible for the appointment of the CEO and the continuing evaluation of their performance. Is the board appropriately resourced to evaluate the performance of the CEO against management of any AI risks that the company incurs?

9. The board should ensure that the organisation communicates with members and other stakeholders in a regular and timely manner, to the extent that the board thinks is in the best interests of the organisation, so that they have sufficient information to make appropriately informed decisions regarding the organisation.

Can the board ensure that communication with stakeholders reflects the realities of how particular customer decisions are being made by the organisation's AI systems?

10. The board's performance (including the performance of its chair, the individual directors and, where appropriate, the board's subcommittees), needs to be regularly assessed and effective action taken to address any issues identified.

Is the performance of the board and its members properly assessed against their ability to ensure control and monitoring of AI decision- making? Is the board suitably engaged with the question of AI decision-making in the organisation?

Clearly, AI brings material challenges to traditional corporate governance. Boards and senior management teams should be concerned, and take steps to address these emerging control and monitoring gaps. While the above list highlights questions a board should be able to answer, management must also take responsible action to ensure good governance from the top. We highlight various activities that management may consider to reduce the control and monitoring gaps identified above, and provide a more detailed analysis of these gaps in the next section, describing specific types of risk, and exploring each in a series of general examples to assist in determining appropriate actions to narrow them.

3. Risks

In this section, we identify, explain and illustrate a range of risks associated with the use of automated decision systems. We also illustrate how each of these risks is linked with the overall loss of traditional models of control or monitoring:

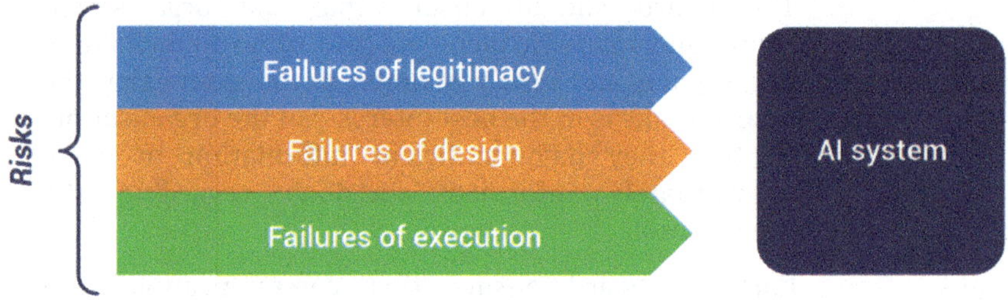

Figure 6.2: Categories of AI risk

As illustrated in Figure 6.2, we fit AI risks into three broad categories: failures of legitimacy, design and execution.

3.1 Legitimacy

Legitimacy is about general acceptance that an authority has the right to exercise power within a certain scope. If a company or government uses its powers illegally, or in ways that customers or the broader society believe is unacceptable, it faces the risk of being sued, losing customers or harming its reputation. In such cases there is a lack of legitimacy.

To illustrate a few themes of how the emergence of control and monitoring gaps can lead to failures of legitimacy:

3.1.1 Unlawful process

The use of AI systems to make decisions previously made by people can increase the chances that the resulting decisions are unlawful. In human systems, we rely on human beings knowing or being trained in the requirements of the law, and avoiding breaking the law; in many cases an unlawful act by a subordinate would be detected by regular monitoring activity, while an unlawful instruction by a manager would be identified by an effective risk or audit function, or a subordinate blowing the whistle. But, as we observed above, both control and monitoring are undermined by AI, potentially reducing the effectiveness of traditional governance measures. An AI system does not know what the law is, and will not observe it unless legal requirements are built in as objectives or constraints; mistranslation of board and manager directives, as discussed further below, can result in illegal actions.

Case Study: **Robodebt**

In 2015, the Australian federal government deployed an automated system to recover welfare overpayments based on data-matching between tax office data and welfare data. Previously, data-matching was used to identify potential discrepancies, a subset of which would be reviewed, as the law required, by a human who would gather more material to establish to their satisfaction that there had been overpayment. The newly introduced system used data-matching to trigger a letter to welfare recipients; if recipients failed to respond, a debt was raised against them. This was unlawful because Centrelink could not be satisfied, based only on data-matching, that there was a debt: assumptions made in the data-matching, in particular that income reported to the tax office was received evenly over the year, were known to be often wrong.

The goal of automating recovery of overpayment in the absence of accurate data on when and how income was earned led to mis-specifying the problem. This led to widespread errors when sending debt notices automatically, causing distress, financial hardship and mental health problems for thousands of people. This was particularly common and upsetting for already disadvantaged individuals with irregular sources of income.

The Robodebt scandal resulted in multiple enquiries by the Attorney General and Senate, and, ultimately, a class action led to the Government agreeing to repay over $750 million dollars unlawfully recovered by the system, as well as $122 million dollars in compensation, and wipe out more than $1.7 billion in outstanding unlawful debts raised by the system.

There are many areas of the law directly relevant to automated decision-making, such as privacy, anti-discrimination and consumer law. When deploying an AI system, an organisation, whether a company or a government department, needs to be as confident that it's not breaking the law as when it is not using AI, and it may have to adapt traditional monitoring and control processes to ensure the legality of its actions.

3.1.2 Lack of Social Licence

Even if a certain use of technology is entirely legal, sometimes organisations have strong incentives to avoid it, because of a lack of public acceptance and concern for reputation. However, control and monitoring gaps driven by automated systems may mean that socially unacceptable systems are still deployed. Not only may there be a lack of understanding across the organisation of the likely impact of a system, but it may also be harder for managers and the board to obtain feedback about its failures. In human systems, socially unacceptable outcomes are in many cases met with immediate feedback from those affected to humans in the frontline, and those monitoring the activity - if effective in that role - will quickly understand this, and act to correct it. AI systems may not be as effective at collecting such feedback, and those affected may be less able or willing to give it, due to concerns that the feedback is unlikely to change the system.

Case Study: Face Recognition

In 2018, researchers demonstrated that the accuracy of the IBM and Microsoft face recognition systems was significantly higher for white people and for men than for women, people of colour, and especially women of colour, for whom accuracy was the most compromised. Public outcry ensued, and in 2019 researchers reassessed the performance of the systems to see if the companies had responded to that pressure. Indeed, the authors found that the performance improved overall and the gaps were reduced, although they were still significant. In this second study, the authors also audited the performance of Amazon's system – which wasn't exposed in the first study – and found that the overall performance was inferior and the gaps much larger. This led the researchers to conclude that public pressure had been more effective in changing the behaviour of the exposed companies. The second study had now exposed Amazon as well, but all companies still had issues with inequitable performance across gender and race.

Automated facial recognition systems for surveillance are often employed differently to their manual counterparts, in a way that jeopardises their social licence. Human operators searching for suspects are incapable of trawling through thousands of hours of footage from hundreds of cameras. As a result, they must use their knowledge of the suspect to refine the search to locations and times they believe the suspect may be present. A potential facial match is supported by other evidence, suggesting that the suspect could be in that location. On the other hand, AI systems make it cheaper and easier for investigators to cast a wide net, and produce potential matches across a citywide network of cameras within minutes. Even a very accurate system will still produce many errors given the large number of candidate faces that it can process, resulting in false arrests and a degradation of trust in the system.

Following ongoing public pressure on the use of face recognition technology, IBM eventually announced in 2020 that it would no longer offer face recognition products. It was soon followed by Amazon, who instituted a one-year moratorium on the use of their technology for policing. Microsoft was next, saying it would not sell face recognition to the police until the government passed federal legislation regulating the technology. In November 2021, Facebook announced it was shutting down its face recognition system[19].

3.1.3 Lack of transparency

Some systems must be opaque to certain parties in order to operate effectively. For example, software to detect money laundering would be ineffective if it were entirely visible to money launderers. However, many decisions are not of this form, and transparency of some form may be required in order for the decision to be legitimate.

Sometimes reasons must be given for a decision, and earlier chapters in this book highlighted the importance of transparency, explainability and accountability. In human systems, this can often be resolved by a conversation with a service agent, but automated systems require substantially different mechanisms to ensure adequate transparency, particularly for effective monitoring.

Case Study: **Drug Dispensing**

NarxCare is a US prescription drug monitoring program: a set of databases and algorithms that track patients' use of potentially addictive drugs. Hospitals and pharmacies use the algorithm to search for patients who are concealing an opioid addiction by sourcing pain management drugs from multiple doctors. For such patients, the system may alert doctors who direct them into a support program, or at the very least prevent an overdose. But for the majority of people presenting with legitimate pain, an erroneous flag may be excruciating if it leads to the doctor refusing to prescribe medication.

The company that makes NarxCare, Apriss, uses a proprietary model and dataset. The algorithms and the features used to train these models are not clearly disclosed to the public or the doctors. Those affected have complained that ambiguous or contradictory information about the medical appointments or past medical diagnoses is used to inform the decision, and may even affect a patient's risk score if they buy medication for a chronically ill pet.

The hospitals subscribing to this tool may believe it frees them from the responsibility of carefully assessing specific patients' circumstances, but doctors are often expected to use the system without knowing its data or training objectives. For example, when it was reported that 20% of the system's erroneous flags are on cancer patients, who would of course require visits to multiple medical specialists, neither the patients nor doctors knew whether the system was compensating for this. These doctors do not have access to guidance on whether they should or shouldn't accept the system's recommendation, but are incentivised to accept it to avoid any liability, and so this ignorance is evidently a monitoring gap.

If the system were run by humans, doctors could demand to know the reasons for the recommendation, allowing them to make an informed decision, but because the system is now automated and lacking in transparency, they must blindly follow the recommendation - a monitoring gap in terms of questionable legitimacy.

3.2 Design

"When you pass from the vague to the precise... you always run a certain risk of error[20]."

A system's goals may be legitimate, and yet they may be poorly designed into a metric that the AI takes action to optimise. This introduces a control gap as the system's objectives are no longer necessarily aligned with the intent behind its creation, potentially resulting in unintended outcomes.

Although all systems are subjected to a risk induced by the inaccurate design and encoding of general intent into metrics that can be operationalised, systems that rely exclusively on human decisions have greater flexibility, and feedback mechanisms that reduce the impact of mis-specified objectives. Simply put, humans may decide that a standard process is wrong, and act unilaterally to correct it, so while this human agency may be a source of problems, it does help to ensure rules are not applied so rigidly as to cause fundamental issues. AI systems, on the other hand, have no in-built moral compass, no understanding of societal norms nor any concern for potential repercussions as a result of any decisions outside of what they have been explicitly instructed to optimise. The computer will do exactly as it has been told - even if there would be broad agreement among people that the decision is wrong.

In this section, we review some of the common factors that contribute to the poor design of an intended objective into an AI System.

3.2.1 Missing normative constraints

Humans are unaware of many common sense constraints and rules they apply when making decisions, so when they specify to a machine what needs to be done, they tend to miss important things without realising it. This is a common, and often serious, control gap.

For example, a marketing campaign for groceries set to maximise sales may determine that the optimal way to achieve this goal is to focus entirely on marketing unhealthy foods. The marketing manager probably didn't intend this outcome when instructing the AI developers to maximise sales, but a limit on the amount of unhealthy foods which can be marketed might lead to healthier outcomes for consumers, and need to be imposed on the system.

Case Study: Biased outcome

In 2015, a misclassification error by Google's photo app applied the racist label 'gorillas' to two black subjects, in line with historical stereotypes that dehumanise black people in western society. All classification algorithms make mistakes, but when designing them we can try to choose which mistakes we most want to avoid. Mistaking a chair for a table is unlikely to have moral significance. But dehumanising black people is profoundly damaging. Humans should know this, and avoid such damage without being told, but machines need to be instructed. Designers can consider the social and historical circumstances of their systems, and apply rules to account for them, but in this case, that may have been the conservative decision to omit labels that correspond in any way with stereotyped depictions of racial minority groups. Still, checking all potentially harmful miscategorisations could well prove a formidable challenge.

Our current technology cannot design a complete set of rules to restrict the behaviour of an AI system – that would amount to the Holy Grail of integrating human values into machines - nevertheless, it's imperative to keep pushing in that direction, and dedicate best efforts to identify critical constraints that prevent the system from causing harm.

3.2.2 Poor proxies

Sometimes we don't have the data we would like. It may be hard to obtain direct access to measurements corresponding to the true amount of interest, so a proxy has to be used, and if there is lack of sufficient care when picking a proxy measure, issues of design may arise, representing a control gap.

Case Study: **Misclassification error**

One study assessing a proprietary algorithm that estimated a patient's health risk for the purposes of directing them to a special care program highlights this issue well: in the absence of detailed biomarkers, the designers of the algorithm used individuals' healthcare costs as a proxy for their healthcare needs when training an algorithm to predict healthcare needs for future patients. This is perhaps intuitive, since sicker patients tend to incur greater healthcare costs, however, the study revealed that, for a given healthcare cost, black patients had a higher true health risk than white patients as measured by biomarkers the researchers subsequently collected. Since the algorithm made triaging decisions based on cost, this meant black patients were denied special care at a higher rate than white patients for the same health risks.

Further investigation revealed a key factor explaining why cost of service was a biased proxy: black patients on average have poorer access to health services than white patients, so the investment in the health of black patients is on average lower for the same health risks. The designers expected cost of service to be an accurate proxy of health, and although they are indeed correlated, it proved to be a biased proxy, and the outcome affected the disadvantaged group perversely.

3.2.3 False causality

In some cases, an AI system may be designed using correlational information, but instructed to act in a manner assuming the information is causal. This is a subtle but potentially devastating control gap. If the AI's actions change the properties of the environment under which its training data was collected, the correlations that it identified may no longer hold, producing wildly inaccurate predictions.

Case Study: **Correlation v causation**

An AI system was developed in the mid-'90s to identify patients that were at high risk of dying from pneumonia on admission to hospital, based on historical case outcomes and information such as the patients' symptoms and their medical history. The idea was to use the predictions to decide whether the patients should be admitted or sent home.

When the data scientists inspected the results of the system, they discovered that if a patient had a history of asthma attacks the system was more likely to predict low risk. This struck the data scientists as odd, because asthma is a potentially fatal pre-existing condition. When the doctors were informed, they realised the reason: asthmatic patients are immediately admitted to hospital and closely monitored by staff, resulting in an even lower death rate than for the healthier ones sent home.

The system should have been designed to explicitly answer the question "what should be done with a patient presenting with pneumonia?" Instead, it was designed in a way that unintentionally answered the question "what happens to a patient presenting with pneumonia?" The design was correlational when it should have been causal. This was a critical control gap that fortunately didn't translate into a disastrous decision due to opportune human oversight early in the process.

Were the triaging system purely human, only humanly understandable criteria would have been used to make the decision of how to triage the patients. These would have been based on known causal factors, reducing the chances of triaging based on spurious correlations.

3.3 Execution

Even with a legitimate objective, and adequate design of a system to deliver on that objective, execution failure can occur. The gaps in control and monitoring driven by AI identified above make operational failures more challenging to address than in traditional, better understood human decision domains. This potential for operational failure is regularly identified in existing guidance on Model Risk Management, for example SR 11-17, issued by the US

Federal Reserve[21].

Organisations must be made aware of the new forms of execution failure associated with automated systems, compared to traditional human systems, and take steps to manage them. Some examples follow:

3.3.1 General failure of monitoring

Modern organisations are used to continuous monitoring of critical IT systems, but traditional human decision-making systems tend to be less strictly observed, precisely because they are human. A monitoring function usually exists, but may operate with a time delay, or review only a small sample of interactions, and the inherent subjectivity of some human decisions also makes such supervision less clearcut than the performance detection of critical IT infrastructure.

When decisions are automated, monitoring systems need to become more IT-like, but, just like IT systems, automated decisioning systems may fail catastrophically and quickly. High frequency trading systems have been regularly implicated in flash crashes.

Case Study: Chatbots

> The Microsoft chatbot Tay very quickly evolved from low-stakes interactions to racism and abuse, when let loose on Twitter. A monitoring system aware of, and looking for the potential for such outcomes might have allowed the plug to be pulled sooner.

The performance of automated systems may degrade over time, and this degradation may be uneven, so it is important to monitor system performance both as a whole and for specific groups, notably vulnerable groups, in order to spot important issues as they occur.

3.3.2 Ambiguous accountability

Certain decisions can be delegated to an AI system, but it certainly cannot be held accountable in the same manner as a human decision- maker. It cannot be disciplined or fired for making poor decisions and, if it is turned off, this does not involve the system taking responsibility or feeling consequences.

Who then is ultimately accountable when an AI system goes

wrong? Organisational leaders should be concerned that this question is regularly asked today. If it is an open question in an organisation, there is a risk that nobody considers themselves accountable, both a control and monitoring failure. Issues can easily fester, becoming ever more serious, when nobody is considered responsible for listening to or fixing them.

The primary gap, in our view, is likely to emerge between junior mid-management and the developers of AI systems, which may be an internal team or could be external for a procured system. Management may feel ill-equipped to take responsibility for a system they do not have the expertise to understand, and try to blame the developers. However, most AI developers are unlikely to believe they should be accountable for the actions of a system in a business domain where they may have little to no expertise, and where the goals of the system were determined by management. This mirrors the historical tension when IT systems were introduced, with traditional management being ill-equipped at the time to understand or govern a new technology. Ultimately this was not a problem pushed onto IT - it led to the creation of executive roles for IT, and general improvements in IT literacy in management teams and boards. Similarly, we feel that improvements in executive and board literacy will be needed for AI, if it is to be governed responsibly.

Failures of this accountability may result in issues festering and escalating, first in seriousness, and then up the hierarchy. Governance failures of this kind are likely to reflect badly on the senior management staff responsible for this area of the business.

A further complication is the probable implicit or explicit delegation or contracting of certain activities out to either developers or vendors of AI systems, which may confuse management, and be particularly problematic for vendor relationships. Like other forms of software, some delegation of responsibility – particularly for functionality – may be expected at this point, however unless otherwise specified, this should always be understood as delegation of a responsibility, not transference or abdication. The manager delegating responsibility for constructing an AI system should not expect to transfer accountability for that system, particularly for large failings. There is a risk though of their misunderstanding this. For external partners, contracts may outline various responsibilities and accountabilities of each party, but ultimate accountability for the decisions made by an AI system – particularly in the eyes of those affected – will usually rest with the original firm. Again, there is a risk that management may not properly understand or accept that accountability – particularly the potential for reputational damage – cannot be transferred, which may lead to monitoring and control failures.

Case Study: Accountability

The recent Australian Royal Commission into Misconduct in the Banking, Superannuation and Financial Services Industry provides a series of case studies in consumer lending that, at least in part, illustrate problems of ambiguous accountability arising from automated systems. In at least two case studies, errors in automated systems were found to persist for a lengthy period, affecting customers without an accountable person taking practical corrective action or even noticing. It seems reasonable to suspect that equivalent errors within a purely human system would have been detected earlier, and corrected more quickly and effectively due to clearer accountability. The Royal Commission specifically noted the absence of – and need for – end-to-end accountability for the design, implementation, marketing, and monitoring of financial products.

3.3.3 Error replication

In traditional systems, a frontline team consisting of human operators acts as both a speed limiter and final sanity check on the overall system's decisions. A single human operator making regular mistakes has limited power to reduce the potential impact of their errors, but even this is removed in AI systems, where a single error introduced into the decision-making process may instantly impact the organisation's entire customer base. The potential volume of affected individuals means that even minor errors may pose a significant reputational or financial risk to the organisation, which increases the need for effective control and monitoring.

3.3.4 Domain creep

It is not uncommon for models and systems developed for specific domains or uses to be applied in other settings which feel 'similar enough', and this is often described as domain creep.

For human decision systems, the duplication of an existing function brings new frontline staff and a new rule book, and people will consult and interact with each other, and use their judgement in order to identify where changes must be made to adapt to the new domain; however no similar controls are in place when we transfer a model or AI system to another domain.

Case Study: Domain creep

In January 2016, Google pushed a software update to its Nest Learning Thermostats, where an error in the code caused many of their batteries to drain, leaving users unable to turn on their heating in the depths of the Northern Hemisphere winter.

Some forms of domain creep may be subtle and challenging for non-expert management to spot, and, perhaps more worryingly, management enthusiasm for rolling out an effective but narrowly tested system can be a primary cause of this form of control failure.

Case Study: Software errors

During the Covid-19 crisis, many researchers attempted to build models to assist with diagnosis and prognosis. Training data for such systems is usually taken from a particular hospital, setting or form of equipment, but there was clearly a human desire to extrapolate use outside this original domain – to other hospitals, settings, equipment types and countries – so, in several studies, it was unclear if models could be expected to perform adequately outside of the narrow domain in which the data was collected.

Ethical failures can arise from domain creep, and models' performance is likely to deteriorate when applied in unfamiliar territory. Biases may also emerge – perhaps models perform better in a new domain than in a newly observed group of people with whom the system is generally unfamiliar.

3.3.5 Input errors

A deceptively simple failure mode, it is critical to identify input errors in automated systems. Human intuition will naturally correct obviously erroneous inputs, but automated systems require specific steps to achieve similar standards of correction, another manifestation of a control gap.

For example, a bank manager approving loans will likely question the applicant if they declare an income which seems unreasonably high or low. The applicant can then correct the input before it is used for a decision. An automated system will need to be specifically instructed to perform these sorts of checks, without which loans may automatically be given to customers unable to repay them, or automatically and unreasonably refused.

3.3.6 Off-the-shelf

Off-the-shelfing means unduly trusting outsourced expertise, such as a client believing, without due diligence, that a vendor has taken appropriate care in the design of an AI tool under procurement and that the tool addresses their needs.

For example, a police department may purchase an AI system that claims to predict crime, and then use it for policing resource allocation. The system may be using past arrests to predict future crime - as if arrests were a true proxy for the real-world incidence of crime, when in fact it is biased by historical patterns of arrest. If the department acts on these predictions without adequately understanding the assumptions that underpin the technology, a feedback loop that reinforces patterns of historical discrimination may be created: that the police only make arrests in communities that the system sends them to, and the system only sends police to communities where they are likely to make arrests[22].

Diffusion of responsibility is another hazard associated with off- the-shelfing: a naive customer is likely to feel somebody else is now responsible because they paid money for the tool, but the deployment of a tool procured from outside an organisation doesn't remove the need to evaluate the consequences of its use.

4. Actions

As illustrated above, there are a range of serious risks to organisational governance driven by the introduction of AI systems, and we believe it is possible to effectively address those risks. In this section, we suggest a series of interventions under three broad themes: people and organisational culture, organisational routines and processes, and technical practices and tools (Figure 6.3). We view these actions as elements of an emerging responsible or ethical AI practice which leads to general improvements in the governance of automated decisions by addressing failures of legitimacy, design and execution.

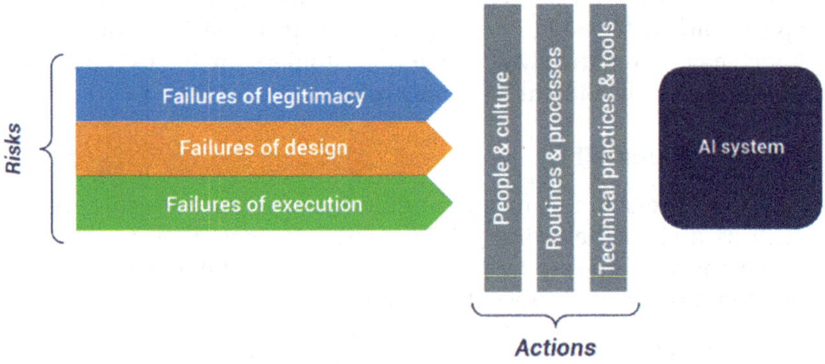

Figure 6.3: Actions to address AI risk

We encourage the reader to adapt and supplement these suggestions to meet the specific needs of their own organisation:

4.1 People and culture

Traditional organisational governance is centred on people, and governance of AI should be no different. Fundamentally, people will be held responsible for any failings, but, as observed above, significant control and monitoring gaps are emerging within AI systems, due to inadequacies in traditional skills, motivations, governance methods and the culture of people within organisations. As such, interventions focused on people and, more broadly, organisation culture, can be effective in narrowing control and monitoring gaps.

4.1.1. Appropriate incentives

> "It is difficult to get a person to understand something when their salary depends on them not understanding it[23]."

Incentives are very powerful interventions, and should not be underestimated. Wise incentive design can have substantial benefits across all areas of risk, but the poor design of incentives may increase risk.

Including explicit objectives to incorporate elements of common sense or morality into an AI system's design in an attempt to avoid failures of design may compromise the business performance of the system (for example reduce profits)[24]. It would be hard for system owners and managers to justify such elements unless leadership explicitly incentivises or requires such ethical objectives or constraints.

For example, a public company may declare simple key objectives like a target profit margin, target revenue, or customer satisfaction, agreed by the board and senior management team, and hyped to shareholders, although such metrics do not adequately describe non- commercial objectives such as ensuring that the AI systems don't make discriminatory or unfair decisions. Within such an environment, a middle manager with direct responsibility for controlling and monitoring a system may find it difficult to accept a lower profit or revenue in order to promote a social or ethical goal. In the worst cases, they may be specifically incentivised to do the opposite by bonuses or promotion rewarding outstanding profits, and instruct their AI developers to pursue a narrow goal in the full knowledge of the ethical failures which may ensue.

We therefore recommend that organisations advocate mechanisms to incentivise the explicit or implicit development and adherence to responsible AI practices among product owners, senior management and AI developers. This will help to foster greater legitimacy, and other stakeholders such as system developers may also become more aware of responsible AI considerations in their work if they understand them to be a key concern for system owners and senior executives.

There are many possible mechanisms to incentivise responsible AI practice for improved governance, such as:

- Characterising loss of potential profit or revenue due to implementation of fairness constraints as an investment in fairness
- Adjusting target metrics to account for a range of objectives that capture not only commercial, but also broader ethical objectives

- Celebrating and sharing the stories of system owners who implement responsible AI processes
- Flagging implementation of responsible AI as a critical factor in annual performance reviews for system owners
- Using key performance indicators that measure customer impacts
- Integrating ethical considerations alongside technical ones in the organisation's development workflow[25]
- Providing specific and meaningful incentives for ethical conduct
- Removing heavily conflicted individuals from key decision-making roles in the system's design
- Incentivising the inclusion of underrepresented groups in key decision-making roles in the system's design.

We encourage the reader to consider the incentive structures in their organisation carefully, the effects of those incentives on management's control function for AI systems, and how they may be adapted to reduce the risks of poor conduct.

4.1.2 Training

The skills required for teams to implement responsible AI come from several disciplines, including social science, political science, ethics, systems thinking and governance, as well as statistics and machine learning, and include concepts only recently developed in academia. It is therefore likely that most employees are underskilled in many areas of responsible AI - even those who are AI specialists.

We recommend that organisations provide training in multidisciplinary approaches for responsible AI to AI developers, system owners, system integrators, business leads and the board, to ensure that they have the expertise and awareness required to govern systems effectively. Greater multidisciplinary training will help to reduce both control and monitoring gaps, and to create clearer lines of communication. Table 6.1 provides an overview of some of the key skills needed in the various roles identified in this chapter.

Role	Skills needed
Developers Data scientists and data engineers developing, deploying and validating AI systems	• Understand link between design decisions and the impacts of AI systems • Communicate the implications of design decisions to non-technical audiences • Quantify non-commercial, ethical objectives into mathematical measures, understand their limitations, and integrate them into the design of AI systems • Identify unintended behavior in AI systems, investigate causes, and apply mitigations • Understand the ways in which AI systems can ingrain existing societal biases • Understand the business domain in which they are operating.
System owners & integrators Business leaders responsible for the operation of the AI systems (either developed in-house or procured	• Understand the novel risks introduced when AI systems replace manual systems • Define both business and ethical objectives for AI systems • Decide how to balance those objectives when they might compete • Deploy AI transparency as appropriate for the system context • Understand and communicate the implications for the system's impact of technical design decisions.
System review committee Cross-disciplinary committee ensuring system owner follows responsible AI process in the design, development and deployment of AI systems	• Assesses the degree to which a system's design and operation aligns with its stated objectives, and the values and priorities of the organisation • Understands the limitations of the system as implemented, and its potential unintended impacts • Ensures the organisation maintains an effective process of responsible AI governance.
Board of directors Governing body that sets management and monitoring policies	• Understands the risks introduced when AI systems replace manual systems • Sets strategic direction on AI use, including when not to use AI • Ensures that the organisation maintains an effective process of responsible AI governance.

Table 6.1: Roles and skills required for effective AI governance

4.1.3 Broad stakeholder engagement and co-design

This intervention addresses failures of legitimacy and design in general. System development should not be done in isolation from those the system may impact. To foster greater legitimacy, a diverse range of stakeholders potentially affected by a system may be given the opportunity to add input into its design and operation. This may use mechanisms of consultation, community juries[26], and other ways to involve people[27], or more structured methods of co-design. Otherwise, less formal methods of iterative design and feedback, possibly via informal design workshops, surveys, testing or prototypes, may be effective.

Whatever approach is adopted, the involvement of a suitably diverse range of stakeholders in the design of a project will tend to reveal designers' blind spots, defeat issues before systems are put onto the market, allow important feedback and monitoring themes to be discovered early, and, ultimately, foster greater legitimacy of the final system. Importantly, these approaches will only work if feedback from stakeholders is used in system design and system governance, and risks once identified are taken seriously. Consultation or co-design that has no discernible effect on outcomes will undermine, not increase, legitimacy. For significant or sensitive systems, mechanisms for ongoing engagement with stakeholders may be necessary.

4.1.4 Role-taking

Role-taking is the socio-psychological concept referring to the ability of an individual to understand others' thoughts, feelings, experiences, and perspectives[28]. An acute sense of the impact of the AI system on people can help reduce the gap in both control and monitoring functions.

The AI sector is responsible for conceiving, designing, implementing, deploying and assessing systems that will shape the lives of diverse populations. However, most demographics, particularly disadvantaged groups, are underrepresented in this sector, which is dominated by a white male workforce. As a result, there is a risk that organisations may miss important or even critical considerations.

In addition to the perhaps obvious and highly recommended intervention of increasing diversity in the sector and relevant professions, progress can also be made with existing professionals.

There is evidence that people from majority groups can improve their role-taking abilities through structured collaborative activities with members of marginalised populations who are empowered as leaders[29]. This opens up the possibility of role-taking training as a valuable intervention for improving the legitimacy of design processes for AI systems. Simple interventions can be introduced internally to improve the team's role-taking, some exemplified below:

- Microsoft's Judgement Call[30] is a roleplaying activity for the design phase of development to cultivate stakeholder empathy by imagining the effects of the system from different perspectives.
- Tarot Cards for Tech[31] is a brainstorming exercise that presents designers with hypothetical futures for the AI system. Participants are encouraged to explore the consequences of these futures with a focus on stimulating discussion on preventing undesirable outcomes.

Because role-taking is necessarily relational, it is crucial that these activities be implemented in collaboration with stakeholders from underrepresented and marginalised groups. These stakeholders should not only participate, but be empowered as leaders in activity sessions, and recognised as experts in their lived experiences.

4.2 Routines and Processes

Standardisation and routine are a powerful mechanism to reduce risk. It may be difficult for management to specify from scratch an effective monitoring approach each time an AI system is deployed, or to ensure the full and complete specification of an AI system to a developer when exercising control without the aid of some standardised processes to guide them.

Standardisation and routine provide a useful default position for the governance of an organisation, fostering baseline effectiveness. Standard methods may be varied – usually enhanced – with good reason, but their existence is still necessary to allow an organisation to effectively maintain a suitable starting point for control and monitoring.

4.2.1 Roles and routines to support accountable persons

As observed in Section 3, organisational accountabilities may become unclear when AI systems are deployed. It is important that management are clear in their accountabilities, and confident that they have the skills and support to exercise them usefully. Improvements in accountability can mirror benefits of appropriate incentive design, since a key component of accountability is sanctionability, a negative incentive. Just like incentive design, roles and routines serving accountability goals have far-reaching effects across all three major categories of identified risks: legitimacy, design and execution.

Primary accountability for the outcomes of an AI system should normally be assigned to the person able to delegate decision-making power to it, who would traditionally be a manager within the company with the power to delegate the task.

However, a manager who is used to delegating and managing people may not be suitably skilled in the risks of AI systems to competently delegate a decision to AI developers and an AI system, so organisations should not assume their managers have this expertise. While individual managers can, and, over time and with training and experience, probably will, become expert in this new domain, in the short term organisations should seek to create roles and routines to support them.

One option is to hire an individual or team specialising in AI governance and risks to create policies or routines for the organisation, offer advice to management and AI developers, and conduct independent reviews of systems.

Another complementary option is to create a dedicated governance committee for an AI system or collection of systems. First, and most importantly, individual accountability for the outcomes of a system may be clarified by the charter of any such committee. Independent advisory or audit specialists like the AI governance or risk specialists noted above may formally discharge their responsibilities within such forums, and other areas of the organisation can input into system design via such forums. The explicit formalisation of ethical considerations and tradeoffs in such a committee is a useful mechanism to ensure they receive sufficient attention from management. Finally, review and escalation protocols can be formalised by the committee's charter, allowing management a clear approach to the upwards reporting of emerging risks or issues.

4.2.2 Independent technical audits

Independent audit is an important function in most organisations, and, in some situations, considered so essential that it is required by law or regulation - published financial statements being a common example. In many cases, it is the independence of the audit process which allows questioning – although, even with justified intent, it is often demanding to critique one's own work, systems and processes. Independent technical audits, depending on their scope, should be able to address a range of potential failures.

For AI systems, independent technical audits serve three important purposes:

First, an audit can find technical flaws in design, construction or operation which were not apparent to the system builders or owners, and which either have the potential to cause issues, or may already be causing them. This allows system designers to correct flaws or remedy problems before they become too acute to solve.

Second, an independent technical audit can make non-technical senior management or board members confident that systems have safe technical oversight, similar to an audit of financial statements - management can rely on the audit process to conduct the technical checks which may be too detailed or complex for them to undertake themselves, and this improves their monitoring function.

Third, an independent audit can be a mechanism for receiving advice and guidance on better practices in the general market, producing continual improvements, and incremental risk-reduction.

Audit teams do not have to be entirely independent of the organisation itself. It may be possible for an organisation of suitable scale to employ an internal audit team, or to rotate construction and audit responsibilities within an analytics function on a project-by-project basis, but with internally staffed audit functions or processes, it is important to manage any conflicts of interest which may emerge, particularly interpersonal relationships.

A variation on a traditional audit is the concept of 'red-teaming', where an independent team challenges the status quo, and attempts to break systems. Adversarial audits of this type are common in areas such as cybersecurity, and of particular benefit in identifying flaws in the design of AI systems.

4.2.3 Buyer beware

Procuring an AI system from a third party does not absolve an organisation from responsibility for its operation. This means that a procured system must satisfy the same standards as one developed internally. The system's explicit objectives and how they are balanced, its limitations and failure modes, must all be available for analysis and review. Systems sold as proprietary solutions expect the system owner to be accountable for the impact of a system whose objectives and constraints they were not responsible for. This action directly addresses the off-the-shelving risk identified in Section 3.3.

Arnold et al. (2018)[32] provides a good starting point for items to seek clarification on, before deciding whether to incorporate a third- party application into an AI system, such as:

- What is the intended use of the service output?
- What algorithms or techniques does this service implement?
- Which datasets was the service tested on? Provide links to datasets that were used for testing, along with corresponding datasheets. Do the datasets have any known biases, and are they relevant/ appropriate?
- Describe the testing methodology
- Describe the test results
- Are you aware of possible examples of bias, ethical issues, or other safety risks as a result of using the service?
- Are the service outputs explainable and/or interpretable?
- For each dataset used by the service: was the dataset checked for bias? What efforts were made to ensure that it is fair and representative?
- Does the service implement and perform any bias detection and remediation?
- What is the expected performance of unseen data or data with different distributions?
- Was the service checked for robustness against adversarial attacks?

- When were the models last updated?

While buyers of AI systems should be responsible for the system, suppliers should maintain a suitable service after the sale and during operation. We suggest that agreements between buyers and suppliers include provisions concerning supplier action to uncover problems, processes for buyers and those affected by systems reporting issues, and clauses requiring prompt corrective action when issues are discovered. Like provisions in many IT service agreements today, this may include a range of incentives for good performance or penalties for poor performance of the supplier in relation to the legal and ethical risks discussed.

4.2.4 Pre-emptive contestability

Contestability of AI decisions is a frequently discussed topic, and often seen as an important element of legitimacy. However, it is a poor outcome for all concerned if an AI system makes an incorrect decision which must then be contested, often via a formal, adversarial process. Where mistakes are expected to occur frequently, a pre-emptive process can be deployed where decisions can be contested before they have affected anyone. This allows many issues to be resolved before they escalate to a full-blown dispute, and can significantly improve the social licence of a system.

One common method for achieving this is to show the data relied on for the decision to the person affected, together with the preliminary decision, and a clear way for them to point out any mistakes before that decision is finalised, which directly addresses the risk of the input errors identified above.

A recent case involving a computer vision algorithm is instructive (the KNITTER case described earlier in chapter 2): a fine was issued incorrectly to a motorist after a number plate detection system mistook text on another person's t-shirt for their car's number plate[33]. The photos of the alleged infraction were shown to the motorist, who was able to call and have the fine cancelled before it was paid. While there are perhaps improvements to be made, this process is far better than a fine being issued without any other information, followed by an adversarial process for the motorist to attempt to prove their innocence.

Organisations deploying AI systems should expect them to make mistakes, and should expect mistakes to be new, unusual, strange and unforeseen. Whereas an organisation will try to find mistakes before customers are affected, it may not be possible to identify all of them, and, in such situations, a clear, non-adversarial mechanism to point out the mistake and have it corrected – before the mistake has a serious impact– is desirable, and often easy to implement. We call this 'pre- emptive contestability'.

4.2.5 Questionnaires and checklists

A large part of risk management is the identification of potential problems. Depending on how specific or ambiguous they are, questionnaires and checklists help by providing a standardised starting point for reflection. Used well, they stimulate imagination and creativity that may identify blind spots within the development team as well as cultivating a more active and engaged attitude towards the risk management process.

We encourage organisations to develop standardised checklists designed to meet their AI scale, nature and needs, and to consider whether the completion of checklists should be mandatory prior to the release of an AI system.

A number of online resources exist to identify potential risks during the design phase and there are three in particular that we'd like to highlight: The Open Ethics Canvas[34], MIT's AI Blindspot[35] tool and The Ethical OS Toolkit[36].

4.3 Technical practices and tools

Interventions focused on people or processes may be ineffective without complementary technical practices or tools designed to suit the situation. In this section, we identify a series of technical interventions which help to improve management's ability to exercise control and monitor AI systems, and suggest these complement many of the interventions listed above.

4.3.1 Dashboards and control panels

The people responsible for a system must understand its consequences if they are to monitor and control it. As these can change over time, managers may benefit from automated visualisation and display of live impacts via a software dashboard. Many such tools currently exist[37], though by default typically report only model performance measures like accuracy. The definition and measurement of an AI system's important effects is a precursor to deploying any impact dashboard, and remains a context-specific challenge to be undertaken by organisations on a per-system basis.

However, even if they understand the system's current impacts, managers cannot effectively control it without also understanding the potential repercussions that could result from changing how it operates. Such lack of visibility is one of the causes of the control and monitoring gaps described above.

The AI impact control panels aim to close this gap by giving managers levers to control a system's impacts in an intuitive way. Like a dashboard, a control panel translates mathematical measures of performance into human-readable summaries of impact, but it also works in the other direction: translating a manager's preferences and intentions for the impact of the system into the mathematical parameters that tune the AI system accordingly. This two-way translation is depicted in Figure 6.4.

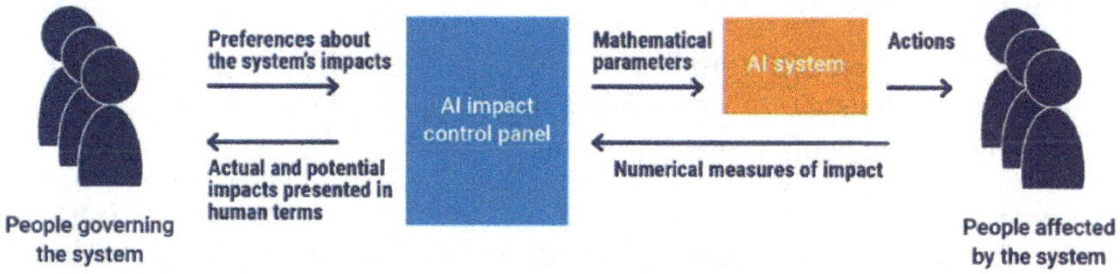

Figure 6.4: AI impact control panel

Tools such as AI impact control panels are especially important when the managers of an AI system do not have the technical background to engage directly with the technical implementation details. A control panel enables them to examine the system's different potential aftermaths without needing to understand which technical details control those results. For example, a manager could examine various potential fairness/revenue trade-offs for their system and select an acceptable balance of these objectives, which the control panel software then translates into the value of the mathematical property that controls the system.

Like dashboards, building an impact control panel for an AI system requires system-specific input and customisation. Unlike dashboards, however, work to develop off-the-shelf software to support their implementation is at an early stage[38].

4.3.2 Technical documentation and transparent development

The life cycle of an AI system from concept through to deployment is complex, and involves numerous consequential decisions made by contributors with different specialisms. Documentation is both an artefact that brings clarity to this complexity, and also a process that, if correctly carried out, integrates responsible thinking throughout the entire system life cycle.

To ensure that everyone developing, monitoring and auditing has a complete picture of the system, organisations should document all of the important design decisions, system objectives, constraints and performance indicators of an AI system in a central register, accessible to all internal stakeholders, although this may make documentation extremely technical and detailed, and unfamiliar to some middle or senior managers, who should encourage it as an effective means of monitoring, and also request a summary of the more pertinent points.

There are a number of resources available giving ways to document the system's development that also place a strong emphasis on governance considerations:

- The ABOUT ML resource library[39] is the ongoing collaborative effort of a diverse range of organisations within the AI community to establish a set of best practices for documentation that industry should adhere to. It contains useful guidance, and examples of transparent development that can be tailored to match the requirements of the stakeholder.
- M. Arnold et al. (2018)[40], T. Gebru et al. (2018)[41], and M. Mitchell et al. (2019)[42] provide useful templates for accessible summaries for AI systems, data and predictive models, respectively.

The public is another crucial stakeholder, and the degree of visibility that it has of the system should be carefully considered. Public visibility in a project helps to ensure its legitimacy, and is an effective method for identifying the development team's blind spots. The New Zealand Government has committed to explaining clearly to the public when their decisions are informed by algorithms[43], and the explanations may include information about the data used and how they are processed as well as clearly identifying a point of contact for public inquiries about the algorithm. However, public transparency should always take into account the privacy of the individuals affected, and potential for malicious actors to game the system.

4.3.3 Explainable AI

While people often make predictions based on causal relationships, AI systems do so by transforming and combining data to discover complex correlations between their inputs and the output variable. Although this approach may provide impressive predictive performance, tracking the AI's internal logic can be very unintuitive to a human.

Explainable tools and models focus on showing why an AI made a certain decision, and making the mechanics of AI understandable improves both the ability to control and monitor it: enabling control by ensuring the system is doing what it is meant to do, and monitoring by alerting people at different levels of an organisation to identify problems, and escalate if necessary. It can also address problems of design and execution, identifying incorrect assumptions made during its design or mistakes in programming that mean it doesn't work, as well as improving legitimacy through better transparency, as illustrated in 3.1.3.

Techniques for gaining insights into the factors that influence an AI's decision vary depending on the class of model, the expertise of the user, and nature of the question. Interpretable Machine Learning by Christoph Molnar[44] provides a comprehensive overview of the common approaches, and the UK Information Commissioner's Office has also published practical advice[45] to help organisations explain the decisions of their AI systems to affected individuals.

It is important to note that most explanations rely on providing a simplified view of models to make them more understandable, although these simplifications make assumptions that may not hold up in certain situations, therefore the interpreter must understand the limitations of the explanation when deciding how to act.

5. Summary

The growing use of AI is challenging traditional methods of corporate governance. AI is increasingly used for consequential decisions, from credit scoring and insurance pricing to marketing, health triage, recruitment, and government services. But when decisions are delegated to machines rather than humans, traditional governance methods of control and monitoring - designed for human decision-makers, not machines - can, and do, come to grief, as current governance structures have failed to control AI. Novel risks created by the use of AI have resulted in systems making unlawful, immoral, discriminatory, opaque and unaccountable decisions, but the human designers of these systems, supposedly in control of their consequences and monitoring their outcomes, are invariably surprised by these failings.

This chapter is intended as a guide to action for organisations considering the risks of using AI systems. It also serves as guidance for policy makers concerned about how to respond to the challenges and risks presented by automated decision systems. We encourage the reader to draw on our general illustrations and suggestions, and adapt them to their own unique context in order to identify, understand and respond to these risks.

Footnotes

1. Proposal for a Regulation of the European Parliament and of the Council on European Data Governance (Data Governance Act), Brussels, 25.11.2020 COM(2020) 767 Final, available at https://eur-lex.europa.eu/legal-content/EN/TXT/?uri=CELEX%3A52021PC0206
2. https://www.camara.leg.br/noticias/811702-camara-aprova-projeto-que-regulamenta-uso-da-inteligencia-artificial
3. Australian Human Rights Commission, Human Rights and Technology Final Report (Australian Human Rights Commission, 2021) available at <https://tech.humanrights.gov.au/downloads>
4. E. Moss, E. Watkins, R. Singh, M. C. Elish and J. Metcalf, Assembling Accountability: Algorithmic Impact Assessment for the Public Interest (June 29, 2021). Available at SSRN: https://ssrn.com/abstract=3877437
5. Acknowledging the standard definition of risk as the effect of uncertainty on objectives, in this chapter we are primarily concerned with downside risks. Hence when using the term risk, this should primarily be taken to mean an exposure to a potential harm or loss, rather than the potential for gain. This matches the colloquial discussion of AI risks, which focuses on downsides. Comparative terms such as 'high-risk', 'low risk' or 'increased risk' should be read as considering the expected loss arising from those risk exposures, rather than other potential measures of risk which could be considered.
6. ISO is currently developing both a risk management standard (https://www.iso.org/standard/77304.html) and a management systems standard (https://www.iso.org/standard/81230.html) dedicated to AI.
7. NIST (the US National Institute of Standards and Technology) has proposed an approach for identifying and managing biases in AI, based on risk: Schwartz, Reva et al, A Proposal for Identifying and Managing Bias in Artificial Intelligence (National Institute of Standards and Technology, 22 June 2021) <https://nvlpubs.nist.gov/nistpubs/SpecialPublications/NIST.SP.1270-draft.pdf>
8. R. C. Williamson, M. N. Raghnaill, K. Douglas and D. Sanchez, Technology and Australia's future: New technologies and their role in Australia's security, cultural, democratic, social and economic systems, Australian Council of Learned Academies, September 2015, https://acola.org
9. Nicholas Crafts, Artificial intelligence as a general-purpose

technology: an historical perspective, Oxford Review of Economic Policy, Volume 37, Issue 3, Autumn 2021, Pages 521–536, https://doi.org/10.1093/oxrep/grab012

10. Commonwealth Ombudsman, Automated Decision-Making Better Practice Guide, https://www.ombudsman.gov.au/publications/better-practice-guides/automated-decision-guide
11. https://www.ombo.nsw.gov.au/__data/assets/pdf_file/0003/138207/The-new-machinery-of-government-special-report_Front-section.pdf
12. Administrative Review Council, Report 46 - Automated Assistance in Administrative Decision-Making 2004, https://www.ag.gov.au/legal-system/publications/report-46-automated-assistance-administrative-decision-making-2004
13. Definitions here are difficult, and language is imprecise. In this chapter, focused on high level guidance, we can afford to be imprecise: we use "automated decision systems" and "AI Systems" interchangeably, as well as "AI decisions" and "automated decisions", or "automated decision making" and "AI decision making". As will be clear from the text, nevertheless, our focus is on forms of automated decision making that create different challenges for traditional governance mechanisms within organisations.
14. This does not mean the resulting decision making system is free of problems. There is ample evidence that human decision systems often exhibit significant bias (Kahneman, D. (2011). Thinking, fast and slow. New York: Farrar, Straus and Giroux) and noise (Kahneman, D., Sibony, O., & Sunstein, C. R. (2021). Noise: a flaw in human judgment. First edition. New York: Little, Brown Spark). Unless appropriate mechanisms are set up to measure and audit issues with human decision making, an organisation may be "in the dark" with respect to the actual quality of those decisions.
15. Often some rules are coded explicitly by the AI developer, but with the increased adoption of machine learning a growing number of rules are now coded by the machine itself (based on a precise mathematical specification of the objective provided by the AI developer).
16. More precisely, the front-line automated systems include both the machine learning algorithms (that generate rules) and the resulting AI models (that execute said rules).
17. When managers delegate to a front-line team, they are often delegating to people with direct and ongoing experience of the issues at the front-line of the domain (whether that is insurance, banking, health or other). On the contrary, when management delegates to AI developers they are delegating to generalists removed from dealing

with customers and front-line issues.

18. Guiding Principles of Good Governance. Australian Institute of Company Directors. https://www.aicd.com.au/corporate-governance-sectors/not-for-profit/not-for-profit.html
19. https://about.fb.com/news/2021/11/update-on-use-of-face-recognition/
20. Bertrand Russell, The Philosophy of Logical Atomism, Lecture 1 1918-19
21. https://www.federalreserve.gov/supervisionreg/srletters/sr1107a1.pdf
22. https://www.brennancenter.org/our-work/research-reports/predictive-policing-explained
23. Sinclair, Upton. I, Candidate for Governor: And How I Got Licked (1935) (original quote edited slightly to use more inclusive language)
24. It won't necessarily be compromised since there may be "profitability plateaux". An AI system may admit several design configurations that lead to essentially the same "maximum profit", and yet some of them may be significantly better than others from an ethical perspective. E.g. see https://ambiata.com/blog/2021-03-22-nba-for-social-good/
25. Microsoft's AI Fairness Checklist, for fairness-specific considerations: https://www.microsoft.com/en-us/research/project/ai-fairness-checklist/
26. https://learn.microsoft.com/en-us/azure/architecture/guide/responsible-innovation/
27. See eg Ada Lovelace Institute, Participatory Data Stewardship (Ada Lovelace Institute, 2021) <https://www.adalovelaceinstitute.org/report/participatory-data-stewardship/>
28. Mead, George Herbert. 1934. Mind, Self, and Society. University of Chicago Press.
29. Love, Tony P., and Jenny L. Davis. 2021. "Racial Differences in Women's Role- Taking Accuracy: How Status Matters." Sociological Science 8: 150-169
30. https://learn.microsoft.com/en-us/azure/architecture/guide/responsible-innovation/judgmentcall
31. http://tarotcardsoftech.artefactgroup.com/
32. Arnold et al. (2018). FactSheets: Increasing Trust in AI Services through Supplier's Declarations of Conformity. arXiv preprint arXiv:1808.07261. https://arxiv.org/abs/1808.07261

33. https://www.theguardian.com/uk-news/2021/oct/18/motorist-fined-number-plate-t-shirt
34. The Open Ethics Canvas is a tool for developers and system owners to initiate conversations with the intention of revealing blind spots in the development process https://openethics.ai/canvas/
35. MIT's "AI Blindspot", a resource to spot unconscious biases and structural inequalities in AI systems: https://aiblindspot.media.mit.edu/
36. The Ethical OS Toolkit is an aid for organising workshops aimed at identifying risks specifically targeted at AI systems. https://ethicalos.org/
37. Prometheus and Evidently AI are two (of many) open-source software monitoring tools: https://prometheus.io and https://evidentlyai.com/
38. See an open-source prototype illustrating the control panel ideas: https://github.com/gradientinstitute/ai-impact-control-panel
39. ABOUT ML https://partnershiponai.org/workstream/about-ml/
40. Arnold et al. (2018). Fact Sheets: Increasing Trust in AI Services through Supplier's Declarations of Conformity. arXiv preprint arXiv:1808.07261. https://arxiv.org/abs/1808.07261
41. Gebru et al. (2018). Datasheets for datasets. arXiv preprint arXiv:1803.09010. https://arxiv.org/abs/1803.09010
42. Mitchell et al. (2019). Model cards for model reporting. In Proceedings of the Conference on Fairness, Accountability, and Transparency (pp. 220-229). ACM.
43. Algorithm Charter for Aotearoa New Zealand https://data.govt.nz/assets/data-ethics/algorithm/Algorithm-Charter-2020_Final-English-1.pdf
44. https://christophm.github.io/interpretable-ml-book/
45. https://ico.org.uk/for-organisations/guide-to-data-protection/key-dp-themes/explaining-decisions-made-with-artificial-intelligence/

Chapter 7
The Responsible AI Index

1. Introduction

A lack of regulation, legislation, and guidelines to monitor AI's development and use increases the risks that AI is developed without a true understanding of responsibility, potentially creating negative outcomes. AI technology maturity appears to be years ahead of legislation or regulation of AI, and therefore organisations should turn to frameworks and guidelines as well as ethical leadership to guide them through developing Responsible AI (RAI). In this context, Fifth Quadrant, Ethical AI Advisory and the Gradient Institute partnered to create the inaugural Responsible AI Index, sponsored by IAG and Telstra (Fifth Quadrant, 2021). Through their survey of attitudes and practices toward RAI, Fifth Quadrant has addressed the difficult task of making an assessment of RAI maturity and, further, identifying the actions that organisations are taking – or not taking – today to address the potential for AI harms.

2. Survey design

In February-March 2021, Fifth Quadrant conducted a fifteen-minute online survey of 416 decision-makers (distinct organisations) for AI strategy. The sample for the survey was drawn from organisations with twenty or more employees based in Australia, who had either deployed AI in their business or were planning to do so within the next twelve months. The sample covered a range of businesses by size, industry and location, and the respondents were AI strategy decision- makers with roles such as chief information officer (CIO), chief technology officer (CTO), and chief data officer (CDO) (Figure 7.1).

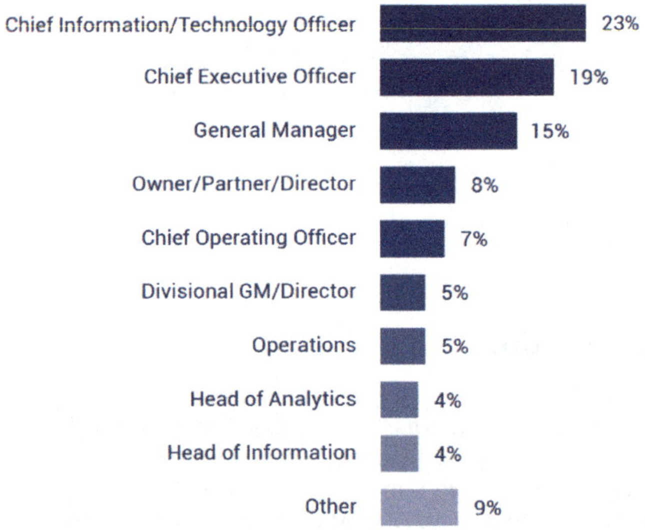

Figure 7.1: Respondents by job title (Fifth Quadrant, 2021)

The survey included organisations from a range of sectors (Table 7.1).

Sector	%
Manufacturing	24
Retail and hospitality	18
Services	16
Public services (incl. NFPs and education)	10
Finance and banking	8
Technology and communications	8
Energy and resources	7
Construction	6
Healthcare and social assistance	3

Table 7.1: Organisations surveyed by industry sector (Fifth Quadrant, 2021)

The maturity model takes account of five dimensions of performance, and the extent to which responsible actions are taken across those dimensions (Figure 7.2). The Index is constructed from a self-assessed performance rating across sixteen statements about Responsible AI, and whether any of thirteen actions had been taken to implement AI in a responsible way. Answers to these questions were combined and weighted to provide a total score out of one hundred.

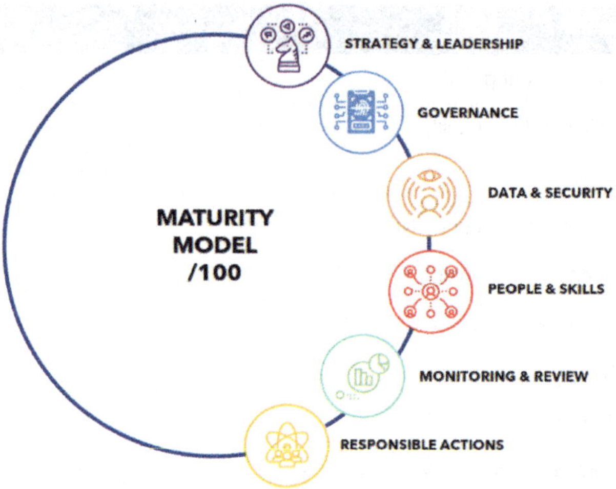

Figure 7.2: RAI maturity model dimensions (Fifth Quadrant, 2021)

3. Results

3.1 The RAI Index

Based on the overall maturity scores, the RAI survey on AI strategy categorises organisations into four levels of Responsible AI maturity: maturing (the most mature), developing, initiating, and planning (the least mature), based on survey questions addressing the five dimensions of performance in Figure 7.2. The report reveals that over half of the organisations studied (54%) are only at the planning or initiating stages of maturity, and fewer than one in ten are at the maturing stage (8%), highlighting the opportunity for business leaders to act on critical AI initiatives such as reviewing algorithms and underlying databases, monitoring outcomes for customers, sourcing legal advice in potential areas of liability, and reviewing global best practice (Figure 7.3).

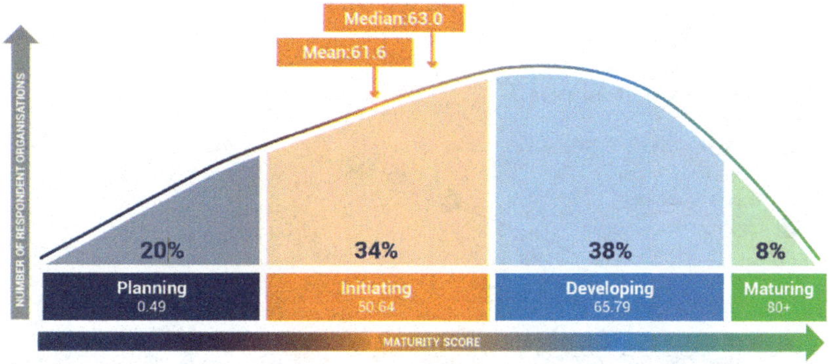

Figure 7.3: RAI maturity (Fifth Quadrant, 2021)

Characteristics of the four stages of maturity are shown in Figure 7.4. At the planning stage, organisations are focusing on business benefits and return on investment. As organisations mature, their focus moves towards developing guidelines for responsible use of AI, and a culture shift from a narrow focus on return on investment to wider ethical issues.

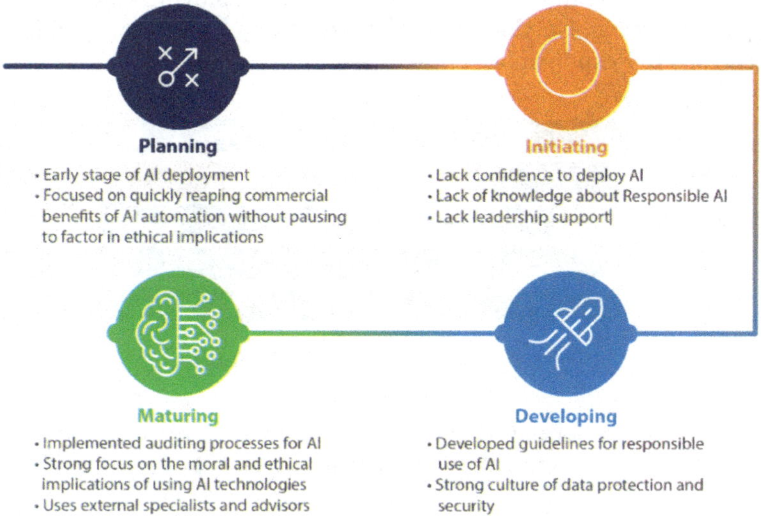

Figure 7.4: Initiating – Lack of confidence and Lack of leadership

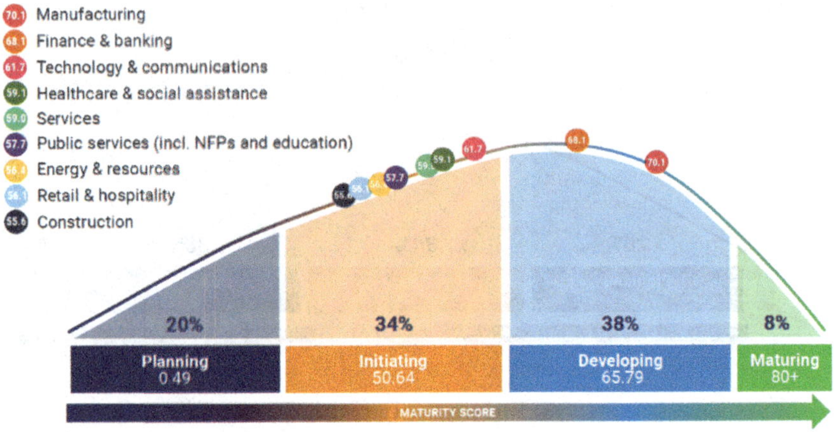

Figure 7.5: RAI maturity by industry sector (Fifth Quadrant, 2021)

In addition, respondents were asked to rate their organisation's overall ability to deploy AI responsibly and ethically. Overall, only 32% gave a high rating - 89% of the Maturing segment, and only 3% of the Planning segment (Figure 7.6). This result indicates that the majority of Australian organisations that are deploying or planning to deploy AI recognise there are significant gaps in their capabilities, according to Responsible AI practices.

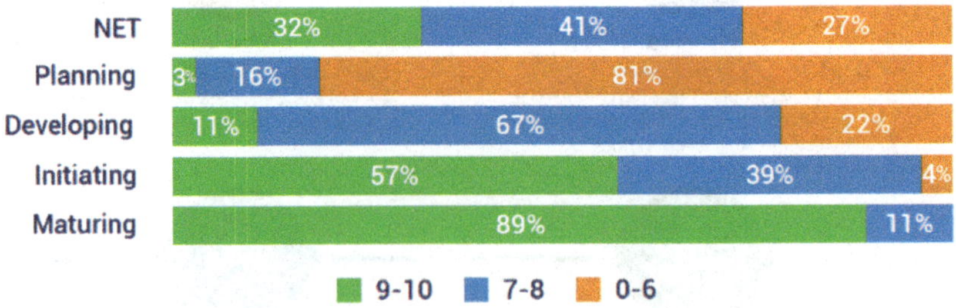

Figure 7.6: Overall rating of ability to deploy AI responsibly and ethically (Fifth Quadrant, 2021)

3.2 Enablers of responsible AI

The results suggest that the lack of confidence in deploying AI responsibly comes down to an overall lack of knowledge and vision, while those who are more confident and mature cite that their greater capabilities are due to the processes they have put in place, as well as consultation with subject matter experts (Figure 7.7). Respondents note that control over the data used by the AI systems gives them the most confidence in their ability to deploy AI responsibly.

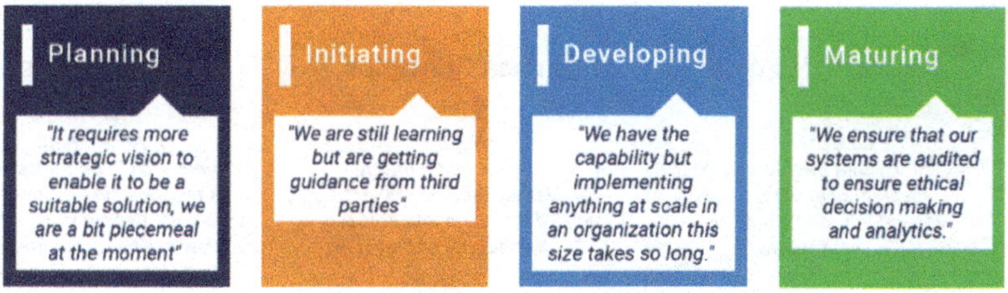

Figure 7.7: Enablers of RAI (Fifth Quadrant, 2021)

3.3 Organisational strategy for AI

Just over half (51%) of the organisations studied have an enterprise-wide AI strategy, and this remains a work in progress for the Planning and Initiating segments where AI capabilities are likely to be more siloed or unevenly distributed (Figure 7.8). To be more mature in responsible AI, organisations need to transition from opportunistic and tactical AI decision-making to a more strategic orientation.

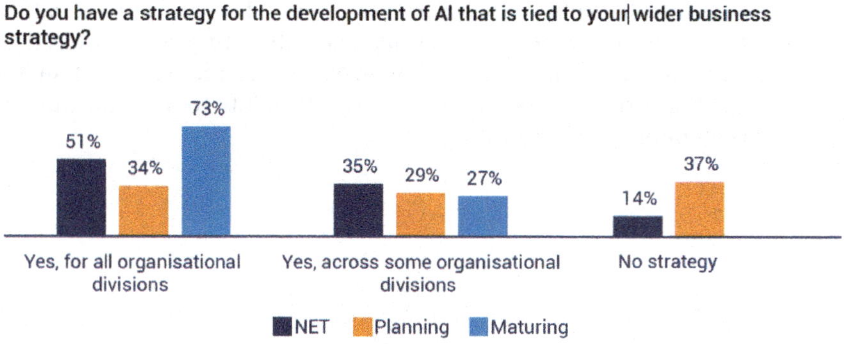

Figure 7.8: RAI strategy (Fifth Quadrant, 2021)

3.4 AI and ethical principles

The elements of the Australia's AI Ethics Principles, developed by the Department of Industry, were incorporated into the survey to identify the gap between attitudes towards Responsible AI and the steps that organisations are taking towards implementing Ethical AI.

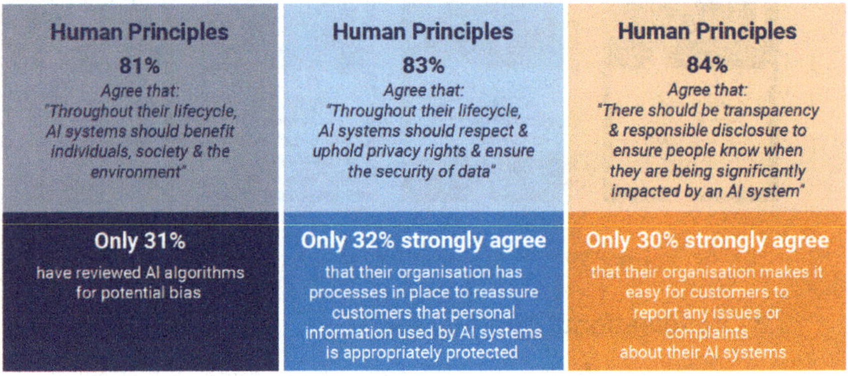

Figure 7.9: Ethical alignment (Fifth Quadrant, 2021)

Awareness of Australia's AI Ethics Principles is much higher in the Maturing organisations (94%) (Figure 7.9). As organisations become more mature in their development and use of AI, they are more likely to have developed their own ethical standards.

Principles relating to social well-being, human-centred values, fairness, data and technical security and integrity are considered by respondents to be important, however this is not reflected in the actions that organisations take. This result points to a significant gap between intent and actions.

Figure 7.10: Actions (Fifth Quadrant, 2021)

3.5 Action-taking

Despite broad agreement with Australia's AI Ethics Principles, this is not reflected in the actions organisations have taken to develop and deploy AI responsibly, indicating a gap between beliefs and behaviour (Figure 7.10).

3.6 Bridging the responsible AI gap

To bridge the gap between current practices and aspirations to Responsible AI, Fifth Quadrant(2021) provided aset of recommendations (Figure 7.11). These recommendations sit comfortably with the proposals made in earlier chapters on AI development and deployment and de-risking of AI decisions.

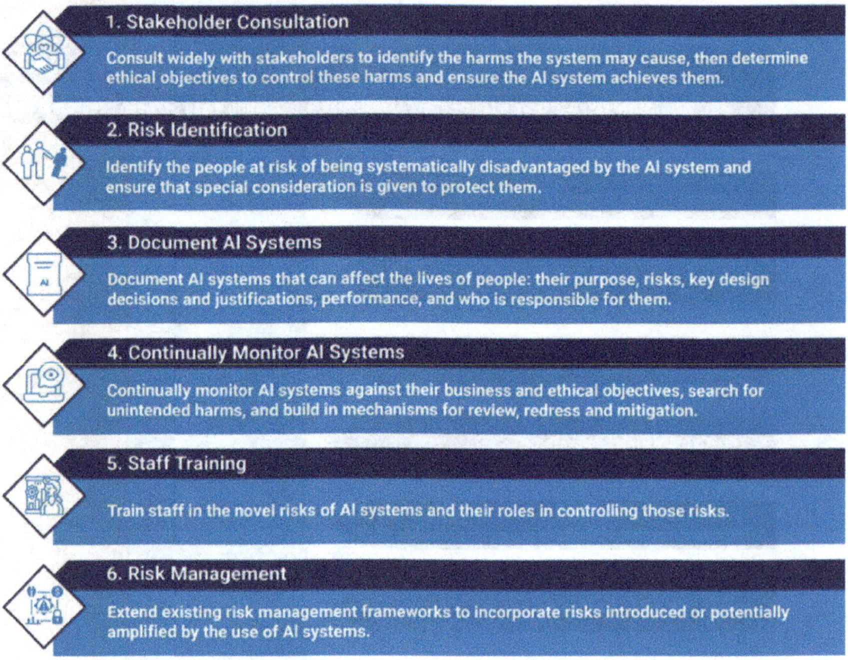

Figure 7.11: Steps to bridging the AI responsibility gap (Fifth Quadrant, 2021)

4. Implications

The RAI index is a pioneering attempt to define and assess RAI maturity. It provides an early state of the nation review of where organisations are today in terms of RAI practices. The survey provides a way of measuring the maturity of an organisation's AI use, as well as a guide to and benchmark for RAI improvement programmes. The survey will be refined and repeated annually as an indication of how RAI practices are maturing and changing. Additionally, RAI software usage will be included in future iterations of the study.

References

Fifth Quadrant (2021). *The Responsible AI Index.* https://www.fifthquadrant.com.au/2021-responsible-ai-index

Chapter 8
Regulation and governance of AI

1. Introduction

How do we regulate to limit, mitigate, and remediate harms caused by using AI? How can the law provide incentives for beneficial developments in AI technology? And to what extent are our laws, our broader regulatory system, and our regulators suited to achieve either of these broad goals?

The relationship between regulation and new technologies has long been challenging. When new technologies create disruption, political and policy decision-makers are confronted with a series of questions: should the technology be banned, controlled, or encouraged? How do existing laws apply? Do existing laws need to be adjusted to achieve their goals better, now that the technological circumstances have changed, or have the goals changed in light of our new capacities? (Bennett Moses, 2017). These questions take on different permutations for different waves of new technologies. The issues raised by gene technology, for example, are different from those raised by nano- technology – and those raised by AI.

In the case of AI, society is still working through the impact of these technologies: what they change about how things work, and what that means for the law. The public and legal discourse has moved beyond "this is a lawless realm" (Australian Human Rights Commission, 2021), and even the assertion that governments should "avoid regulation, it will stifle innovation". Now we are well and truly involved in a more nuanced discussion, one that recognises that some regulation already applies, albeit some reform is required. But where there is still a debate over both application and reform, how does the law apply, and how should it be reformed?

It is already clear that AI's need for, and extensive use of data as the basis for prediction and action are putting new pressure and importance on the regulations that govern our data, the privacy law in particular. AI's capacities to distinguish between people, and infer and make decisions that affect social groups differently, spotlight the role of anti-discrimination law, and other rules that require everyone to be treated fairly. And the capacity to program machines to take actions without human intervention raises very interesting questions about whether, and when, such automation is acceptable, and who is accountable for automated actions.

2. What law and regulation do

Before getting to the questions of how we regulate AI and its use - or how we should regulate AI and its use - we need a crash course in what the law does, and how it works. Even if we are just focused on laws backed and enforced by the power of the state, there are so many different ways that the law can impact on the development and deployment of general use technologies like AI. Understanding some of the differences helps us think, in a more nuanced and sophisticated way, about how the law limits, mitigates and remediates harm, and encourages beneficial developments in AI technology, its uses, deployment and its governance.

2.1 What do we mean by the law?

In thinking about the way that AI and its use are regulated, we first need to consider what we mean by regulation. When we talk about what regulates a technology or its use, the universe of possible regulators can be drawn broadly or narrowly. This chapter takes mostly a narrower view, focusing only on authoritative rules and rulings issued by one of the three branches of government (Parliament, Executive, or Judiciary). This means legislation passed by Parliament, and regulations issued by the Executive (executive and ministerial directions, the legislatively authorised and enforceable orders of a regulator or other enforcer of the law like the police), and judgments issued by the courts. Other regulating forces – norms, ethics, and privately-framed incentives within firms, are mentioned in other chapters.

There are differences between all of these as means to regulate. Legislation, written by government but scrutinised and passed by Parliament, has greater claims to legitimacy than any regulation, but is slower to pass and often, although not always, less detailed than regulations, which can be written by ministers and their departments at any time, and are often used to fill in the gaps, or details not included in legislation. Court judgments are different again: they generally resolve only real and not hypothetical disputes before the court.

Governments have other ways to try to influence the development and deployment of AI: for example increasing use of guidelines and ethical or other principles. In some cases - like Australia's AI Ethics Principles - these are no more than recommendations or principles that people and companies can, and, as argued earlier in this chapter, should choose to follow. Another example is the NSW Government's Smart Places Customer Charter. In other cases, regulators may issue guidance on how they interpret rules - like the guidelines issued by Australia's Office of the Australian Information Commissioner that outline how the OAIC interprets privacy rules. Guidelines of this kind lack legal authority, and may or may not hold if ever put to the test in a court. But they have the advantage of flexibility: they can be published and amended at any time in response to new developments, and firms that follow regulator-endorsed approaches are less likely to be pursued by that same regulator.

Governments also influence development through contracts and procurement rules that apply to the significant technology acquisitions that they themselves make. The NSW Government, in late 2021, released an AI Assurance Framework, a structured set of questions, designed to be considered by government project teams and surface risks. From March 2022, new AI projects have included a mandatory assessment under the framework, with potential for review by an expert AI Review Body. Governments also use co-regulation to influence behaviour: encouraging or even requiring firms in an industry sector like banking to develop their own codes of practice and dispute settlement systems. Or governments can adopt other industry-developed rules by calling for companies to comply with technical standards developed by the IEEE, ISO or other similar standards bodies. The proposed EU AI Act, for example, would make compliance with standards a way to fulfil the requirements of the law (European Commission, 2021 art 40).

Governments aren't the only influences on technical development and deployment of AI: social norms, voluntary standards developed by standards organisations[1], or even the inherent capacities of technology, which theorists call affordances, see Davis, 2020, impose external constraints on what can be done with a given technology, or how it can be built. But the law is special, and there is an important difference between mere influences, and state-issued rules that demand or exact certain responses from people, and back that up with the potential for enforcement, drawing on the state's unique coercive powers to imprison, expel from the country, and take property, deregister companies, deny licences to operate, or otherwise impose lasting and rigid discipline on people and companies (Hildebrandt, 2020). A focus on law, therefore, is more than enough to be going on with.

2.2 Different kinds of law

The law also comes in different varieties, with different spheres of application, and different goals. One key element is jurisdiction: the question of who enacts the law, and where, and to whom it applies. The law mostly applies to people and activities within the physical jurisdiction of a government, and for this reason people sometimes assume that truly global phenomena, like AI as a series of technological fields, and/or the multinational companies that often develop and deploy it, are beyond the reach or influence of national legislatures. Also relevant are subnational laws in federated countries like Australia or the US, international laws like trade agreements and treaties that apply between countries, albeit with only limited mechanisms for enforcement, and supranational law, such as

European law that applies to members of the European Union, and can be enforced by European institutions including the Court of Justice of the European Union).

There are certain challenges when national laws and regulators take on global technology that we should not dismiss too readily. National legislatures can and do write laws that are costly to breach: consider the US$5 billion settlement Facebook paid following the Cambridge Analytica scandal, where Facebook had allowed third parties to access extensive personal data contrary to its own policies. Consequences can be imposed on local employees and managers; compliance with local laws is in many cases a condition of operating in a country.

Some laws have global impact beyond their official jurisdiction. In relation to data, and AI in particular, Europe has become quite adept at using the force of its size, and relative wealth to influence standards of behaviour for firms globally. European privacy law (the General Data Protection Regulation, or GDPR) applies to any processing of the data of European citizens, meaning firms outside the EU must comply with its rules (European Commission, 2016, and see Appendix C). The EU is currently trying to use the same 'Brussels effect' to write global rules for AI, via the proposed EU AI Act (European Commission 2021). The Act would apply to providers placing on the market or putting into service AI systems in the EU, users of AI systems located within the EU, and providers and users of AI systems located in a third country, where the output produced by the system is used in the European Union (Article. 2).

Nationally, lawyers also distinguish between public, private or private and commercial - and criminal law (Hildebrandt 2020, Ch 3). Without getting deep into the weedy debates over definitions and boundaries, public law involves the power of the state as a state: it dictates the powers of government (constitutional law) and accountabilities to people for government decisions that affect people (administrative law, freedom of information), as well as providing general protections (regulating governments and the private sector) for important human rights (anti-discrimination law), and other important standards such as environmental standards (environmental law). Governments, which spend public money and wield considerable powers accorded them by the people, are accountable to those they govern. They are held to higher standards of transparency than private individuals and organisations through freedom of information laws, and have obligations to justify decisions impacting individuals through administrative laws that impose requirements to accord natural justice, such as a fair hearing, and to give reasons for their decisions. These principles can preclude the use of automated/AI systems where decisions cannot be explained in at least some government contexts (NSW Ombudsman, 2021).

Private and commercial laws lay down the rules governing interactions between people and organisations, as well as governments acting not as governments, but, say, acquiring goods on the market. Historically, private actors have often not been required to explain how they make internal decisions, or to give reasons for their decisions; instead, much of private and commercial law provides a framework for private transactions: setting basic entitlements, facilitating transactions, and establishing standards of behaviour and the outer limits of acceptable behaviour in private dealings. Different areas of private law set out who owns what, and how property is transferred (property law, including intellectual property laws), how people make binding bargains, and how benefits, risks, and responsibilities are allocated between parties to a transaction (contract), who owes duties to avoid harming others, and when one party must compensate another for harm they have caused (tort, including the tort of negligence), standards of behaviour that businesses must observe in their dealings with individuals, and in producing and offering products and services (consumer protection laws).

Competition law imposes controls against misuse of market power. Company law makes companies into legal persons capable of acting in their own name, and managers accountable through directors' duties, issuing rules for governance, and allocating power within the firm. Privacy law governs personally identifiable information, and is particularly important in regulating AI. It can be hard to categorise as it straddles both public (protecting human rights, constraining what government can do with data) and private/commercial law (setting rules for private sector transactions involving data collection).

Criminal law is distinct again: it adds moral condemnation and additional consequences such as fines, imprisonment and other kinds of long-term societal exclusion, from limits on entering other countries to legal prohibitions. Serious breaches of standards in both public and private law may bring criminal penalties.

2.3 Things that law does

Governments use law and regulation to achieve all kinds of goals, and to shape the development and governance of AI it can:

1. Assign rights and entitlements generally, or in certain interactions or transactions with governments, other people or businesses - rights in data and algorithms, and rights against discrimination
2. Establish requirements for undertaking certain kinds of business or activities : for example, experience in data analysis in order to access certain data sets, or data security standards for companies wanting access to certain kinds of sensitive data, or requiring risk/ impact assessments to be undertaken prior to undertaking a project
3. Set positive standards of behaviour or action like the Australian requirement that financial services firms treat customers 'efficiently, honestly and fairly' (Corporations Act 2001 (Cth) s 912A)
4. Set positive standards that must be met: like safety standards for products and services, or requirements that AI systems do what they are advertised to do and/or come with certain guarantees and warranties
5. Prohibit or restrict activities considered harmful or undesirable, such as misleading or deceiving consumers, and discriminating against people on the basis of protected attributes such as race, gender or sexuality
6. Impose transparency obligations, for example requiring firms to report on the performance of their systems against certain measures of fairness. Possible obligations relating to fairness in AI could take inspiration from Australian laws that require firms above a certain size to report on their performance against measures of equal pay by gender
7. Allocate or reallocate responsibilities such as who is responsible for preventing certain wrongs or harms, and controlling certain technologies by giving company officers particular responsibilities, or determining which firm within a data/AI ecosystem must comply with privacy obligations.

If we think about all these different modalities the law can use to influence the direction of development and deployment of AI, we can have a more nuanced discussion of where we go from here, or how the law, specifically, can best contribute to the development and deployment of responsible AI. There is more than one way to regulate, and which modality we choose matters.

Earlier chapters in this book have outlined justified concerns about unfair AI systems disproportionately denying credit or job interviews to people from minority populations (see the earlier chapter on AI harms). Technical tools to detect and correct gender or race- disparate impacts exist, and, although we know that not all quantified measures of fairness can be met simultaneously (Australian Human Rights Commission, 2020), there are still various ways that the law may be called upon to promote fairer, more responsible systems for allocating credit and job interviews. We could:

- **Prohibit discrimination,** and give people the right not to be discriminated against, with means to enforce that right through a dispute resolution system such as the courts. One problem with this is that individuals denied credit or interviews may not be able to find out if the cause is discrimination or something else. It is difficult to detect discrimination from a single instance of an automated decision.
- **Set positive requirements,** either for building systems (fairness by design, or requirements for commercial AI systems to meet standards of fairness) or users of systems (obligations to treat/take active steps to treat potential customers/job applicants fairly). This could create incentives for developing and incorporating fairness by design, although it does raise some questions about what the standard then is: do firms have to achieve a certain measure of fairness? Take reasonable steps? Adopt the best technology? Does it apply to all firms, or only those of a certain size, or in certain industries?
- **Mandate transparency,** requiring firms to report statistics on loans or interviews by different metrics. This would stimulate competition, and enable public monitoring and reporting, but be hard to do well, especially since numerous measures of fairness, and numerous protected attributes; reporting can have unintended consequences[2].

Which of these (or which combination of these) we choose matters a lot. Our instinct is often to prohibit the things we don't want, leaving maximum room for flexibility and freedom of individuals and commercial actors. But proving that a prohibition has been breached can be extremely difficult, especially when activities are spread throughout a large organisation or network of organisations collecting data, cleaning data, developing AI systems, deploying systems, and providing oversight. Proving a breach is especially difficult in the private sector, where actors rarely need to explain themselves or their decisions. In this context, it is perhaps not surprising that large jurisdictions which have recently written AI-specific regulations – Europe, Brazil, and China are increasingly looking to risk-based approaches, and effectively requiring firms to take positive steps to manage risks.

2.4 Things the law doesn't do

The reader may notice something missing from the list above: the law can also require remediation - imposing fines, requiring the payment of compensation or ordering someone to take action for failures to meet standards, or for wrongfully causing harm to other people or businesses. But with very few exceptions[3], the law does not intervene in every case where X causes harm to Y. The law imposes no general duty to avoid harming others, and it is not enough to recognise a harm, such as those identified earlier in this book, and then look to the law to provide a remedy. It is the failure to comply with legal rules, or legally required standards, that takes on liability.

Consider the notorious Australian example known as Robodebt, where the Australian government deployed an automated (although not AI) system to recover alleged welfare overpayments. This example is also given in the chapter on AI risk. The system used data-matching between income reported to the Australian Tax Office, and income reported via the welfare system, to trigger a letter to welfare recipients; if recipients failed to respond, a debt was raised against them. The data-matching, in order to identify discrepancies, assumed that annual income would have been earned evenly over the course of a year, a wildly inaccurate assumption for people working in casual positions or who had periods of unemployment punctuated by short-term positions. As a result, thousands of inaccurate debt notices totalling around $1.7 billion were sent out, causing serious distress and financial hardship to already disadvantaged people. A class action led to the government agreeing to repay over $750M, cancel other outstanding debts and pay $122M in compensatory damages. There is much that is interesting – and appalling - about Robodebt.

But it is important to note here that the ways the obvious moral wrongs of Robodebt, and its attendant widely-reported harms, intersected with the ability of those harmed to assert a legal case and obtain a remedy. The plaintiffs faced serious challenges in framing their case, as is evident from the trial judge's reasons when accepting the settlement of the class action: Prygodicz v Commonwealth of Australia (No 2) [2021] FCA 634, describing the debacle as 'a shameful chapter in the administration of the Commonwealth social security system and a massive failure of public administration'. But the judge also noted challenges for the plaintiff of two types:

The first set of challenges related to proof and evidence: while it was clear that responsible officials should have known the system was unlawful, it was "quite another thing to be able to prove to the requisite standard that they actually knew that the operation of the Robodebt system was unlawful". This should give us pause, when considering the regulation of AI, as it is often easy to frame a law or regulation in terms of a wrongful act we wish to prohibit, but wrongs framed to require culpable knowledge on the part of a human may be difficult, even impossible, to prove when that human is operating an inscrutable, automated AI system.

The second set of challenges in Prygodicz was framing the legal wrong that corresponded to the obvious public administration wrong. It was clear that, under the legislation, the Commonwealth could not put the onus on welfare recipients to prove they had not been overpaid simply on the basis of the data-matching. This made the debts unlawful, meaning plaintiffs could recover any money paid with interest. But the plaintiffs also argued that the Commonwealth had been negligent, had breached its duty of care, giving rise to a claim, not just for the money, but also damages for 'stress, anxiety and stigma' associated with the request or demand for, and threatened or actual recovery of, their asserted debts. Untutored, you might think that the government was under some kind of duty of care when asserting big debts against vulnerable welfare recipients. The trial judge, however, stated that he thought the argument for a duty of care was weak, and, even if it did succeed, there was uncertainty whether damages for distress caused would succeed. Law, in the end, granted a remedy, but not a remedy for all harms, and perhaps not in the ways a non-lawyer might expect.

3. Law and AI

3.1 Law already regulates AI: but how well?

The need to show a legal wrong, and not just harm, as the basis for recovery is one of the ways in which new technologies like AI challenge the law. When technologies, potentials, business models and modes of operation change, sometimes it takes time for everyone to determine what this means legally. Many of the AI harms identified in the taxonomy presented earlier are harms that have long existed in various forms, and that the law has responded to. Physical harms such as misdiagnosis are dealt with through approval systems for medical devices and tort law, in particular the tort of negligence. Mental and emotional harms created through workplace surveillance are addressed in workplace privacy laws. Financial harms that could arise through people being manipulated or misled by AI systems are, to some extent, addressed by consumer protection law, which prohibits misleading, deceptive, and unconscionable conduct. The question is whether those laws still hold, and whether they are still adequate, in light of AI.

Often our existing laws do still hold. Not every issue arising from or exacerbated by technology creates problems for the application of law. Quite general rules are often drafted, and adjusted incrementally by courts and other decision-makers to suit new circumstances. As Bennett Moses has argued (Bennett Moses, 2020; Guihot and Bennett Moses 2017), the key is to distinguish between:

- Situations where we can simply apply well-established rules to a new technology
- Situations where we can apply well-established principles to the new technology, although details of the rules may need reforming, because they incorporate certain assumptions about the way things work
- Situations demanding a significant rethink, either because there is a genuinely new problem, or because shifts in technology have made us more aware of an old problem.

Some - many in fact - of our existing legal rules, standards, and rights are written in such a way that they apply regardless of new or expanded technologies like AI or automation. Consumer protection law prohibits misleading or deceiving consumers, and it doesn't matter whether the deceitful content is delivered automatically or by a person, as both Google and Trivago learned in important cases brought by the Australian Competition and Consumer Commission (Australian Competition and Consumer Commission v Google LLC (No 2) [2021] FCA 367; Trivago N.V. v Australian Competition and Consumer Commission [2020] FCAFC 185; 384 ALR 496).

Dynamically changing systems can make it harder to prove breach - but not impossible. Banks' duties to treat customers efficiently, honestly and fairly under s 912A of the Corporations Act 2001 (Cth) still apply in an AI context, and the recent Banking Royal Commission in Australia was highly critical of banks' failures to exercise sufficient oversight over some automated systems (Commonwealth of Australia, 2019), and some use of tools for modifying behaviour – such as social proofing – have been condemned by the courts (ASIC v Westpac [2019] FCAFC 187). In the US, the Federal Trade Commission has increased its enforcement of consumer protections in the digital context, and warned AI companies that promising 'unbiased hiring decisions' without factual basis could be deceptive (Federal Trade Commission, 2021), suggesting that firms promising to abide by ethical standards may, at least to some extent, be held to those standards.

For governments and organisations, this means it is important to understand the laws that already regulate their activities – current obligations that they must treat consumers and citizens fairly and honestly – and ensure that the introduction of AI systems does not lead the organisation or government to breach those existing laws.

3.2 Thinking about where law is more likely to see reform

In other cases, legal standards written with human processes and human decision-making in mind can and should be reformed. Consider anti-discrimination law. The principle that people should not be treated less well on the grounds of their race, gender, or other protected category is clearly a sound one, well-grounded in international human rights law, but how we put that into operation probably needs to change (AHRC, 2021). When humans make decisions about whether to hire a certain person, or grant a loan, one way to avoid discriminating against a certain race is to avoid including that information in the decision- making process – i.e. race-blind consideration of applications. Anti- discrimination laws and organisations' compliance systems have been built around that assumption. A machine learning system, however, learning from past discriminatory decisions, may infer race, even if that information is deliberately left out of a dataset (for example, from some combination of where someone lives, their name, or where they went to school). Adjustments to law - whether legislation, or interpretation by courts – could help clarify the position, and ensure the law meets its goals. Notably too, anti-discrimination law is focused on a small number of protected categories, prohibiting unfair treatment of people based on a small number of features, such as gender, age, and race. It does not provide a remedy where people are treated unfairly based on their socio-economic status, where they live, or what profession they hold. How far the law should go to proscribe unfair treatment – and just when treatment is unfair – is a matter of ongoing debate, for example in the context of consumer protection law.

Other situations demand closer attention. Consider transparency and explainability, ideas at the cornerstone of many sets of AI principles, and even good practice, but which are only imperfectly required by law. In chapter 5 we identified transparency and explainability as a gateway both for responsible AI, and for the conception of people's rights and responsibilities in relation to AI. At present, in many countries this is only imperfectly reflected in the law as government's basic – but not universal - obligations to consider relevant information, or give reasons when making decisions about citizens (NSW Ombudsman, 2021), although a range of clarifications and tweaks have been suggested (Australian Human Rights Commission 2021; NSW Ombudsman 2021). What precisely this means in the context of AI use is unclear, as it may be that in some cases, these obligations preclude government use of purely black box systems. The situation is even more murky in the private sector, where as a rule entities are not usually required to explain their decisions to the public at all (at least, not unless and until there is formal litigation, when a court could well require some kind of explanation of how technology works). Article 22 of the GDPR, discussed in an appendix to this chapter, provides an example of a law that imposes basic transparency obligations in relation to AI and automated decision-making, including in the private sector.

More generally, consider the democratic harms identified earlier in the book, and the potential of AI to change the relationship between government and the governed. AI's capacity to make fine-grained predictions about people's behaviour – and then intervene on the basis of that prediction, potentially in an automated way – challenges our systems for holding government accountable (Johns, 2021; Dencik 2019). New capacities to create large linked datasets of government data, coupled with ubiquitous dashboards that visualise data, may encourage a different kind of governing that is more immediate and experimental. Rather than establishing widely applicable rules, applying them over an extended period, and undertaking review after a defined period, dashboard-driven (or just data-driven) governing encourages incremental, real-time or immediate and experimental interventions with the expectation of ongoing feedback and amendment (Johns 2021). The ability to drill down into data also encourages interventions aimed at smaller and smaller subgroups with particular features. Our usual methods for holding governments and decision-makers accountable for their actions do not necessarily work in this in-between space of incremental policies, and policies that target small subsets of the population:

- Parliament can exercise oversight only at the highest level by establishing broad principles. Any oversight is likely to occur at extended intervals and at a high level.
- Individuals can contest the application of individual decisions that apply to them through appeal, for example to the NSW Civil and Administrative Tribunal, or the Administrative Appeals Tribunal (Cth), but not the formulation of even narrowly targeted policies or interventions.

It should be acknowledged that there are few situations that warrant banning. Consider, for example, activities that the European Commission proposes to bar in its new Proposal for an EU AI Act (European Commission 2021, art 5). The first two proposed prohibitions in the Draft Art 5 are:

1. The placing on the market, putting into service, or use of an AI system that deploys subliminal techniques beyond a person's consciousness in order to materially distort a person's behaviour in a manner that causes or is likely to cause that person or another person physical or psychological harm
2. The placing on the market, putting into service or use of an AI system that exploits any of the vulnerabilities of a specific

group of persons due to their age, or physical or mental disability, in order to materially distort the behaviour of a person pertaining to that group in a manner that causes or is likely to cause that person or another person physical or psychological harm.

These prohibitions could address harms highlighted earlier in this book. One can legitimately query (as Bennett Moses did in a recent keynote) why such conduct should be prohibited only when AI is used. If AI were not used, but there was manipulation of behaviour causing psychological harm, or exploitation of vulnerability, isn't that still the kind of thing we want to prohibit? Or is it that AI increases the speed and scale, requiring intervention where it was previously unwarranted?

In other cases, it is arguable that specific kinds of AI technology should be subject to regulation, moratorium, or even outright ban: where the nature of the technology creates new, seriously problematic harms which may not be outweighed by any apparent benefits. While the details are beyond the scope of this chapter, AI technologies that fit in this category include some highlighted earlier in this book:

- One to many facial recognition or other forms of real time, remote biometric identification systems for government or law enforcement purposes
- Autonomous weapons
- Emotion detection systems or affect recognition.

It is beyond the scope of this brief chapter to trace in detail the way that various laws intersect with AI. This is an extraordinarily fast-moving space, evidence that we are in a phase, not of lawlessness or a regulation free zone, but one where regulators and courts are getting down to the hard work of applying the law to control the harms and risks engendered by AI. For book-length expositions, we recommend Guihot and Bennett Moses (2020) (Australian law), or Chesterman (2021) (international law).

3.3 Law enables AI, and shapes its possibilities and its limits

A final point to make about where we are now is that laws have shaped what is possible in AI development. Legal systems globally have imposed few limits on information gathering by observing people, and this has allowed firms to gather and use information about people with relatively few constraints, enabling the business models of large platforms. Different choices could have been made: gathering extensive information about people's online activities could have been treated as a form of illegal surveillance; we could have decided that putting information files (cookies) on people's devices to allow tracking across multiple websites was a form of trespass, which would have meant the large platforms had to develop quite different business models to support their activities (Zuboff 2019; Cohen, 2019).

The absence of any obligation of large firms to share their data with competitors entrenches the advantage of first movers, and this too is a legal choice. We could have decided - and still could - on exceptions to commercial secrecy to enable public interest research[4] or private sector competition. We have seen some moves in this direction with Europe's introduction of data portability (GDPR, art 20), and Australia's Consumer Data Right (CDR) Competition and Consumer Act 2010 (Cth) Part IVD). The CDR, which has commenced in the banking industry, and which is expected to expand, explicitly gives consumers the right to have other commercial parties access data about them, potentially to offer a superior or better tailored product. As noted below, negotiating the availability and control of data are emerging as two of the next significant fights that may indeed shape the future developmental trajectories of AI.

Privacy laws are continuing to shape the direction of AI's development. Privacy regulators globally and consumer protection regulators are paying increasing attention to cases where firms have breached their own privacy policies by gathering, sharing or using data in ways that they did not disclose. There have been or are lawsuits against both Facebook (in relation to Cambridge Analytica) and Google (in relation to its use of geolocation data), and people are paying more attention (see OAIC 2020), but privacy law can be evaded in an AI world. Having been developed after World War II to constrain governments' use of their citizens' data, twentieth-century privacy laws are in some jurisdictions confined to government use, and commonly applied only to personal information - that is, information about an identified or identifiable individual. Twentieth-century laws are also focused on the security of such personal data, and preventing disclosure. The impact of privacy law, and concerns about privacy, seem to be factors pushing large data collectors and users to move towards de-identified, cohort- level data (see Google's now abandoned FLOC, and Zoltan, 2021) and encouraging more concentration of data.

Other aspects of the law have shaped where we are, and the uses that can be made of AI. The law's tolerance for contracts and privacy notices where people click their consent to make enforceable numerous lengthy and elaborate conditions that no one could possibly have read or understod has enabled more efficient business dealings, but also one-sided deals that favour the businesses that get to write the terms of the deal (Cohen, 2019). Again, we could (and some recent shifts in consumer protection law have started to) ban particularly one- sided terms.

A key point here is that while AI developments have been assisted by existing legal settings, especially a generous allowance for data gathering, governments can change these baselines in the future. The current set of rules and entitlements around data favours data collection and the use of AI, and has enabled the larger players who have been able to amass, themselves or through acquisition, vast data caches. At any point, governments can mostly change these settings - although moves to lock in settings allowing for free movement of data via trade agreements should be noted. In short, the law as it relates to AI is presently a site of very significant contestation and change. The question is, what is the direction of such change, and what may be missing?

4. Where is the legal regulation of AI headed?

A theme of this chapter is that we are in a great regulation phase in relation to AI. This is observable in the substantial increase in activity by legislators and regulators, and in court cases applying existing law to AI/automated systems. In addition, we would draw attention to two steady trends in law and regulation affecting the development, and deployment of AI:

4.1 Risk management

The first is a focus on risk and impact assessments (see the earlier piece for an organisational perspective on risk). At the time of writing, major new proposals for regulation of AI are on the table in Europe (European Commission, 2021), and also in Brazil[5] and China[6] - all different, but each incorporating a risk-based approach to regulating AI. The European proposal divides very broadly defined applications of AI into prohibited activities, high risk uses, and low risk activities. High risk activities are listed in Annex III, and range from systems for biometric identification and categorisation of people to certain specified uses in employment services and education, for allocation/ assessment of welfare and social services, and much more. For higher Risk AI systems, a risk management system should be created and maintained throughout the lifecycle of the system. The idea is to eliminate or reduce risks in design and development as far as possible, and mitigate or control remaining risks (European Commission 2021, art 6, 9 and Annex III). Approaches seeking to identify and design away from or mitigate harms in advance of implementing a system are also evident in Australia - the Australian Human Rights Commission proposed such a requirement, and the NSW Government has recently implemented its own AI Assurance Framework.

The shift towards regulation based on risk management is a smart move away from seeking to remedy legal wrongs ex post towards a positive and pre-emptive approach. It carries some clear benefits, and many firms already have risk and compliance processes that can serve as a model. Standards bodies are developing guidelines for risk assessment and risk management in AI, and ex ante risk management and ongoing monitoring should mesh more easily with existing internal and external oversight mechanisms, and be easier for regulators to audit than relying on external actors identifying legal wrongs. Much has yet to be worked out, but it is worth noting that a critical element of any risk-based approach is the ability to properly identify harms, which will need to be well done and incorporate a broad range of perspectives (see the discussion in chapter 5 on AI development and deployment).

But there may be something else missing, apart from the obvious challenges of enabling a serious rather than a checkbox process of risk management, and of identifying the full range of risks. Two questions about the focus on risk management and the mitigation of harms are worth mentioning:

First, requiring risk management does nothing about power imbalances. On the contrary, risk management assumes there is a power imbalance (X has the power to create harms to Y), but seeks to manage the harms without addressing the power imbalance, and it implies that the activity is ok, even if people don't want it, provided that harms are identified and mitigated.

Second, a risk management approach suggests that AI developers or those deploying such systems have no positive obligation to ensure that their systems are beneficial to or promote the interests of AI subjects or other stakeholders - an approach that addresses neither power imbalances nor potential benefits for a broader range of stakeholders than could be gained using AI is incomplete as a vision of what AI could do for us.

4.2 The future of data

The second great trend is the emerging battle over the future of data: what we do about data, who owns data, who has a say about data, who supplements data, who accesses data, how we assure quality and relevance, how we acknowledge the gaps. Even the casual observer of developments globally over the past couple of years could not have failed to notice the exponential growth in discussions over data. Europe has a series of initiatives building on the GPDR, including a proposed Data Governance Act to address data use and sharing. Australian governments are also moving towards sharing more data between departments, and between governments, and constructing persistent data assets - linked (perhaps federated) datasets that can be used, reused, and applied to new problems over an extended period for policy development or research. Governments are looking at how they can share more government-held data with researchers and others, and privacy law is under active review and discussion. At the same time, as noted earlier in this chapter, there is much discussion about access to commercially held data, and how that can be opened up to improve competition across a range of sectors. Given the importance of data to AI, how all of these assorted issues are resolved will do much to influence how AI can be developed in the future.

5. Summary

For organisations, the basic message of this chapter is clear, and corresponds with the whole book: we are well and truly beyond the stage - if, indeed, we were ever in it - where organisations could take the view that harms are outside the reach of the law simply because they occur through the use of AI. Organisations that are deploying AI must be sure to do so in ways consistent with their existing legal obligations - whether they are government organisations accountable for treating people according to the requirements of public law, or private sector organisations bound by a wide range of consumer protections and standards to meet duties of care under existing tort law. Organisations developing and deploying AI in relation to individuals also need to be aware of their obligations under anti-discrimination law, and privacy rules governing the data they use, so they can be confident about the provenance of data, and their right to use them for purposes such as training and deploying AI.

Further reform to the legal and regulatory framework is needed, and it seems increasingly likely that, in the not-too-distant future, organisations developing and applying AI will be subject to more rules. In this context, another message from this chapter for both policymakers and organisations involved in policy debate is that AI regulations need to be nuanced and fit in with the many approaches to legal regulation. Imagination will be required if the law is to contribute to a positive vision of what AI can contribute to society, and address the questions of power and justice raised by AI.

Note: research reflected in this chapter has been supported in part by philanthropic funding and the Australian Research Council Centre of Excellence on Automated Decision-Making and Society.

Footnotes

1. International standards bodies are currently working on various standards related to the governance of AI and control of AI-related risks: e.g., the US National Institute of Standards and Technology (NIST) in 2021 launched a draft AI risk management framework.
2. Concerns have long been expressed, for example, that reporting, say, surgery success rates or the test scores of students of a given teacher or school can lead to gaming, cheating, or professionals refusing to take 'hard cases' for fear of the impact on their 'scores' (O'Neil, 2016).
3. Occasionally a law will require a party to take remedial action even in the absence of any proof of fault. One example comes from copyright law: internet service providers can be required to block access to infringing sites, even where they are not liable for authorising the infringement involved. Such cases might be seen, however, as a 'condition of doing business' - a necessary mitigation of known risks (of copyright infringement) involved in a certain line of business (providing internet services).
4. A wide range of Bills have been proposed in the US Congress aimed at providing individuals with more rights in data, and also providing better access to data for researchers: see, for example, the proposed Platform Accountability and Transparency Act which proposes requiring social media companies to provide vetted, independent researchers and the public with access to certain platform data. Such proposals are a response to concerns about disinformation spread on large social media platforms, longstanding but largely unsuccessful efforts by researchers to negotiate better access, and recent action taken by Facebook in particular to shut down independent research efforts, such as action taken against NYU's Ad Observatory project.
5. https://www.camara.leg.br/noticias/811702-camara-aprova-projeto-que-regulamenta-uso-da-inteligencia-artificial
6. https://carnegieendowment.org/2022/01/04/china-s-new-ai-governance-%20initiatives-shouldn-t-be-ignored-pub-86127

References

Australian Human Rights Commission, Human Rights and Technology Final Report (Australian Human Rights Commission, 2021) <https://tech.humanrights.gov.au/downloads>

Australian Human Rights Commission, Using Artificial Intelligence to Make Decisions: Addressing the Problem of Algorithmic Bias (Technical Paper, Australian Human Rights Commission, 2020)

Lyria Bennett Moses, 'Regulating in the Face of Sociotechnical Change', in Roger Brownsword, Eloise Scotford and Karen Yeung (eds), The Oxford Handbook of Law, Regulation and Technology (Oxford University Press, 2017), 576

Chesterman, Simon, We, the Robots?: Regulating Artificial Intelligence and the Limits of the Law (Cambridge University Press, 2021)

Cohen, Julie E, Between Truth and Power: The Legal Constructions of Informational Capitalism (Oxford University Press, 2019)

Commonwealth of Australia, Royal Commission into Misconduct in the Banking, Superannuation and Financial Services Industry, Interim Report, Volume 2 (2019) https://www.royalcommission.gov.au/system/files/2020-09/volume-2.pdf pp 64-68, pp 74-82

Davis, Jenny L, How Artifacts Afford: The Power and Politics of Everyday Things (MIT Press, 2020)

Dencik, Lina et al, 'The "Golden View": Data-Driven Governance in the Scoring Society' (2019) 8(2) Internet Policy Review 1

European Commission. Regulation (EU) 2016/679 of the European Parliament and of the Council of 27 April 2016 on the Protection of Natural Persons with Regard to the Processing of Personal Data and on the Free Movement of Such Data, and Repealing Directive 95/46/EC (General Data Protection Regulation) 2016

European Commission. Proposal for a Regulation of the European Parliament and of the Council Laying Down Harmonised Rules on Artificial Intelligence (Artificial Intelligence Act) COM/2021/206 final (2021). https://eur-lex.europa.eu/legal-content/EN/TXT/?uri=CELEX%3A52021PC0206 .

Federal Trade Commission, 'Aiming for Truth, Fairness, and Equity in Your Company's Use of AI | Federal Trade Commission', Federal Trade Commission Business Blog (19 April 2021) <https://www.ftc.gov/business-guidance/blog/2021/04/aiming-truth-fairness-equity-your-companys-use-ai>

Guihot, Michael and Lyria Bennett Moses, Artificial Intelligence, Robots and the Law (LexisNexis, 2020)

Hildebrandt, Mireille. Law for Computer Scientists and Other Folk. Oxford: Oxford University Press, 2020. https://academic.oup.com/book/33735 .

Johns, Fleur, 'Governance by Data' (2021) 17(1) Annual Review of Law and Social Science 53

NSW Ombudsman, The New Machinery of Government: Using Machine Technology in Administrative Decision-Making (NSW Government, 29 November 2021) <https://www.ombo.nsw.gov.au/__data/assets/pdf_file/0003/138207/The-new-machinery-of-government-special-report_Front-section.pdf>

Office of the Australian Information Commissioner, Australian Community Attitudes to Privacy Survey 2020 (2020) 121 <https://www.oaic.gov.au/assets/engage-with-us/research/acaps-2020/Australian-Community-Attitudes-to-Privacy-Survey-2020.pdf>

O'Neil, Cathy, Weapons of Math Destruction: How Big Data Increases Inequality and Threatens Democracy (Crown Publishing Group, 2016)

W, Shanika and Zoltan, Miklos, 'A Complete Guide To Google FLoC - What It Does and How It Works - How FloC Affects Privacy', Privacy Affairs (23 July 2021) <https://www.privacyaffairs.com/google-floc/>

Zuboff, Shoshana, The Age of Surveillance Capitalism: The Fight for a Human Future at the New Frontier of Power (Profile Trade, Main edition, 2019)

Conclusions

> "Algorithmic pollution is a new form of social pollution which denotes the unjustified, unfair, discriminatory, and other harmful effects of automated algorithmic decision-making for individuals, their families, groups of people, communities, organisations, sections of the population, and society at large."
>
> (Marjanovic et al., 2021a, p. 397)

Without doubt, AI applications will be developed and adopted. These applications will also bring considerable benefits to citizens and society, as well as AI-related harms, both intentional and unintentional. To conclude we present a cohesive response to the challenge of AI and (automated) algorithmic decision-making, (A) ADM, arguing that responsible AI (RAI) is an issue that must be addressed by citizens, organisations, society at large, and governments.

Networks of algorithms, unintended and emergent consequences at the societal level, and the possibility of existential risk all suggest that a broader perspective than RAI practices and legislation and regulation of organisations is needed. Drawing on developments in handling pollution, we propose a three-pronged response: curative, preventive, and precautionary. The curative approach addresses AI harm after the fact, the preventive approach attempts to stop it happening in the first place, and the precautionary approach takes a wider and more circumspect view of AI risk, centring on the potential for catastrophic outcomes and existential AI risk. We then frame these three concepts in the larger context of regulation, legislation and civil society institutions.

Addressing AI harms

The pollution literature mainly focuses on environmental pollution, for example in farming where practices that damage the natural environment are not reflected in the price of food paid by the consumer. We consider three approaches to tackling AI pollution, working from the premise that algorithmic decision-making (ADM) – and automated ADM (AADM) in particular – can and do cause tangible harm to individuals, groups, and society.

Three principles of pollution have been advanced: curative, preventive, and precautionary (de Sadeleer, 2020). We use these principles to provide a response to algorithmic harm in support of a wider aim of achieving algorithmic justice.

Curative principle

The curative principle is concerned with externalities, in which a polluter is responsible for the costs generated by their activity. If the polluter absorbs all of the external costs, then internalisation is complete; if part of the cost of their activity is borne by the community, then it is incomplete. In the case of environmental pollution "[there are two ways to ensure that prices reflect the true cost of production and consumption: taxation that corresponds to the estimated economic value of the environmental damage, and regulatory standards to prohibit or limit the damage associated with an economic activity." (de Sadeleer, p. 32). The curative principle is often reduced to the 'polluter pays principle' (PPP).

The PPP places an obligation on project owners to mitigate, repair or provide compensation for the consequences of their activities: "In other words, to internalise the environmental costs of their projects." (Cordella, 2017, p. 169). Based on transaction cost theory (Coase, 1960), it can be argued that, where information is reciprocally available, the rights of the parties are clearly defined, and the cost of information available to all parties is low or zero, it is "as efficient to allow the victim of pollution a right to compensation as it is to recognise the polluter's right to pollute" (de Sadeleer, p. 32). Discounting the transaction cost view as an unrealistic set of conditions, the PPP approach requires intervention by public authorities, since self-regulation is not sufficient, and a regulatory body is required to ensure that the polluter does indeed pay. One such body is the European Union.

The PPP approach is not without difficulties, such as the identification of the polluter (a particularly difficult issue when data and decisions are shared between organisations), the assessment of the harm, establishing a threshold for harm, and specifying compensation for victims of AI harm.

In chapter 5, AI development and deployment, we proposed an AI gateway in which an organisation's responsibilities for transparency, explainability, and contestability are matched with an AI subject's rights of awareness, understandability, and disputability. Any such AI approach will likely need to be supported and strengthened through legislation and regulation.

Preventive principle

The preventive principle (PvP) is concerned with preventing pollution with due diligence before it happens. The curative approach of the PPP can be used to remediate damage, but is very much a 'bolting the stable door' approach. The PvP is concerned with the identification and management of risk. Such an approach requires knowledge of the risk, and understanding of the nature and significance of the harm. Further difficulties arise in the location of the activity, for example algorithms deployed and hosted in countries that have weak AI regulation.

The PvP has been dominant in the treatment of AI, starting with broad principles to guide the development and use of AI. In chapter 5, we presented a curated set of principles and definitions for responsible AI practice, which include fairness, human-centredness, well-being (human, social, and environmental), accountability, safety, privacy, transparency, explainability, and contestability. Such principles have been proposed by many bodies (Leslie, 2019; European Commission, 2019; DISER, 2020), and while they are beneficial (who would want an AI system that is not fair, not safe, or not contestable?), without regulatory backup, such principles lack teeth. In chapter 6, "De-risking automated decisions", we proposed initiatives for organisations to manage and govern their AI risk profile. Thus, the PvP approach focuses on prevention, due diligence, and the management of risk.

Precautionary principle

The origins of the precautionary principle (PcP), can be traced back to the notion of Vorsorgeprinzip, developed in the 1970s as part of German environmental policy. The component parts of Vorsorgeprinzip are Vor (before), Sorge (care), and Prinzip (principle), so it is the principle of taking care before we act (Adams, 2002). Under the PcP, authorities intervene before damage occurs, such as with genetically modified organisms (GMOs). The PcP views threats as tangible in situations that can quickly become critical, and is an anticipatory approach where we prepare for uncertain and hypothetical threats with no proof that they will materialise, in contra-distinction to the PvP, which is based on the notion of certain risk (de Sadeleer, 2020). In the PcP, we act first and then ascertain facts, accepting multiple possibilities, contingencies, and plausibilities. By its very nature, such an approach must be able to cope with conflict, controversy and contested ground.

Miller and Engemann (2019) identify the strengths of applying the PcP: to avoid catastrophes such as the use of asbestos in insulation, to level the playing field of corporate power, like Monsanto's stranglehold on farming, through GMO patents, and to create incentives to pursue safer technologies, such as limiting pesticide use, which has led to innovations in organic farming (pp. 268-269). Critics argue that the PcP eliminates the benefits arising from technology, leading to stasis (e.g., banning drones for commercial use), and stifles innovation (e.g., not approving a new drug), which may move innovation to regions with less stringent regulation, and be used to further commercial and political objectives (for example, a delivery service company might want to slow down drone deployment) (p. 269). Despite the vagueness and lack of definition surrounding the PcP (Clarke, 2005), four elements are generally accepted (DeFur and Kaszuba, 2001):

1. A threat of harm, either credible or known
2. A situation in which lacks scientific certainty or evidence
3. Cause and effect relationships are not proven
4. There is a necessity or duty to act (p. 157).

While the PcP is, in a sense, concerned with risk, it differs from PvP in that these risks are surrounded by a greater degree of uncertainty, so that they are not sufficiently well-defined to be amenable to the risk management techniques of the PvP. At the heart of the PcP is decision- making in its broadest sense, requiring input from multiple disciplines and multiple stakeholders, including civil society at large. Adams (2002) argues that the PcP is usefully viewed as a "boundary object" (Star and Griesemer, 1989), and "a space in which protagonists encounter each other, and in which they sustain the sense of a common debate, even when the interests at stake are fundamentally opposed"(p. 302).

The PcP is particularly relevant in situations of uncertainty, such as AI, where the long-term effects are unknown, as seen in chapter 4, Existential risks of AI.

Responsible AI framework

In developing the Responsible AI framework, we build on all three pollution principles:

- *curative* for the redress of AI harm that has occurred;
- *preventive* to reduce the risk of AI harm occurring;
- *precautionary* to mitigate against catastrophic outcomes of AI.

Initiatives to tackle AI pollution will ultimately need the implementation of regulation and legislation – we do not believe that voluntary approaches, such as codes of practice and industry bodies, will be sufficient (see chapter 8, Regulation and governance of AI).

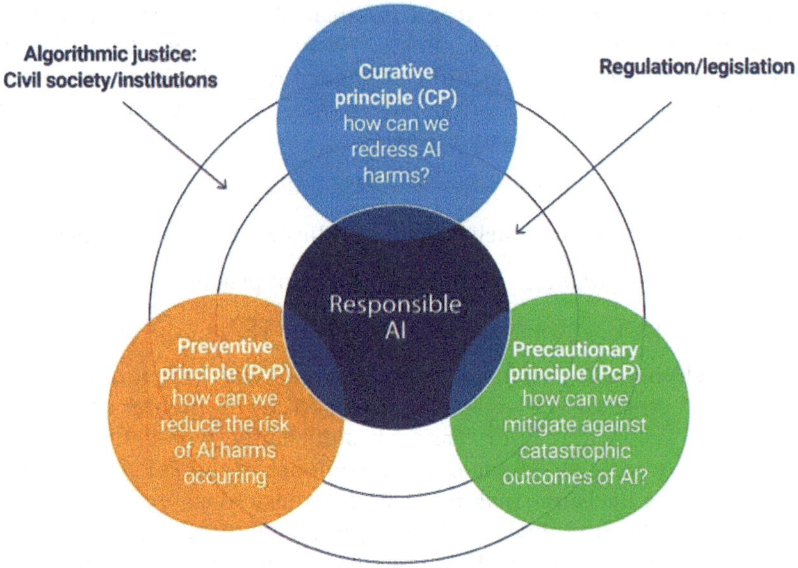

Figure C.1: Responsible AI framework

In the outer loop of the RAI framework (Figure C.1), we propose the establishment of AI civil society and institutional tracks in support of algorithmic justice (Marjanovic et al., 2021b). The civil-society track is important for raising issues of injustice through grassroots movements, activism, citizen forums, etc., but does not have the power to introduce policies, regulation, or binding decisions (Fraser, 2010, p.415). Both tracks are needed, leading Fraser (2010) to posit that the relationship must be dialogical (the two tracks, civil society and institutional, being mutually shaping). Taken together, the five elements of the RAI framework provide a cohesive and systemic approach to living fairly and safely with AI.

Recommendations

In developing a framework for RAI, we have been inspired by the different approaches used in addressing environmental pollution, and taken a three-stranded approach of curative (making redress for AI harms), preventive (stopping AI harms from occurring in the first place), and precautionary (addressing the larger risk of AI for catastrophic/ existential consequences) responses. Most importantly, we argue for a broad view of AI and algorithmic decision-making in which civil-society and institutional tracks work together dialogically to inform, shape, and monitor the impact of AI on individuals, society, and the physical environment.

Our investigations lead us to these essential recommendations:

1. All organisations using AI to support algorithmic decision-making should implement an AI gateway to provide transparency (awareness that AI is being used), explainability (understanding how AI is used, and how an individual decision is reached), and contestability (a channel for AI subjects to dispute AI-supported decisions).
2. As well as rights, AI subjects have responsibilities, and should be willing to engage with AI in an active way: to understand what it is, how it is used, to contest its use by organisations, to be aware of its individual and social impacts, and to be willing to join grass roots movements, lobby government, and boycott organisations that are not using AI in a responsible or ethical fashion.
3. Legislation and regulation are required – nationally and internationally – and must be led by government organisations. For example, this may include the establishment of a Technology and Human Rights Council with an AI and Metaverse Human Rights Commissioner.
4. The potential for the emergence of invisible networks of harm needs to be addressed. These networks are fuelled by data sharing, where the results of an AI-based decision are passed as input to another AI decision-making process, leading to intensification of the datafication process.
5. Organisations must implement effective governance of business AI systems, which should include governance

structures, reporting standards, AI maturity assessment, and active C-suite engagement. This governance must be grounded in clearly articulated ethical principles, and can be further cemented within the organisation through the use of techniques such as the business ethics canvas.

6. Organisations should implement effective risk management processes, such as a risk register, risk monitoring, and impact assessment. De-risking the AI development and deployment process is a fundamental aspect of responsible AI that should be consistent with and promote the ethical values of the organisation.

7. Data scientists employed in AI development and deployment should be professionalised. For example, sign-off of an AI application by a chartered data scientist may be required before an AI application is developed, and then again before it is deployed. This would be analogous to chartered accountants signing off a company's annual accounts.

8. Organisations should be particularly concerned about the role of AI and automated decision-making in the design of their business processes. Organisations must consider the 'human in the loop' and build in checkpoints and fail-safes as appropriate.

9. As a society, we must promote the formation of dialogical civil- society/institutional arrangements that promote open debate and oversight, and effective interaction between institutions such as governments, regulatory bodies and civil society to review and mitigate AI risks and harms. This includes grappling with the potential for catastrophic and existential risks.

We believe that if the recommendations presented in this book are followed by individuals, managers, organisations and governments, together we shall be in a good position to steer AI to support humans to be more productive, more effective and fairer and more creative, and make better decisions. While recognising that Responsible AI is a fast- moving area, the recommendations above provide a useful platform for thinking about where the future research efforts of academics and practitioners might be directed. Developing Responsible AI is a key step to developing Responsible Technology, Responsible Infrastructure, and, in particular, a

Responsible Web3 and metaverse. We encourage all readers to step into the role of a Responsible AI Leader, and hope the content of this book will assist you to do this.

References

Adams, M., (2002). The precautionary principle and the rhetoric behind it. *Journal of Risk Research*, 5(4): 301–316.

Clarke, S., (2005). Future technologies, dystopic futures and the precautionary principle. *Ethics and Information Technology*, 7:121–126.

Coase, R., (1960). The Problem of Social Cost. *Journal of Law and Economics*, 3: 1– 44.

Cordella, E., (2017). Public Interest Regulation? The Polluter-Pays Principle in Environmental Impact Assessments: A Case of "Bipolar" Regulatory Failure. *Environmental Policy and Law*, 47(5-6): 169-180.

deFur, P., and Kaszuba, M., (2001). Implementing the precautionary principle. The Science of the Total Environment, 288: 155–165.

DISER (2020). Australian Government, Department of Industry, Science, Energy and Resources. *AI Ethics Principles.* https://www.industry.gov.au/science-technology-and-innovation/technology/artificial-intelligence

European Commission (2019). *Ethics guidelines for trustworthy AI.* https://digital-strategy.ec.europa.eu/en/library/ethics-guidelines-trustworthy-ai

Fraser, N. (2010). Who Counts? Dilemmas of Justice in a Postwestphalian World. *Antipode*, 41(s1), pp.281–297.

Leslie, D., (2019). *Understanding artificial intelligence ethics and safety*. Alan Turing Institute. https://www.turing.ac.uk/sites/default/files/2019-06/understanding_artificial_intelligence_ethics_and_safety.pdf

Marjanovic, O., Cecez-Kecmanovic, D., and Vidgen, R., (2021a). Algorithmic pollution: making the invisible visible. *Journal of Information Technology*, 36(4): 391–408.

Marjanovic, O., Cecez-Kecmanovic, D., and Vidgen, R., (2021b). Theorizing algorithmic justice. *European Journal of Information Systems.* Published online 6 June 2021.

Miller, H., and Engemann, K., (2019). The precautionary principle and unintended consequences. *Kybernetes*, 48(2): 265-286.

De Sadeleer, N., (2020). *Environmental Principles: From Political Slogans to Legal Rules*. Second edition. Oxford University Press.

Star, S.L. and J. R. Grisemer, (1989). Institutional ecology, translations and boundary- objects: amateurs and professionals in Berkeley's museum of vertebrate zoology 1907–1939. *Social Studies of Science*, 19(3): 387–420

Appendix A

Frameworks for the responsible use of AI/ADM

European Commission

https://digital-strategy.ec.europa.eu/en/library/ethics-guidelines-trustworthy-ai

Human agency and oversight: AI systems should empower human beings, allowing them to make informed decisions and fostering their fundamental rights. At the same time, proper oversight mechanisms need to be ensured, which can be achieved through human-in-the-loop, human-on-the-loop, and human-in-command approaches

Technical Robustness and safety: AI systems need to be resilient and secure. They need to be safe, ensuring a fall-back plan in case something goes wrong, as well as being accurate, reliable and reproducible. That is the only way to ensure that also unintentional harm can be minimized and prevented.

Privacy and data governance: besides ensuring full respect for privacy and data protection, adequate data governance mechanisms must also be ensured, taking into account the quality and integrity of the data, and ensuring legitimised access to data.

Transparency: the data, system and AI business models should be transparent. Traceability mechanisms can help achieving this. Moreover, AI systems and their decisions should be explained in a manner adapted to the stakeholder concerned. Humans need to be aware that they are interacting with an AI system and must be informed of the system's capabilities and limitations.

Diversity, non-discrimination and fairness: Unfair bias must be avoided, as it could could have multiple negative implications, from the marginalisation of vulnerable groups, to the exacerbation of prejudice and discrimination. Fostering diversity, AI systems should be accessible to all, regardless of any disability, and involve relevant stakeholders throughout their entire life circle.

Societal and environmental well-being: AI systems should benefit all human beings, including future generations. It must hence be ensured that they are sustainable and environmentally friendly. Moreover, they should take into account the environment, including other living beings, and their social and societal impact should be carefully considered.

Accountability: Mechanisms should be put in place to ensure responsibility and accountability for AI systems and their outcomes. Auditability, which enables the assessment of algorithms, data and design processes plays a key role therein, especially in critical applications. Moreover, adequate an accessible redress should be ensured.

Turing Institute

https://www.turing.ac.uk/sites/default/files/2019-06/understanding_artificial_intelligence_ethics_and_safety.pdf

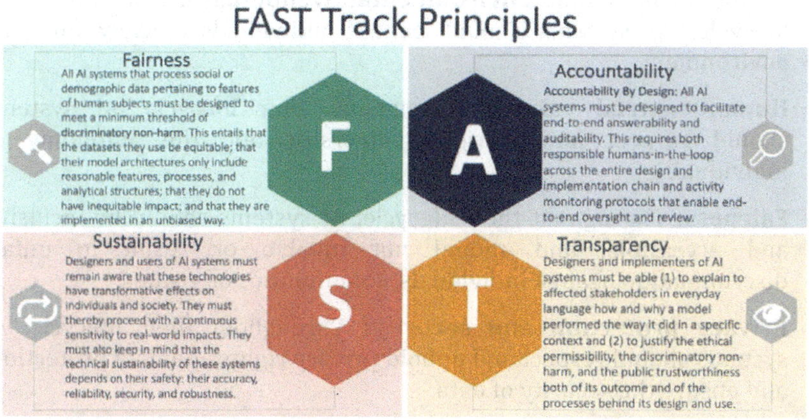

Australian Government – AI Ethics Principles

https://www.industry.gov.au/science-technology-and-innovation/technology/artificial-intelligence

Human, social and environmental wellbeing: Throughout their lifecycle, AI systems should benefit individuals, society and the environment.

Human-centred values: Throughout their lifecycle, AI systems should respect human rights, diversity, and the autonomy of individuals.

Fairness: Throughout their lifecycle, AI systems should be inclusive and accessible, and should not involve or result in unfair discrimination against individuals, communities or groups.

Privacy protection and security: Throughout their lifecycle, AI systems should respect and uphold privacy rights and data protection, and ensure the security of data.

Reliability and safety: Throughout their lifecycle, AI systems should reliably operate in accordance with their intended purpose.

Transparency and explainability: There should be transparency and responsible disclosure to ensure people know when they are being significantly impacted by an AI system, and can find out when an AI system is engaging with them.

Contestability: When an AI system significantly impacts a person, community, group or environment, there should be a timely process to allow people to challenge the use or output of the AI system.

Accountability: Those responsible for the different phases of the AI system lifecycle should be identifiable and accountable for the outcomes of the AI systems, and human oversight of AI systems should be enabled.

OECD AI Principles

https://www.oecd.org/digital/artificial-intelligence/

The Recommendation identifies five complementary values-based principles for the responsible stewardship of trustworthy AI:

- AI should benefit people and the planet by driving inclusive growth, sustainable development and well-being.
- AI systems should be designed in a way that respects the rule of law, human rights, democratic values and diversity, and they should include appropriate safeguards – for example, enabling human intervention where necessary – to ensure a fair and just society.
- There should be transparency and responsible disclosure around AI systems to ensure that people understand AI-based outcomes and can challenge them.
- AI systems must function in a robust, secure and safe way throughout their life cycles and potential risks should be continually assessed and managed.
- Organisations and individuals developing, deploying or operating AI systems should be held accountable for their proper functioning in line with the above principles.

The OECD Principles on Artificial Intelligence promote artificial intelligence (AI) that is innovative and trustworthy and that respects human rights and democratic values. They were adopted in May 2019 by OECD member countries when they approved the OECD Council Recommendation on Artificial Intelligence. The OECD AI Principles are the first such principles signed up to by governments. Beyond OECD members, other countries including Argentina, Brazil, Costa Rica, Malta, Peru, Romania and Ukraine have already adhered to the AI Principles, with further adherents welcomed.

The OECD AI Principles set standards for AI that are practical and flexible enough to stand the test of time in a rapidly evolving field. They complement existing OECD standards in areas such as privacy, digital security risk management and responsible business conduct. In June 2019, the G20 adopted human-centred AI Principles that draw from the OECD AI Principles.

Appendix B
Risk identification checklist

Each process in the AI development process model raises risks and responsibilities for practitioners and organisations engaged in building and deploying AI solutions. These risks are informed by the AI principles adopted by the organisation, turning abstract notions into a concrete checklist. We also recognise a higher level of risk assessment that pertains to the project as a whole, i.e., is the project of high or unacceptable risk? We address this topic as part of our broader response to AI harms. With regard to Figure 5.1 and Table 5.3:

AI algorithm development (0)

Algorithm development entails arriving at a set of rules for making predictions. A goal (objective) needs to be set, such as to reduce the risk of making bad loans that are not repaid. The goal may involve constraints and trade-offs, such as the requirements imposed by the GDPR (general data protection regulation – see the chapter on regulation) in relation to the use of customer data. The goal dictates the answers that the algorithm will be fed when learning. Algorithms are trained using the data of existing customers and driven by goals established by the organisation.

Risk 0.1: are the AI development goals acceptable? [human- centred, privacy, well-being]

Risk 0.2: is accountability for the project and the working of algorithm in business clearly specified? [accountability]

Risk 0.3: is AI developer bias present? [fairness]

Risk 0.4: is the training data representative? [fairness]

Risk 0.5: how accurate is the model? What are the costs of false positives and false negatives? [safety]

Risk 0.6: are the ethical implications of the algorithm explored, for example with a business ethics canvas (Vidgen et al., 2020)? [well-being]

Risk 0.7: is the algorithm developed in-house or sourced externally? If external, does the supplier's governance and ethical position align with the organisation? Is the use of the solution allowed in the deployer's country and industry? [safety, well-being]

Data acquisition (1)

Data acquisition is triggered by events. Events happen all the time. Some events are sensed and captured as data, which may be processed into information, i.e., in a form that is usable for decision-making by humans and machines. The prevalence of sensing and data capture have exploded in volume (there is a lot more of it), velocity (it is moving quickly and often in real-time) and variety (data includes audio, images, and video as well as numbers and text). This explosion in data has been further amplified through the use of 'things' to gather data automatically via the Internet of Things (IoT) (e.g., fitness trackers, weather stations, logistics) and user generated content via social media. Events sensed and captured might include missed payments and a loan going into default. Some events won't be sensed. For example, the bank might not be aware of the emotional state of a customer following an instance of poor service or if they have just been made redundant.

Risk 1.1: are appropriate, relevant, required events being sensed and captured? [privacy]

Risk 1.2: does the organisation have permission to collect and store the data? [privacy]

Risk 1.3: are the rights of subjects infringed? [human-centred]

Risk 1.4: have subjects given informed consent to the collection, storage, and use of this data? [human-centred]

Data processing (2)

In data processing, the company will collect some data about the consumer and combine it with other external data, such as a credit score. The raw data (the result of events that are sensed) are processed into data that has meaning, which we label 'information'.

Through data, we build an image of an AI subject (this process is called 'datafication') in which a wide range of data points can be used to build a composite view of the subject.

Risk 2.1: is the data defined (dictionary) and managed? [safety]

Risk 2.2: is the data of sufficient quality (e.g., accurate, timely)? [safety]

Risk 2.3: is the data stored securely? [safety, privacy]

Risk 2.4: what internal and external data is being combined with the captured data? [privacy]

Risk 2.5: is the combined data being used for purposes beyond those it was authorised for? [safety, privacy]

Predictive modelling (3)

Once the model has been developed it can be deployed within an organisation's business processes to make predictions. Thus, the model will be used to predict outcomes on acquired data (e.g., a new application for a credit card loan).

Risk 3.1: does the model work accurately and effectively? [safety]

Risk 3.2: are the predictions and associated decisions recommended by the AI models auditable? [explainability]

Risk 3.3: are the AI predictions biased? [fairness]

Risk 3.4: are the AI predictions likely to further inequality or inequity? [fairness, well-being]

Decision-making (4)

The decision-making process might be fully automated or involve the input of human intelligence, as to what action to take, e.g., an offer of improved contract terms, or the making of a one-time free offer. Where both human and machine intelligence are drawn on in making decisions, we have collaborative intelligence. Humans have always drawn on machines in some form, whether it is an Excel spreadsheet or a hand- written ledger of transactions. At first glance it seems that machines can make decisions – and enact them – without human involvement. However, the human hand is always present in specifying the goals, designing the predictive models, building the processes in which the algorithms are embedded. While machine and human intelligence appear separated, they are always intertwined.

Risk 4.1: is there an appropriate balance of machine and human decision-making (collaboration of human and machine)? [human-centred]

Risk 4.2: if decision-making is automated, is there human oversight of decision-making? [human-centred, well-being]

Action-taking (5)

Action-taking results in an AI touchpoint for an AI subject, who may or may not - be aware that they are the subject of ADM. This action-taking might be machine-driven, such as an IT system generating an email offer to at risk customers automatically or a human calling the customer to assess customer satisfaction (or a combination of both).

Risk 5.1: how much of action-taking is automated? [human- centred, well-being]

Risk 5.2: does the AI subject know that ADM is being deployed? [transparency]

Risk 5.3: can the results of an AI decision be understood by the AI subject? [explainability]

Risk 5.4: can the results of an AI decision be challenged? [contestability]

Monitoring (6)

Monitoring requires going beyond individual decisions to look at larger patterns of performance and potential bias.

Risk 6.1: are the generated predictions being recorded and continuously monitored? [fairness, well-being]

Risk 6.2: are the AI models out of date (i.e., trained on data that is no longer current or representative of the current state of affairs). [safety]

Risk 6.3: are the goals of the algorithm still appropriate? [human-centred, safety]

Risk 6.4: has the algorithm learnt from new data and introduced new bias? [fairness]

Risk 6.5: are there unintended consequences? For example, emergent impacts on social justice, the natural environment [well-being]

Data sharing (7)

The deployer of the algorithm will record the action outcomes resulting from their use of AI. They then have the option of whether they engage in data sharing of this new data with other organisations.

Risk 7.1: are results of algorithmic decision-making shared outside the organisation? [privacy]

Risk 7.2: is the privacy of the individual protected? [privacy, well-being]

Appendix C

General Data Protection Regulation (GDPR)

Adapted from Vidgen et al., 2019.

An example of regulation is the GDPR – general data protection regulation. The GDPR defines and strengthens data protection for consumers and harmonizes data security rules within the European Union (EU). The GDPR came into effect on May 25, 2018 and regulates how organisations collect, store and process personally identifiable information (PII) about EU citizens. Any company that stores or processes data on EU citizens must comply with the GDPR legislation, including US, Asian, Australasian companies that sell goods and services in the EU. Companies must now seek consent if they are to store and process personal data. In the UK, this regulation is overseen by the Information Commissioner's Office (ICO). The analogy of AI and guns provides additional insight. Although gun ownership is legal in the US, a US citizen bringing their gun into Europe is highly illegal. Thus, AI applications developed in one country may be illegal in other countries, as we have found with data practices and the GDPR.

Specifically, individuals have the right to be informed about the collection and use of their personal data; organisations must provide individuals with information, including the purposes for processing their personal data, retention periods for that personal data, and who it will be shared with. This privacy information must be provided to individuals at the time personal data is collected. Where personal data is collected from other sources, organisations must provide individuals with privacy information within a reasonable period of obtaining the data and no later than one month (ICO).

The GDPR legislation also provides individuals with rights to explanations, i.e., a meaningful explanation of the logic and consequence of automated decision-making systems (e.g., customer profiling). Articles 13 to 15 of the GDPR stipulate that the data subject possesses the right to access "meaningful information about the logic involved, as well as the significance and the envisaged consequences" of automated decision-making systems. This indicates that companies should provide sufficient transparency regarding the logic of their machine learning systems that use personal data. Thus, explaining how an algorithm has come to a decision is an essential requirement, and algorithms that cannot be audited effectively (e.g., some AI and deep learning applications) should not be used.

Without a doubt, there will be calls for self-regulation, industry codes of conduct (such as that used by the newspaper industry and the banking standards board in the UK) and professional codes of conduct. However, we expect to see new initiatives in government regulation in the arena of AI, particularly with respect to automated ADM. This may include a requirement to register algorithms with a central agency, to demonstrate the safety of those algorithms, and to obtain a licence for algorithm use. Failure to use AI and ADM responsibly may result in fines (e.g., see BBC, 2021) and criminal prosecution of managers deemed to be responsible (similar to the case today in many countries with respect to corporate manslaughter).

Companies must now seek consent if they are to store and process personal data. According to the UK's Information Commissioner's Office (ICO):

> "Consent means giving people genuine choice and control over how you use their data. If the individual has no real choice, consent is not freely given and it will be invalid. This means people must be able to refuse consent without detriment and must be able to withdraw consent easily at any time. It also means consent should be unbundled from other terms and conditions (including giving separate granular consent options for different types of processing) wherever possible." (https://ico.org.uk/for-organisations/guide-to-the-general-data-protection-regulation-gdpr/consent/what-is-valid-consent/)

Further, data collected for one use should not be repurposed for other applications that have not been authorized by the individual.

The GDPR contains further provisions that speak directly to

information ethics. For example, Article 9, paragraph 1, of the GDPR states:

> "Processing of personal data revealing racial or ethnic origin, political opinions, religious or philosophical beliefs, or trade union membership, and the processing of genetic data, biometric data for the purpose of uniquely identifying a natural person, data concerning health or data concerning a natural person's sex life or sexual orientation **shall be prohibited**." (emphasis in the original, http://www.privacy-regulation.eu/en/article-9-processing-of-special-categories-of-personal-data-GDPR.htm).

Paragraph 2 of Article 9 says that this does not apply "if the data subject has given explicit consent to the processing of those personal data for one or more specified purposes".

Before we announce the GDPR-induced death of business analytics we should first recognize that in many instances of big data analytics do not involve personal data at all (e.g., transport, supply chain, weather data) and that other applications may be able to work with anonymized data from which individuals cannot be identified.

Dinsmore (2017) argues that GDPR affects data science practice in three areas:

1. it imposes limits on data processing and consumer profiling;
2. it creates a "right to an explanation" for consumers subjected to automated decision-making;
3. it holds firms accountable for bias and discrimination in automated decisions.

Dinsmore (ibid.) recommends that organizations using machine learning for profiling and automated decision-making should:

- Limit access to personally identifiable information (PII) about consumers;
- Implement robust anonymization, so that by default analytic users cannot access PII. Define an exception process that permits access to PII in exceptional cases under proper security.

- Identify predictive models that currently use PII.

For those models that use PII, the organization should ask (Dinsmore (ibid.):

- Is this data analytically necessary?
- Does the PII provide unique and irreplaceable information value?
- Does the predictive model support a permitted use case?

The organization should make an inventory of their consumer-facing automated decisions and identify decisions that require explanations and implement procedures to handle consumer questions and concerns (e.g., requests for explanation). To establish a data science process that minimizes the risk of errors and bias, organizations should (Dinsmore (ibid.):

- Implement a workflow that ensures proper model development and testing;
- Consider the possibility of bias "built-in" to training data;
- Rigorously test and validate predictive models;
- Implement peer review for an independent assessment of every model.

Dinsmore (ibid.) concludes by saying "Even if your organization is not subject to GDPR, consider implementing these practices anyway. It's the right way to do business."

While the GDPR provides a measure of protection concerning how data is collected, used, and shared with others (the fuel for the AADM engine), it does not consider how the harms caused by AI decisions, such as refusal of parole, can be contested and remedied. Current proposals in the European Union – notably the Proposal for an AI Act – are more directly focused on harms, with a graduated series of rules: prohibitions for some uses of AI; and then differing levels of regulation for 'high risk' and 'low risk' uses. At the time of writing, the proposal is the subject of ongoing negotiations within Europe, including over how to frame which activities count as high or low risk, or ought to be prohibited outright.

References

BBC (2021). *EU artificial intelligence rules will ban 'unacceptable' use.* BBCNews, 22 April, https://www.bbc.co.uk/news/technology-56830779

Dinsmore, T., (2017). *How GDPR affects data science.* KDNuggets, July 2017, https://www.kdnuggets.com/2017/07/gdpr-affects-data-science.html

Vidgen, R., Kirshner, S., & Tan, F., (2019). *Business Analytics: a management approach.* Red Globe (Macmillan Higher Education).

Made in the USA
Monee, IL
03 November 2026

67385937R00174